THEORISING SPECIAL EDUCATION

The field of special education is well established. However, although it continues to develop in exciting and controversial ways, involving some of education's leading thinkers, many people feel it is lacking a coherent theoretical analysis of its own.

Students and practitioners, looking for some solid theory to reinforce their own study or practice, commonly have to borrow from other disciplines, such as psychology and sociology. This is because there has been no attempt to provide a theoretical foundation for the special needs community. This book does exactly that, bringing together contributions from key names in the field from the UK and beyond.

Catherine Clark, Alan Dyson and **Alan Millward** work in the Special Needs Research Centre in the Department of Education at the University of Newcastle. Catherine Clark is Lecturer in Education, Alan Dyson is Professor of Special Needs Education and Alan Millward is Senior Lecturer in Education.

THEORISING SPECIAL EDUCATION

Edited by Catherine Clark,
Alan Dyson and Alan Millward

London and New York

First published 1998
by Routledge
11 New Fetter Lane, London EC4P 4EE

Simultaneously published in the USA and Canada
by Routledge
29 West 35th Street, New York, NY 10001

©1998 Catherine Clark, Alan Dyson and Alan Millward, selection and editorial
matter; individual chapters, the contributors

Typeset in Goudy by Routledge

Printed and bound in Great Britain by Creative Print and Design (Wales) Ebbw Vale

British Library Cataloguing in Publication Data
A catalogue record for this book is available from the British Library

Library of Congress Cataloguing in Publication Data
Clark, Catherine
Theorising special education/Catherine Clark, Alan Dyson and Alan Millward.
1. Special education–Great Britain–Philosophy. I. Dyson, Alan.
II. Millward, Alan. III. Title.
LC3986.G7C53 1998
97–43773
371.9'0941–dc21
CIP

ISBN 0–415–14750–6 (hbk)
ISBN 0–415–14751–4 (pbk)

CONTENTS

CONTENTS

CONTRIBUTORS

Mel Ainscow is Professor of Special Needs and Educational Psychology, and Dean of the School of Education at the University of Manchester. His current research is concerned with the development of inclusive education.

Julie Allan is a Lecturer in education at the University of Stirling and a part-time tutor with the Open University. She has been involved in a number of major research projects in special education, including a study of special school and multiple policy innovations and a comparison of mainstream and special schools. She is currently writing a book, based on pupils' accounts of inclusion.

Derrick Armstrong is a Lecturer in the Division of Education at the University of Sheffield. He is currently researching the history of special education from a life histories perspective.

Felicity Armstrong is a Lecturer in the Division of Education at the University of Sheffield. She has a particular interest in policy, change and special education in a comparative framework.

Jeff Bailey is Professor of Special Education at the University of Western Sydney, Nepean and Director of the Children's Hospital Education Research Institute, New Children's Hospital, Sydney, NSW, Australia. His research interests include inclusive schooling and students with chronic illness. With Done Rice, he has just published a book on Attention-deficit Hyperactivity Disorder.

Len Barton is a Professor in the Division of Education at the University of Sheffield. He is currently working on a socio-political perspective on disability issues. This includes the development of a comparative approach.

Phil Bayliss is the Course Director for the Masters programme in special education at the University of Exeter. As a practitioner, he has taught in both special and mainstream provision. His research interests focus on the theory and practice of the inclusion of disabled children and adults.

Tony Booth is a senior lecturer in education at the Open University. He has been teaching, researching and writing about special and inclusive education for the last twenty years. Currently, he is engaged in a comparative research and development programme on inclusion policy and practice.

Sally Brown is Deputy Principal and Professor of Education at the University of Stirling. She was formerly Director of the Scottish Council for Research in Education and a past President of the British Educational Research Association. Her involvement in educational research over the last 25 years has produced many publications in a wide variety of areas. Most recently her work and research interests have been in the nature of teaching, special educational needs and pre-school provision.

Catherine Clark is Lecturer in Education at the Special Needs Research Centre in the Department of Education at the University of Newcastle. She is the co-author (with Alan Dyson, Alan Millward and David Skidmore) of *New Directions in Special Needs* (1997, Cassell) and the co-editor (with Alan Dyson and Alan Millward) of *Towards Inclusive Schools?* (1995, David Fulton).

Alan Dyson is Professor of Special Needs Education at the Special Needs Research Centre in the Department of Education at the University of Newcastle.

Jeff Lewis is Principal Lecturer in Special Education in the Rolle School of Education, University of Plymouth. He has published articles on listening to children with SEN and contributes papers to a range of educational and philosophical conferences.

Alan Millward is Senior Lecturer in Education at the Special Needs Research Centre in the Department of Education at the University of Newcastle.

Sip Jan Pijl is senior researcher at the Institute for Educational Research, GION, University of Groningen, The Netherlands and staff-member of the Interuniversity Centre for Educational research

(ICO). He works part-time for the European Agency for Development in Special Needs Education located in Denmark. He specialises in research in special education and is involved in studies on the integration of students with special needs in regular education.

Patricia Potts is a Senior Lecturer in Education at the Open University and is writing up a study of inclusive policy and practice in China since the late 1970s.

Sheila Riddell is Professor of Social Policy and Director of the Strathclyde Centre for Disability Research at the University of Glasgow.

Roger Slee is Chair of Teaching and Learning and Dean of the Faculty of Education at the University of Western Australia, and is the foundation Editor of the *International Journal of Inclusive Education*.

Gunnar Stangvik is Professor of Education at Finnmark College, Alta, Norway. He has published in the areas of efficacy of special education, self-concept development, quality of life and special education didactics. He is currently involved in a project studying the practice of special education.

Kees van den Bos is an Associate Professor of Special Education at the University of Groningen, The Netherlands. The emphasis in his research and teaching activities is on learning disabilities.

1

INTRODUCING THE ISSUE OF THEORISING

Catherine Clark, Alan Dyson and Alan Millward

This book arises out of a symposium of the same title organised by the editors at the International Education Congress in Birmingham, UK, in 1995. Our own professional backgrounds are first as teachers in a range of mainstream and special educational settings, then as teacher trainers and finally as researchers in the field of special education.[1] Over a period of years, however, we have noted how our own somewhat pragmatic concerns have become permeated by theoretical issues, and how theoretical questions have continually forced themselves upon our attention. It seems impossible to consider issues of educational failure (the child's or the school's?), of disability (personal tragedy or public issue?), of inclusive schooling (ethically necessary or educationally damaging?) from a purely pragmatic perspective. Questions of fundamental values, of assumptions about learning and learners, of conceptualisations of difference and deviance seem to arise at every turn.

Alongside our growing concern was a sense that the state of theorising in special education was complex, not to say confused. On the one hand, the certainties which underpinned the pioneering work of Burt and Schonell seemed to have disappeared. In their place had arisen a multiplicity of positions ranging from the powerful advocacy of new approaches to difference based on an unequivocal commitment to principles of equity and inclusion to subtle deconstructions of special education based on sophisticated theories of organisational types, or of professional learning or of social interests. On the other hand, much practice and research in the field of special education seemed to be proceeding on a pragmatic basis, as though these newer ideas simply did not exist. Above all, it was clear that, if a single reliable theory on which special educational practice could be based had ever existed, no such simple and universal relationship between theory and practice was now possible.

In view of this situation, it seemed to us that the time was ripe for issues of theory in special education to be placed centre stage. In convening the Birmingham seminar – and in the additional work which is incorporated in this book – we asked our contributors to address three questions:

- Do we need a theory of special education?
- What should such a theory look like?
- What are the implications of such a theory for practice and research in the field of special education?

Such questions may well be simple to the point of naïveté; indeed, some of our contributors have not been slow to problematise the whole project of theorising, much less of seeking a single theoretical account of a field which itself is highly problematic and diffuse. Nonetheless, we felt – and continue to feel – that these questions open up perspectives on special education which would be difficult to find and address in other ways. Although, therefore, each contributor has addressed these key questions in different ways, we hope that readers will be able to trace these themes in each of these chapters and will find their own engagement with these questions enriched by so doing.

Is this book *really* necessary?

It is evident that the project of theorising special education is important to us and, indeed, in very different ways, to our contributors. But is it important beyond that? Does it matter to practitioners and policy-makers, or, indeed, to the learners who are the supposed beneficiaries of special education?

Our answer is that, whether this particular book is important or not, the business of theorising is not simply necessary in special education, but is inevitable. Following Schön (1983a, b), we would argue that any form of purposeful action at the very least *implies* a theory. Simply in order for that action to be purposeful – to be directed at making a difference to the world in order to achieve some goal or other – there must be a set of assumptions of the order of : 'this part of the phenomenal world is such that action of the sort y is likely to produce outcome x'. Such assumptions are theoretical in the very basic sense – but a sense that we accept – that they move beyond a simple description of observed phenomena towards an explanation of how those phenomena come to be, how they interact, and how they might be changed.

Such implicit 'theories in action' may, of course, be made more or less explicit. They may be articulated as the relatively unproblematised assumptions of individual or social groups about their worlds. They may be subsequently developed into local theories which might, for example, suggest how to organise a school, or how to teach particular children. These theories may be further extended in their range, their precision and their coherence so that they become what we might call 'theory proper' – the sorts of theories which offer accounts and explanations of particular 'types' of special needs, for instance, or which seek to explain the historical origins of special education, or which account for special education as the product of professional self-interest.

The diversity of these types of theories is enormous. What is important for us, however, is that, whilst the development of 'theory proper' is optional, the process of theorising itself is not. Moreover, we share with Skrtic (1995) the prejudice (and it may be no more than this) that 'naive pragmatism' – the basing of action on implicit or relatively unproblematised local theories – is dangerous. The development of 'theory proper' is optional, as indeed, is the grounding of action in such theory. However, if action is ultimately to be rational in the sense that its purposes and its means of achieving those purposes are to be opened to principled and methodologically rigorous scrutiny, then the construction of 'theory proper' is essential. This is one way in which we are able to interrogate the assumptions and values which are implicit in our actions.

However, we also believe that we have to be careful with the notion of 'theory proper' as an 'explanation' of phenomena. The question is not whether theory should or should not attempt such explanations (it is difficult to see what else a theory – at least 'theory proper' – might be), so much as whether *single* and *consensual* explanations are possible. As readers progress through this book, they will become aware of the shift in thinking which sometimes calls itself post-modernism (see, for instance, Best and Kellner, 1991; Cooper and Burrell, 1988; Hassan, 1987; Lather, 1990) and which problematises the notion of 'foundational' knowledge. It is not simply that theoretical explanations can be 'wrong' in the sense that they break their own rules of evidence in explaining phenomena, but that different sorts of explanations call upon different rules and sorts of evidence, or see different sets of phenomena as calling for explanation. Within our own field, the prime example is the sort of shift to which we alluded earlier, and to which we shall return in the final chapter. That is the shift from an attempt to explain children's difficulties using the natural scientific rules of (some sorts of) psychology and medicine towards an explanation of them in terms of social processes of construction and production, using the rules of interpretivism or radical–structuralist sociology.

It follows from this that theoretical explanations do not formalise what we know for certain, but, rather, formalise what we believe we know and wish to know at any one time. As our interests and priorities shift, so does the nature of our knowledge and of the theories which formalise that knowledge. Moreover, those shifts arise neither entirely arbitrarily nor entirely out of the internal dynamics of rational knowledge production. Because knowledge is produced by particular people at particular times and in particular places, those shifts arise also out of the social, cultural and historical contexts within which knowledge is produced. Within our own field, therefore, the knowledge about educational difference produced by the pioneer educational psychologists of the first half of the twentieth century is different from the knowledge produced by the sociologists of the 1960s and 1970s or the inclusion advocates of the 1990s – with each form of knowledge reflecting its time and place.

3

The assumptions on which this book is based, therefore, are that theorising is an ongoing process which is an inevitable concomitant of action; that the explication of this process in terms of 'theory proper' is highly desirable; and that the process of theorising is socially and historically located. The clarification of these assumptions is important if the reader is to understand what this book does and does not attempt to achieve. In the first place, it does not attempt to develop a single 'theory of special education'. The diversity of types of theory, the nature of theorising as a process, and the dependency of that process on the assumptions, interests and priorities of particular contexts make such a venture meaningless.

Second, this book does not attempt to produce an encyclopaedic handbook or typology of theorising in this field. There is a real temptation to systematise the current multiplicity of theory – a temptation to which we have partly succumbed in the final chapter. However, such systematisation runs the risk of ignoring the insights that emerge within individual contributions. Moreover, it suggests some external standpoint from which the system can be developed and on which it can be based, glossing over the extent to which any such standpoint is itself part of the ongoing process of theory construction. Readers who wish for a more systematic perspective on theory than that offered here are referred to Skrtic's recent (1995) comprehensive work – though we would counsel them to be alert in their reading to the dangers to which we have alluded.

Third, and perhaps most important, this book makes no pretence to be anything other than historically and socially located. The contributors are certainly different from each other in terms of their interests, views and, indeed, national origins. However, we are remarkably similar to each other in terms of our professional backgrounds. We write, without exception, as academics and therefore as members of a rather privileged social group for which theorising has traditionally been a key professional function bringing a range of personal and professional rewards. Whatever our past histories and however else we might identify ourselves in other contexts, we do not write here primarily (if at all) as members of other key stakeholder groups in special education. We do not, for instance, write as teachers or parents or disabled people or as disaffected school students.

This is important because, in recent years, the growing awareness of the social location of knowledge production has led to claims in some quarters that it is only disabled people or those who identify closely with their interests who can legitimately comment on special education (Ballard, 1994, 1995; Barton, 1994; Clough and Barton, 1995; Oliver, 1992a). Readers will find that some contributors to this book tackle this issue directly. Our own position is to acknowledge the homogeneity of our backgrounds as contributors and to accept the legitimacy of questions about ways in which that background shapes the knowledge which we produce. Whether that knowledge can be reduced to or invalidated by that background is, of course, another matter which we leave to the reader to consider. Suffice it to say that there are other positions from which our work can be critiqued and from which very different books might be written. We welcome and invite such projects and hope that by reading the following contributions individuals are stimulated to join us in the ongoing process of theorising.

In the spirit of the above comments we have not sought to summarise, systematise or in any way order the contributions that follow. By not attempting to impose any order or interpretation on these contributions we are not abrogating an editorial responsibility but acknowledging, without necessarily wholly subscribing to, the relativism implicit in post-modernism. Each of these contributions 'speaks' with its own authentic voice. As editors we do not wish to impose our dominant voice or impose an artificial structure on these contributions. We trust the reader to chart their own course through these contributions and to exercise their own judgement about any sequence or grouping which may or may not exist. If they share with us the same view of the field, they will not find this unduly unnerving or indeed surprising; if they are convinced that the complexity and confusion are illusory, then they will impose their own choice regardless of any structure we might offer.

We end this introduction almost at the point that we began by musing on the extent of the complexity and apparent confusion that exists in the state of theorising in special education. If we appear to be reluctant to address this confusion, it is because we believe there is a need for a continued debate. Our hesitancy in this respect may be viewed with scorn by those who believe they have found an unequivocal position which enables them to speak with certainty on these matters. We are content to reserve judgement on such certainties. We prefer instead to see the debate flourish, recognising that there is a possibility that dangerous limitations are ultimately exposed in absolutist positions. We suggest that any uncertainty we have is a reflection of the actual complexity that exists within the field. Confusion is not, therefore, necessarily symptomatic of incoherence or doubt but a recognition of the real diversity that exists within the field. We would not wish to claim that the contributions in this book would necessarily lead to an ending of this complexity. What we would hope is that by bringing together a number of contributions into this one volume we can create a point of reference for those who share our belief that the process of theorising in special education remains underdeveloped.

We have, however, made an editorial decision regarding the ordering of the chapters and exercised one prerogative enjoyed by the authors of most edited collections. Rather than struggling to find a purely random order for the chapters which might, however carefully we sought to construct it, be interpreted as having some underlying structure, we have opted for a sequence which is alphabetic. We have also opted to make our contribution in the form of a final chapter. In this chapter we will articulate our own views on the nature of theorising in special education and suggest that it is 'time to move on'. We, of course, have had the benefit of reading the other contributions – an opportunity that was not available to the other authors. The reader must view our contribution in that particular light.

Note

1   As always in fields which are in some turmoil, terminology is a problem. For our purposes here, 'special education' is taken to refer to any form of educational provision which is regarded within its own context as being 'special'. This embraces both provision which is made in special settings (special schools, units and so on) and 'special' provision which is made in mainstream settings. It also includes the various attempts to reconstruct special education, most notably inclusive education. We freely acknowledge, however, the difficulties both of defining what is 'special' and of applying the unreconstructed terminology of special education to the supposedly reconstructed inclusive education.

2

WOULD IT WORK IN THEORY?

Arguments for practitioner research and theorising in the special needs field

Mel Ainscow

There is a story of a famous professor who, though he had written a number of significant papers about quality in education, had not visited a school for over twenty years. A new young colleague persuaded him to visit a local school that had acquired a reputation for the excellence of its work. On the journey back from the visit the young lecturer asked the professor to comment on what he had seen. After a moment's silence the professor replied, 'I'm just thinking, would it work in theory?'

In many ways my own work addresses the same question. Perhaps the major difference between me and the famous professor, however, is that I continue to spend significant periods of my working hours in schools. Over the last few years in particular, I have been involved in a series of initiatives in schools, in this country and abroad, that have provided me with endless opportunities to reflect upon and engage with questions about how schools and classrooms can be developed in response to student diversity (Ainscow, 1995a). How far these experiences represent what others regard as research in a formal sense is a matter of debate. What they have stimulated is a process of learning as I have sought to find meaning in and understand what I have experienced.

This chapter provides some personal reflections on all of this, leading to an argument that what is needed is a much greater recognition of the power of practitioner research and theorising in the special needs field. I will argue, however, that such a move requires significant changes in thinking in the field about the nature of educational difficulties and how they should be investigated. It also has major implications for the ways in which researchers go about their business.

Rethinking the special needs task

Over recent years my involvement in a number of development initiatives, particularly the UNESCO teacher education project 'Special Needs in the Classroom', which has involved work in many different countries (see Ainscow, 1994a for a detailed account of the research associated with this project), has heightened my awareness of the ways in which different perceptions of the special needs task guide and shape the responses of practitioners. This awareness leads me to assume that concepts of educational difficulty are socially constructed and must, therefore, be regarded as being highly problematic. As I have engaged with these complexities I have found my own position shifting in ways that are, to say the least, both disruptive and disturbing. Inevitably these changes in thinking are apparent in what I have written – thus, perhaps, leading those who read what I write to experience their own feelings of distur-bance

Some time ago Susan Hart and I attempted to map out some possible perspectives on educational difficulties in order to assist ourselves (and possibly others) in gaining a better understanding of our own current positions (Ainscow and Hart, 1992). In this context I take perspectives to mean those basic assumptions that determine our attitudes, values and beliefs, and lead us to predict the nature and meaning of incoming information (Nias, 1987). So the perspectives we defined are attempts to characterise alternative ways of looking at the phenomenon of educational difficulty, based on different sets of assump-tions that lead to different explanations, different frames of reference and different kinds of questions to be addressed. In this sense they lead to assump-tions that provide the basis of different theoretical positions.

We defined three overall perspectives. The first of these, we suggested, seeks to explain educational difficulties in terms of the characteristics of individual pupils. This remains the dominant perspective in the special needs field, where the nature of educational difficulties is explained in terms of particular disabili-ties, social background and/or psychological attributes. The frame of reference created by this perspective is the individual child, and responses are chosen that seek to change or support the child in order to facilitate participation in the process of schooling. Traditionally responses have taken the form of removal of the child from the mainstream curriculum for specialist help. However, more recently, responses have begun to develop which allow help to be provided in the context of the regular classroom.

The second perspective explains educational difficulties in terms of a mismatch between the characteristics of particular children and the organisa-tion and/or curriculum arrangements made for them (e.g. Wedell, 1981; Dessent, 1987). Here support may be directed towards helping the child to meet the demands and expectations of the system, if this is assumed to be fixed or – for the time being at least – unchangeable. Or it may be directed towards making modifications to the system in order to extend the range of pupils that can be accommodated. In many respects current 'state of the art' responses (e.g. whole-school approaches, differentiation) are informed by this perspective. Further, it is a perspective that is seen as arising as a result of dissatisfaction with the first perspective, which is seen as being a 'deficit model' (Dyson, 1990).

The frame of reference in this interactive perspective once again focuses attention on individual pupils but this time is concerned with the ways they interact with particular contexts and experiences. So much so that those adopting this perspective have, in recent years, tended to argue for the use of the term 'individual needs' rather than 'special needs' (e.g. Ainscow and Muncey, 1989). Responses chosen in the light of this perspective include curriculum adaptations, alternative materials for pupils, or extra support in the classroom. Sometimes, these responses are also seen as being of benefit to pupils other than those designated as having special needs.

The third perspective explains educational difficulties in terms of curriculum limitations, using the term curriculum in a broad sense to include all the planned and, indeed, unplanned experiences offered to pupils. Thus, in this perspective, there is a concern with what can be learnt from the difficulties experienced by some children about the limitations of provision currently made for all pupils. The assumption is that changes introduced for the benefit of those experiencing difficulties can improve learning for all children (Hart, 1992a, b). Those adopting this perspective are critical of the limitations of an individual frame of reference, even where this is used to raise questions about the adequacy of curriculum organisation and practice as currently provided for individual pupils. They argue that a wider frame is needed, focusing on curriculum organisation and practice as currently provided for all pupils. The task involves continually seeking ways of improving overall conditions for learning, with difficulties acting as indicators of how improvements might be achieved (Ainscow et al., 1994b). Those who adopt this perspective are likely to favour approaches that encourage inquiry as a means of achieving improvement, e.g. various forms of partnership teaching, action research.

It is important to recognise at this stage in the argument that whilst the adoption of a particular perspective tends to encourage the choice of certain types of organisational and curriculum responses, the responses are in themselves often neutral as to their orientation. So, for example, support teaching, which has become a very fashionable response to special needs in recent years, might be used by teachers favouring any of these three perspectives. In this case, those adopting a characteristics perspective would see support teaching as a means of providing an individual pupil with extra teaching, albeit in the context or framework of regular classroom activities; those who take an interactive view, on the other hand, would see support teaching as a way of making modifications to existing arrangements in order to accommodate certain pupils experiencing learning difficulties; whereas the curriculum limitations perspective would encourage the idea that additional adults could facilitate the review and development of existing arrangements in the light of a scrutiny of the difficulties experienced by certain pupils.

I can now relate this general map of perspectives to my own work, including my continuing involvement with teachers and schools in the various projects with which I am involved, particularly the UNESCO project. In that context I am continually provoked into reconsidering my own thinking and practice as a result of being confronted by what seem strange situations. In particular I find that the unusual contexts that I meet as I work in different countries have the effect of making the familiar seem strange. This seems to be consistent with the view of Delamont (1992) who argues that familiarity can act as a barrier when carrying out research, suggesting that it is possible to make use of national differences in educational experience and organisation to illuminate features that might otherwise be taken for granted.

As the UNESCO project has developed I have gradually become aware that my position has changed from one that I had previously characterised as being based upon an interactive perspective to one that can be seen as being informed predominantly by a curriculum limitations view (Ainscow, 1995b). At the heart of this shift was a growing concern about the limitations and, indeed, potential dangers of an individual frame of reference when addressing educational difficulties. In particular, I saw this as leading to a narrowing of opportunity and lowering of expectations for children, not least in that it masked possibilities for developing practice.

Much of current thinking regarding the improvement of work in the special needs field, set within the context of what I am describing here as an individual frame of reference, treats educational difficulty as primarily a technical issue (Iano, 1986). Consequently, solutions to problems of academic underachievement and exclusion tend to be formulated in methodological and mechanistic terms, dislodged from the wider contextual realities that shape them. As a result, the special needs task is often reduced to a search for the 'right' teaching methods, strategies or packaged materials that will work with those pupils who do not respond to the teaching arrangements generally made.

Whilst it is, of course, important to identify useful and promising strategies, I wish to argue that it is erroneous to assume that systematic replication of particular methods, in and of themselves, will generate successful learning, especially when we are considering pupils that historically have been alienated in or excluded from schools. This overemphasis on searching for effective methods often seems to distract attention from more significant questions such as why, in a particular society or, indeed, school, do some pupils fail to learn successfully?

Consequently, it is, I believe, necessary to shift away from this narrow and mechanistic view of educational difficulties to one that is broader in scope and takes into account wider contextual factors, including both cultural and structural dimensions (Ainscow, 1995a). In particular it is important to reject what Bartolome (1994) refers to as the 'methods fetish' in order to work towards the creation of learning environments informed by both action and reflection. In this way, by freeing ourselves from the uncritical adoption of so-called effective strategies, we can begin the reflective process that leads to the recreation and reinvention of teaching methods and materials in response to the reactions and feedback of children.

In seeking to move in this direction it is important to bear in mind that a teacher's methods are social constructions that grow out of and reflect taken-for-granted assumptions that may obscure greater understanding of the pedagogical implications of power relations within an education system.

Teachers and those involved in working with them must remember that schools, like other institutions in society, are influenced by perceptions of socioeconomic status, race, language and gender. Consequently, it is important to question how such perceptions influence classroom dynamics. In this way the present methods-restricted discussions can be broadened to reveal deeply entrenched deficit orientations towards 'difference'. As educators we need to be constantly vigilant and ask how the deficit orientation has affected our perceptions of pupils who come to be seen as being special.

As I have argued, teaching strategies are neither devised nor implemented in a vacuum. Design, selection and use of particular teaching approaches and strategies arise from perceptions about learning and learners. I contend that even the most pedagogically advanced methods are likely to be ineffective in the hands of teachers who implicitly, or explicitly, subscribe to a belief system that regards certain pupils, at best, as disadvantaged and in need of fixing, or, at worst, as deficient and beyond fixing.

In recent years, of course, this deficit model has been subject to massive criticism in the special needs field. Consequentially we have seen some changes in thinking that seek to move explanations of educational failure away from the characteristics of individual children and their families towards the process of schooling. As I have explained, this has led to the introduction of approaches based upon an interactive view of educational difficulties. However, my involvement in schools during this period leads me now to argue that, despite good intentions, approaches informed by this perspective and the frame of reference it encourages often give rise to a kinder, more liberal, and yet more concealed version of the deficit model that views 'special children' as being in need of special teaching, i.e. approaches that other children do not require in order to achieve in school. Thus, despite moves towards the integration of children seen as having special needs, with an emphasis on approaches such as curriculum differentiation and additional adult support in the classroom, the deficit orientation towards differences continues to be deeply ingrained in many schools and classrooms.

For these reasons I have come to the view that progress towards the creation of schools that can foster the learning of all children will only occur where teachers become more reflective and critical practitioners, capable of and empowered to investigate aspects of their practice with a view to making improvements. Only in this way can they overcome the limitations and dangers of deficit thinking; only in this way can we be sure that pupils who experience difficulties in learning can be treated with respect and viewed as potentially active and capable learners. This analysis indicates, therefore, a need to consider what forms of inquiry are relevant to this task.

Investigating practice

The reconceptualisation of the special needs task that is implicit in my argument so far necessitates the use of forms of inquiry that will enable those involved to investigate aspects of their existing practices as a basis for further development. Unfortunately, the dominant tradition of research in the field is, I will argue, unsuitable for this task. Once again, therefore, what is needed is a radical change, following the advice of others who have argued for the introduction of new approaches to research in the special needs field (e.g. Barton, 1988a; Iano, 1986; Schindele, 1985; Skrtic, 1986).

Traditionally research in special education has been influenced by theories derived from psychology and biology. This was largely consistent with the idea of special education being seen as a search for effective methods to solve a technical problem (Iano, 1986). As a result, the aim was to establish, through carefully controlled experiments, the existence of generalised laws that teachers could use as a basis for their interventions. Indeed much of teacher education, particularly in the special needs field, is based upon this orientation. Teachers attend courses to learn about theories derived from such research in order that they can then use these to inform the development of their practice.

The emphasis within this dominant research tradition is on the use of experimental or, more likely, quasi-experimental designs of a quantitative type. Typically these involve the study of the relationship between sets of variables with a view to making generalisations that apply across settings (Harre, 1981; House et al., 1989). So, for example, research might be carried out in order to consider the impact of teachers' use of praise upon the social conduct of pupils.

The aim would be to demonstrate relationships between the two variables, praise and behaviour, in order to establish the existence of laws that would apply in the classrooms of other teachers.

Such investigations are based upon a number of assumptions that remain matters of dispute (e.g. Heshusius, 1989; Iano, 1986). In particular they assume that variables such as praise and social conduct can be defined in ways that could be said to apply across different contexts, times and people. The problem with this is that classrooms are complex places, involving numerous social encounters, the significance of which comes to be understood separately by each participant. So much so that the idea of generalisable interpretations are always subject to doubt, at least (Bassey, 1990).

Whilst special education was framed as a series of technical tasks concerned with finding solutions to the problems of particular children or groups of children seen as sharing similar characteristics and, by implication, experiencing

12

similar difficulties, this dominant research tradition seemed to provide a good fit. Although issues of methodology, not least to do with rigour, continued to encourage argument, the idea of seeking to establish laws of cause and effect that could be used to make generalisations about classroom life seemed appropriate. The arguments I have outlined above, however, argue that progress in the field will be more likely if the task is reformulated in order to pay attention to the uniqueness of contexts and encounters. Thus, the focus is on specific children as they interact with particular people, at a particular time and in a particular situation. The idea of establishing predictions across people, time and contexts is, therefore, to say the least, inappropriate. Rather, what is needed is a deeper understanding of the nature and outcomes of individual educational events and situations. In this sense reality is assumed to be something that is created in the minds of those involved in the event or situation, rather than something that can be defined objectively, observed systematically and measured accurately. This change in orientation is, of course, indicative of a shift from the positivist to the interpretative paradigm, and assumes very different ideas about the nature of reality and the relationship of 'knower' to the known (Lincoln and Guba, 1985).

In the light of these arguments my own research has involved an exploration of forms of inquiry that have the flexibility to deal with the uniqueness of particular educational occurrences and contexts; that allow social organisations, such as schools and classrooms, to be understood from the perspectives of different participants, not least the pupils; and that encourage teachers to investigate their own situations and practices with a view to bringing about improvements (e.g. Ainscow et al., 1995). Similarly, within my work in higher education I have encouraged course participants to carry out school-based assignments based on these ideas whilst, at the same time, addressing issues of direct relevance to the development of their classroom practice (Ainscow, 1989). Indeed, the overall aim of this work has been to encourage teachers to see themselves as 'reflective practitioners', skilled in learning from experience and, as a result, more responsive to the feedback offered by members of their classes.

Action research and reflection

As I have continued to work in these ways, encouraging teachers to study aspects of their own practice, I have gradually come to recognise the significance of this experience for my own learning. In this respect my experience seems to mirror that of Lanzara, who, as a result of a similar process, notes: 'To my surprise, I discovered that as I was helping my partners to reflect on their own practice, I was also reflecting on my own' (1991: 287).

In my own case the recognition of this process was stimulated as a result of keeping a research diary as a means of recording procedures adopted and decisions made as part of the ongoing evaluation of the UNESCO project

(Ainscow, 1995a, b). Here I was following the advice of Burgess (1982) and Lincoln and Guba (1985) who emphasise the value of diaries to researchers and provide helpful guidelines as to how they might be kept.

Within the project the idea of the research diary is combined with the notion of a learning journal (Holly, 1989) which is used by all participants as part of continuous evaluation of their professional development. Consequently, this places considerable emphasis on the value of writing as a means of making sense of experience.

Initially, despite my good intentions, I found it difficult to establish the discipline of writing in the journal on a regular basis. I found that there were phases during which I was regularly making entries but then at other times long periods would occur when the journal was ignored. Over time I also became aware that the nature of my engagement with the journal changed. Whilst I was continuing to record events and decisions, I also found that I was using the journal to hold conversations with myself. Comments about personal feelings started to appear, as did expressions of confusion or uncertainty. I also began rereading earlier entries and annotating them with afterthoughts. In this way I gradually became involved in what Lanzara (1991) refers to as a process of 'self-study', using what he calls 'backtalk' in order to reconsider events and situations that had previously occurred in order to explore the kinds of knowledge that might emerge.

Lanzara notes that in more conventional forms of research backtalk might be seen as feedback to be used as a corrective device or control mechanism in order to achieve a more rigorous account. However, in what he characterises as 'second order inquiry' it performs a more radical function as a reflective mechanism to interrogate the categories and procedures used in generating earlier accounts. In his work he extends the idea of backtalk to involve other participants and, indeed, my continued interaction with colleagues and participants in the UNESCO project can be seen as providing a similar function.

What then is the nature of second order inquiry? How does it fit into overall thinking about educational research? Indeed, how far does it qualify as a legitimate form of research at all? All of these questions are complex and I am aware that my engagement with them remains uncertain and somewhat tentative. Nevertheless, my experience of this way of working so far has convinced me of its potential for informing the development of thinking and practice, whether or not we choose to regard it as research in a formal sense.

The approach I am describing bears much resemblance, of course, to action research, a form of inquiry that in its original form sought to use the experimental approach of social science with programmes of social action in response to social problems (e.g. Lewin, 1946). More recently action research has come to refer to a process of inquiry undertaken by practitioners in their own workplaces. Here the aim is to improve practice and understanding through a combination of systematic reflection and strategic innovation (Kemmis and McTaggart, 1982). Action research is sometimes dismissed as not being 'proper' research by researchers working within more traditional research paradigms. Others, whilst acknowledging it as a worthwhile activity for practitioners, are anxious that claims for the validity of findings should not be made beyond the particular contexts in which the investigation is carried out (e.g. Hammersley, 1992).

Proponents of action research, on the other hand, have responded to these criticisms by rejecting the conceptions of rigour imposed by traditional social science, and by mounting their own counter-criticism of the methodology and assumptions about knowledge upon which these conceptions of rigour are dependent (e.g. Winter, 1989). They claim, for example, that the notions of rigour to which both positivist and interpretative researchers aspire are oppressive, restrictive and prescriptive, designed to perpetuate the hierarchical divisions between the producers and users of research (Iano, 1986).

Many of those who argue for action research see it as an alternative to traditional forms of research which, they suggest, have been notoriously unsuccessful in terms of bringing about improvements in schooling (e.g. Kemmis and McTaggart, 1982; Eliott 1981; Ebbutt, 1983). Action research, it is claimed, leads to improvements in the quality of education because teachers themselves take responsibility for deciding what changes are needed, and teachers' own interpretations and judgements are used as a basis for monitoring, evaluating and deciding what the next stage of the investigation will be. Thus, action research addresses the crucial issue of 'ownership' over the process of change in schools.

Drawing attention to the limitations of research carried out within positivist and interpretative paradigms, some writers have argued that action research could become a new paradigm in itself (Carr and Kemmis, 1986; Winter, 1989). This new paradigm assumes a different view of professional knowledge and of the relationship between theory and practice. As I argued earlier in this chapter, traditional social science research seems to assume a relationship between theory and practice within which practice involves the application of theory in specific applied contexts. The overall effectiveness of practice is thus limited by the adequacy of the available theory, plus, of course, the practitioner's understanding and skill in applying it. By implication, improvements in practice will follow from the development of more adequate theory, enabling practitioners to apply it effectively. Those who see action research as an alternative paradigm argue that this is a model based on knowledge in the natural sciences and that teachers' professional knowledge cannot be applied with the same degree of certainty – not because the body of knowledge is less adequate but because the process of application of knowledge is of a different order (Winter, 1989).

Action research tends to assume that all knowledge produced through a reflective process of inquiry is necessarily provisional, and that the relationship between theory and practice is dialectical rather than prescriptive. This means that practice is not treated as dependent upon theory to tell it what to do, but that both theory and practice confront and question one another in an ongoing dialogue. Consequently, all judgements and interpretations are regarded as open to question and, therefore, the practitioner–researcher's accounts are accorded no privileged status over those of other participants in the situation under investigation. All are regarded as 'data', i.e. as resources for reflection and critique.

Inevitably within the field there are different viewpoints, even amongst those who are generally sympathetic to the idea of action research. For example, Adelman (1989) argues against 'overblown claims' for action research as a new paradigm. He also argues that it lacks an adequate theory of learning that is capable of explaining how new insights come to be generated through the research process. Furthermore he suggests that the methodology of action research has become a substitute for an adequate account of how learning occurs through the action research cycle. Action research that aims for improvements in practice but does not confront the values implicit in these goals 'may have no more intrinsic educational significance than much of the psychostatistical research to which [it] is seen as a radical popular alternative' (Silver, quoted in Adelman, 1989). What counts as an 'improvement' in understanding? How do we know that we have really learnt something through the action research process and not simply confirmed our existing prejudices or interpretations?

Writers such as Carr and Kemmis (1986), Lather (1986) and Winter (1989) have begun to address these questions, suggesting that central to an understanding of the process of reflection must be the notion of 'critique'. Carr and Kemmis proffer the concept of critical self-reflection, suggesting that the process requires collaboration as a basis for exploring and questioning interpretations within a 'critical community of enquirers into teaching'. Winter also invokes collaboration as an essential element, but goes further in terms of elucidating the process itself as 'questioning what is taken for granted by reconsidering neglected possibilities' (Winter, 1989: 44) and developing in some detail a set of principles derived from a non-positivist theory of knowledge for understanding and carrying the process through.

My own experience leads me to endorse the shift in emphasis which can be detected in recent thinking on teacher development generally towards reflection on practice as the basis for development, rather than reliance on procedures of 'research' (of whatever complexion). Action research offers one means of enabling this to happen, but once the emphasis shifts from research to reflection it becomes clear that teachers' working contexts offer many more. Incidental observations, examples of children's work, instances of misunderstanding or miscommunication, can all provide a stimulus for reflection, without the constrictions associated with traditional research procedures or the predetermined stages of a cycle of the sort recommended in the action research literature. Most significant of all in terms of the agenda of this chapter, challenges posed by pupils experiencing learning difficulties can create an ever-present opportunity to 'reconsider neglected possibilities', provided the difficulty is treated as an occasion for professional development and learning.

It is important to add that the outcomes of traditional social science can also provide important resources for reflection on practice and, therefore, for professional development. The significant difference is that the research is treated by a 'reflective practitioner' (Schön, 1983a) not as a prescription for practice but as a contribution to the resources upon which teachers can draw in order to generate knowledge and understanding through processes of reflection.

Understanding schools from the inside

In the light of the analysis described in this chapter I have found it essential in my own work to engage in forms of inquiry that are to a large degree located within schools and classrooms, and that require me to work in partnership with teachers. The overall aim is to understand difficulties experienced in schools from the points of view of insiders and to explore together how these can be addressed in ways that attempt to support the growth of those involved. In this concluding section I provide a brief account of one ongoing study which illustrates what this involves and, at the same time, gives a flavour of the potential advantages and difficulties of such ways of working.

During the last few years I have worked with a group of colleagues in a project known as Improving the Quality of Education for All (IQEA). The aim has been to explore how schools can develop in ways that support the learning of all students (Hopkins *et al.*, 1994). I see this as contributing to understandings that are central to the field of special needs in that the concern is with how schools can become more inclusive. As part of this research programme we have recently been scrutinising developments that have occurred in a small group of secondary schools over a period of years, focusing in detail on the perceptions and interpretations of insiders. Our detailed knowledge of these developments represented a starting point for the study but we were keen to enrich our understandings and, indeed, have our outsiders' accounts challenged by accounts constructed from the inside. What we were confident about was that all these schools had gone through a period of at least five years of sustained attempts to bring about organisational restructuring and developments in classroom practice, and that there was evidence that actual changes had resulted.

The aim of the study was, therefore, to find ways of 'digging deeper' into the experiences of the five schools. However, we also wanted to make use of methods of inquiry that would enable us to follow their developing stories over those years from the perspectives of different participants. We were conscious that our own impressions and interpretations had probably been influenced, if not shaped, by the relatively small group of people we normally meet during our school visits. This study would, we hoped, sensitise us much more to different interpretations of the same range of events, as well as giving richer accounts of the social and cultural complexities that influence change efforts. Finally, we were very committed to the use of methodologies that would be helpful to our colleagues within the schools as they continue their improvement efforts. To quote our own rhetoric, we wanted to 'work with the schools, not on them' (Ainscow and Southworth, 1996).

In devising a suitable methodology we were aware of others who have attempted to follow a similar path. For example, Poplin and Weeres (1992) report a study called 'Voices from the Inside', carried out by students, teachers, administrators and parents in four schools. Here the aim was 'to create strategies that allowed everyone at the school site to speak and insured that everyone be heard'. Thus, the research allowed all participants to be both the researchers and, at the same time, the subjects of the research. Since the study began with the assumption that academics had already 'misnamed the problems of schooling', the roles of outsiders had to be rethought so that those on the inside could come to know and articulate the problems they experience. The use of this process was reported to have led to many changes in the schools, although it was also found to be extremely time-consuming.

Two other studies also seemed to be near to what we had in mind. First of all, in their 'School Change Study', Wasley and her colleagues (1996) used what they call 'collaborative inquiry' to study the work of five schools that had taken part in the Coalition of Essential Schools Project for at least four years. Their interest was in how the schools had used the project ideas and values to drive change; how they had sustained and developed the process; and whether the changes made were having an impact on the educational experiences of students. In addition to a large external research team, a teacher in each school was paid to act as a co-ordinator for the study and two students at each school were paid to write weekly journals. The stated aim of all of this was 'to bridge the worlds of practitioners and scholars'. However, whilst there was clearly insider involvement in the research process, the locus of control remained with the outsiders. Finally, Levin's (1993) account of his use of what he calls 'empowerment evaluation' as part of the Accelerated Schools Project seems to have many similarities with our approach, particularly his emphasis on the idea of widespread involvement as a school is 'taking stock'.

In designing our own study we too were keen to develop a way of working that might be characterised as 'collaborative inquiry'. At a meeting of representatives of the five schools a set of ground rules was worked out. In our summary of these ground rules we stated that 'the intention is to produce rich, authentic descriptions of individual "cases" as a basis for subsequent analysis and comparison'. It was agreed that each school would form a team of three to five members of staff to carry out the inquiry. The team was to be reasonably representative of 'different levels and viewpoints in the school'. It was also agreed that each account would attempt to include the full range of views available within and around the school, including, if possible, those of students, parents, LEA officers and governors. In the final accounts it was not necessary to reconcile or judge the value of the various perspectives.

All matters of policy within the study were openly debated with the school teams and on a number of key issues our original plans were subject to substantial modifications. As Wasley *et al.* (1996) found, 'even when a collaboration works, it is full of surprises'. So, for example, we were keen to use a series of research techniques, known as 'Mapping Change in School', developed by members of our group (Ainscow *et al.*, 1995). During discussions, however, the teams, which included the headteachers of four of the schools, resisted our proposals, agreeing only to consider the possible use of some of these approaches if they proved to be relevant at a later stage.

The initial phase of the study, involving the collection of data and the production of the initial accounts, took about a year to complete. During this period the approaches used gradually took on very different forms in each of the schools. Such diversity is, of course, somewhat disturbing to a research team attempting to carry out some form of cross-site comparison. It does, however, seem inevitable in a study that is seeking to allow insiders to conceptualise their own versions of what has occurred. In a more positive sense, of course, these diverse formulations are in themselves interesting in that they provide an illustration of how a school goes about getting things done. Furthermore, they illustrate the dangers of researchers attempting to reduce these differences between schools into some form of cross-site, generalised explanation.

At the time of writing all the draft accounts have been read by the inquiry teams in the five schools and debated during a whole-day meeting in which they all took part. This in itself led to some very interesting discussions, with individuals using the experiences of other schools to reflect on their current understandings of their own situations. It also confirmed our view that, despite the vast differences in the ways in which data were collected, analysed and reported, the case studies provide rich, complex and, at times, challenging accounts, based on an impressive range of perspectives in the schools. In addition, as a result of these experiences we are now considerably clearer about both the advantages and, of course, the difficulties involved in carrying out such a study.

In terms of advantages, from the point of view of the schools there is strong evidence that those involved have found the process to be both informative and stimulating. Specifically they have found that the need to engage with multiple interpretations of events in their schools has forced them to think much more deeply about their own perceptions. Furthermore, exploring ways of valuing points of view that they might more usually ignore, or even oppose, also seems to have stimulated them to consider previously ignored possibilities. At the same time they found the process to be affirming, giving them an opportunity to celebrate many achievements in their schools.

Turning to difficulties, the experience of this study has highlighted some of the problems that can occur when practitioners take on the task of carrying out what might be referred to as insider research. We found, for example, that despite the commitment to reporting a wide range of opinions, some of the accounts revealed little evidence of alternative voices, thus giving the impression of what seemed to us a most unlikely level of consensus. There was also very little evidence presented from students and parents, gaps that seem particularly regrettable when we read the findings of Poplin and Weeres's (1992) study, reported earlier. All of this may explain, in part at least, the comment of one headteacher who, after reading the account of his own school, felt that it failed to reveal the 'soul of the place'.

Finally, there remain concerns about confidentiality. Specifically, as the accounts are read by more people in the schools, can we be sure that the views of certain individuals will remain anonymous? And, in one case in particular, we remain anxious that some of the views expressed could lead to considerable distress to at least one colleague in one of the schools.

From our own point of view, as we have explained elsewhere (West et al., 1997), the accounts lead us to question some of the assumptions we have been making about these particular schools. They also throw up more general questions about processes of school and teacher development that we will want to pursue. In particular, they suggest a series of contradictions which will need to be addressed in our subsequent work.

Coda

The experience of this study, and a number of others that involve the use of a similar orientation, has confirmed my commitment to the argument I have developed in this chapter for a much greater emphasis on practitioner research in the special needs field. Specifically it leads me to believe that greater understanding of how educational contexts can be developed in order to foster the learning of all children is most likely to emerge from studies in which outsiders, such as myself, work alongside teachers as they attempt to determine 'what works in theory'. As we have seen, however, such an orientation is fraught with difficulties. On the other hand, the potential benefits are enormous, not least in that the understandings gained may have an immediate impact on the development of thinking and practice.

3

PERMISSION TO SPEAK?

Theorising special education inside the classroom

Julie Allan, Sally Brown and Sheila Riddell

Introduction

We have reached a crisis in special education where theorising has at best proved inadequate for understanding individuals' experiences and at worst has been alienating because it has made them, not participating subjects, but objects upon which research is done. Researchers seem unable to shake off the 'methodological individualism' inherent in positivist social research (Oliver, 1992a: 107) and consequently, there have been many calls over the last fifteen years or so for research in special education which is more sensitive to the experience of learning difficulties (Schindele, 1985; Clough and Barton, 1995).

In this chapter we examine two main strands of theorising about special educational needs and disability – social constructionist and social creationist perspectives – and question their contribution to understanding the experiences of disabled people. We also consider how current market-led educational policies have reinforced individualistic, rather than social, theoretical models. Our sense of 'theoretical crisis' is fuelled by objections from disabled people to researchers' alienating practices. It is clear that researchers need to establish theoretical perspectives which do more than pay lip service to the involvement of disabled people and must, as Oliver (1992a) contends, change the social relations of research production. We offer an alternative perspective for theorising children's experiences of special education provision, which uses Foucault's 'box of tools' (Foucault, 1977a: 205) to analyse discourses, and, finally, we explore the implications of an approach of this kind for research and practice in special education.

Theorising special education from the outside

Two polarised models have tended to predominate theorising within special education and disability. An individualistic model attributes difficulties to *within child* factors and has tended to be associated with medical and charity discourses. A social model, on the other hand, looks for features *outside* the child and reflects discourses on rights (although medical and charity discourses can undermine these). Individual and social models of disability might also be characterised as 'personal troubles' or 'public issues' (Wright Mills, 1970; Borsay, 1986).

Several writers (e.g. Oliver, 1988; Barton, 1993a) consider special education theorising to have become more advanced in recent years. They argue that individualistic and deficit views of disability (expressed in the language of categories and needs) have been criticised and analysed in terms of 'power, control and vested interests' (Barton, 1993a: 236) and have given way to social theoretical models, such as social constructionism and social creationism. Rights discourses, characterised by 'self reliance, independence and consumer wants (rather than needs)' (Fulcher, 1989), more obviously pervade the latter of these. Others (e.g. Reindal, 1995) have questioned whether these perspectives have served the interests of disabled people or enhanced understanding of their experiences. A further group of commentators (e.g. Riddell, 1996) have suggested that the post-Warnock era has been marked by a reversal from social towards individualistic theories of disability, with, for example, demands for statements or records of needs and representations from voluntary organisations invoking categorisation. The social constructionist and the social creationist perspectives are examined more fully below, before considering the possibility that theorising is returning to a more individual model.

Social constructionist perspective

A social constructionist view dismisses individualist notions of disability and attributes the causes to environmental factors, including the teaching approaches used and the attitudes of those who interact with the child. Within this perspective, symbolic interactionists (e.g. Goffman, 1963) examine how individuals try to cope with their labels and control the information the public receives about them through strategies such as 'passing' as normal. Abberley (1993) contends that whilst this is helpful in looking beyond the child, we are left with a sense that 'shameful difference' is inevitable.

Social constructionists aim to discourage the use of all labelling or categorisation (a major criticism of individualistic models). However, the anti-labelling stance of some social constructionists has been criticised by Soder as dangerous:

> This well meaning denial of the problems of disabled people is developing as a professional ideology in a time when service structures are undergoing changes that in themselves tend to make the needs of disabled persons invisible. Segregation is abolished and integration, deinstitutionalisation and decentralisation is being implemented. The driving forces behind this development are twofold. First there is the well intentioned ideological commitment: not to label and treat sepa-

rately, but to integrate. Second the financial crisis of the state that motivates the search for less expensive alternatives.

(Soder, 1989: 255)

Booth (1991), in a now legendary public argument in the *European Journal of Special Needs Education*, accused Soder of misrepresenting anti-labelling as an attempt to deny the reality of disability. Oliver (1992b) attributed this dispute to onanism, rather than to a genuine commitment to disabled people. Abberley argues that disabled people are disadvantaged by the failure to recognise their 'special, *abnormal* requirements' (Abberley, 1993: 111), while Oliver is highly critical of a 'linguistic attempt to deny the reality of disability' by referring to disabled people as 'people with disabilities' (Oliver, 1992b: 21).

Social creationist perspective

Abberley (1993) and others (e.g. Fulcher, 1989; Oliver, 1990b) advocate an alternative perspective, which they define as a social creationist:

> The essential difference between a social constructionist and a social creationist view of disability centres on where the 'problem' is actually located. Both have begun to move away from the core ideology of individualism. The social constructionist view sees the problem as being located within the minds of able-bodied people, whether individually (prejudice) or collectively, through the manifestation of hostile social attitudes and the enactment of social policies based upon a tragic view of disability. The social creationist view, however, sees the problem as located within the institutionalised practices of society.
>
> (Oliver, 1990b: 82–3)

A social creationist perspective views disability as oppression and takes account of the material, environmental, social and psychological disadvantage experienced by disabled people. The aim, according to Abberley, is to connect 'the common features of economic, social and psychological disadvantage with an understanding of the material basis of these disadvantages and the ideologies which propagate and reproduce them' (Abberley, 1993: 244).

Whilst condemning the social production of impairment, the social creationist perspective asserts the value of disabled living and demands 'that difference not be merely tolerated and accepted but that it is positively valued and celebrated' (Oliver, 1992b: 25). It is overtly political, demanding changes in state and welfare provision to improve the material conditions for disabled people.

The rights of disabled people to articulate their wants rather than needs is also a fundamental part of the social creationist perspective. There is, however, a plurality of voices among the disabled and able bodied and there is no guarantee that a social creationist view will allow all of them, particularly the least articulate and powerful, to be heard. It may not be possible or appropriate to establish a single theory of special educational needs which achieves the aims cited by Abberley (op. cit.) for all disabled people and Corbett (1993) warns against merely replacing one form of dominant discourse with another.

The extent to which this perspective has actually challenged the oppression of disabled people has been questioned by some writers. Jenkins (1991), for example, criticises social creationists as reductionists who fail to recognise disability as a social class in its own right. This, argues, Fulcher (1989), is insufficient to account for oppression. Reindal (1995) goes further to suggest that this perspective could itself be oppressive since, taken to its extreme, 'prevention of impairments' might imply an eradication of people born with impairments (e.g. through gene therapy or abortion).

Social constructionist and social creationist perspectives, then, have been criticised for failing to improve our understanding of the experiences of disabled people and their progressiveness (in terms of tackling oppression) has been questioned. Finkelstein prefers not to make these distinctions within the 'social model' (Finkelstein, 1996: 1), but notes the emergence of two versions: active and passive. The former focuses on the removal of disabling barriers created by a world designed for able-bodied living. The latter, of which he is fiercely critical, is concerned with the way disabled people reflect upon, and react to, disabling barriers. Finkelstein argues that 'focusing on experiences rather than disability is the surest way to return to the confusion between impairment and disability that bedevilled the *medical model*' (ibid.: 3; original emphasis). Where these experiences are treated in an essentialist way (by giving them their own external reality), he has a point, but this can be avoided. A further challenge to social models of theorising comes from the current political climate in which special educational needs provision operates.

The post-Warnock era: back to individualism?

Warnock has entered the market place (Riddell and Brown, 1994), and as Barton (1993b) notes, competition and choice are the slogans for the 1990s. Government policies, such as the delegation of resources, opting out, the publication of exam results and local government reorganisation, seek to reward individual success (of schools and pupils) and to punish the losers. The impact of these policies on children with special educational needs has clearly been devastating, leading, for example, to high exclusion rates of children with emotional and behavioural difficulties (EBD) (Pyke, 1992) or a reconstruction of such children as 'disturbed' (Armstrong and Galloway, 1994: 179). Furthermore, there is little doubt that the huge increases in recording and statementing reflect a desire to protect the interests of vulnerable children by ensuring their needs are recognised. At the same time as government policies undermine justice and equality (Barton, 1993b) the drive for recording and statementing reinforces individualistic models of disability.

Parents are also instrumental in reinforcing individualistic models of disability. They may well find the assessment of their child's special educational needs discomfiting since it is primarily a political and social process (Galloway et al., 1994). As members of voluntary organisations, however, parents are able to exert considerable influence over local authorities. These organisations tend to represent parents of children within particular categories, such as autism, Down's Syndrome or deafness, and their advocacy seldom reaches beyond, for example, to pupils within other categories. Individual parents may choose to take on a local authority over the assessment, placement or resourcing of their child. These parents are unlikely (understandably) to be sympathetic to the needs of other pupils in their quest for recognition of their case. There is also a growth of parents who are searching for acknowledgement among professionals that their child has a particular problem hitherto unidentified. Success for these parents is marked by an acceptance that their child has dyslexia (rather than having problems with reading), or has dyspraxia (and is not clumsy) or has an attention deficit disorder (instead of being hyperactive). Recognition of these may well bring additional resources; it certainly reinforces individualism.

Theories in crisis? Or are the researchers to blame?

Theorising in special educational needs could be considered to be in crisis in three respects. First, its social perspectives have done little to understand the experiences of individuals. A second problem is political and relates to the dominance of the consumer culture within education (Riddell and Brown, 1994). This seems to be encouraging a return to individualistic models of special educational needs and the reinforcement of deficits or categories. The third and perhaps most serious element of this crisis concerns researchers, whose work has proved 'alienating' (Oliver, 1992a). Disabled people, in this context, have been treated as objects (ibid.) and Barton (1993a) notes the increasing anger among disabled people over disabling practices (e.g. Morris, 1991; Finkelstein, 1993). Writers such as Finkelstein (1980) have suggested a principle of no participation (in research) without representation, while others (e.g. Oliver, 1992b) have questioned whether the able bodied should be researching or theorising about disabled people's lives at all.

One response to this crisis from the researchers could be to alter radically the social relations within which they operate:

> Disability research should not be seen as a set of technical, objective procedures carried out by experts but part of the struggle by disabled people to challenge the oppression they currently experience in their daily lives. Hence the major issue on the research agenda for the 1990s should be: do researchers wish to join with disabled people and use their expertise and skills in their struggles against oppression or do they

wish to continue to use these skills and expertise ways which disabled people find oppressive?

(Oliver, 1992a: 102)

A new approach, according to Oliver, would be centred on principles of reciprocity, gain and empowerment. Shakespeare (1996), however, points out that 'while it is possible to make the research process more balanced, grandiose claims for its revolutionary potential seem . . . over-optimistic' (Shakespeare, 1996: 118). What is also required (perhaps before research can contribute to emancipatory knowledge) is scrutiny of the power and knowledge relations within which identities and experiences are constructed and a surveying of the 'closure in our own thinking' (Roth, 1992). Foucault's contribution to this process is discussed below.

Foucault's 'box of tools'

A Foucauldian perspective allows for an analysis of the ways in which disabled identities and experiences are constructed. At the same time, however, it avoids viewing these experiences as 'essences', with their own external reality, which threatens to return to 'a previously discredited and sterile approach to understanding and changing the world *out there* that is disabling' (Finkelstein, 1996: 3; original emphasis). Foucault demonstrates how individuals are constructed as social subjects, knowable through disciplines and discourses. He offers a methodology or a 'box of tools' (Foucault, 1977a: 205), which makes it possible to analyse both the official discourses on special educational needs and those operating within schools and classrooms (Allan, 1996).

Foucault demonstrates how discourses (both formal and informal) construct individuals as subjects in two senses: as subject to someone else, through control and restraint and as a subject tied to their own identity by their self-knowledge. 'Both meanings suggest a form of power which subjugates and makes subject to' (Foucault, 1982: 212). Embedded within discourses are, according to Foucault, complex power/knowledge relationships and 'disciplinary techniques', for example, 'the medical gaze' which serves to construct the patient or the madman. To this we can easily add the child with special educational needs.

Techniques of surveillance are so sophisticated, argues Foucault, that 'inspection functions ceaselessly. The gaze is everywhere' (1977b: 195). Foucault identifies three mechanisms of surveillance.

Hierarchical observation 'constructs a perfect gaze, making it possible to see everything perfectly' (Foucault, 1977b: 173). Children with special educational needs are placed under constant surveillance, as are those entrusted with their supervision. Auxiliaries, teachers, specialists, headteachers and parents are all caught within the network of the gaze. Surveillance of pupils with special educational needs enables professionals to show concern for their welfare and acquire knowledge about their disability and the process they are making:

This form of power applies itself to immediate everyday life which categorises the individual, marks him by his own individuality, attaches him to his own identity, imposes a law of truth on him which he must recognise and which others have to recognise in him. It is a form of power which makes individuals subjects.

(Foucault, 1982: 212)

Normalising judgements enable professionals to distinguish between children with special educational needs and the generality of pupils. The 'cut-off' point, where a child is or is not deemed to require a record of needs or a statement, is in no sense clearly defined, however, and variations in levels of recording and statementing have been a source of concern to administrators and others. Some children who are not recorded, but who are seen as having special educational needs by parents or professionals, are thought to be disadvantaged by not having a label which distinguishes them clearly from normal pupils. In a climate of resource constraints, distance from the norm has become valued.

The multidisciplinary assessment or *examination*, according to Foucault, 'establishes over individuals a visibility through which one differentiates them and judges them' (Foucault, 1977b: 184). It holds individuals in a 'mechanism of objectification' (ibid.: 187), classifies them and establishes them (and their parents) as 'cases', which may require to be 'trained or corrected, classified, normalised, excluded etc.' (ibid.: 191).

Following the assessment, the child with special educational needs is marked out for perpetual surveillance throughout the remainder of his or her school career and beyond. Parents and professionals also come under scrutiny as part of the continuous review of the recorded child's needs. All are caught by a gaze which is 'always receptive to the deviant' (Foucault, 1976: 89) and the very existence of 'abnormalities' such as special educational needs provides a further rationale for surveillance of the general population (Ryan, 1991).

Foucault's 'box of tools' lets us examine the complex discourses operating within special education. Archaeology, which characterised much of Foucault's earlier work (e.g. 1967, 1973), facilitates a 'descriptive' account of discourses, essentially a history of statements that stood for the truth (Davidson, 1986). This requires illumination of the discontinuities and oppositions within the special education discourses. Genealogy (Foucault, 1976, 1977) focuses on power/knowledge relations within institutions and reflects a shift of Foucault's interests from discourses to 'discursive practices' and from a macro- to a micro-level of analysis. Both archaeology and genealogy are concerned with the limits and conditions of discourses but the latter takes into account political and economic concerns (Shumway, 1989). The final dimension of his work, ethics (e.g. Foucault, 1987, 1988), is concerned with individual agency and the 'technologies of the self' (1988: 18), which inform choices and action.

Foucault in the classroom

Discourse analysis has now become a respectable occupation which has brought fresh political insights (Fairclough, 1994; Maclure, 1994). However, this has largely been confined to macro or formal discourses. Foucault argues that in order to study power, it is necessary also to look at discursive practices within institutions and he calls for an analysis of the 'micro-physics of power' (Foucault, 1977b: 29). It is only by searching for 'points of resistance', he contends, that power can be discerned (Foucault, 1976: 95). The difficulty for researchers is that Foucault left little guidance on how this might be achieved. His own theorising has been criticised for remaining at a global level, although Fairclough (1992) points out that he does claim to be talking about practice.

A Foucauldian analysis of special education needs to examine both formal and informal discourses on special educational needs. It entails understanding how children's identities and experiences are constructed both at an official level, in policy statements and in records of needs or statements, and through their daily encounters with teachers and peers. As Foucault contends, however, these power/knowledge relations can only be observed at their points of resistance. The researcher, therefore, needs to look for evidence of individuals challenging identities or opting for alternative experiences. The following example (Allan, 1995) illustrates the kind of analysis of the informal discourses which is possible within a Foucauldian framework.

Seventeen-year-old Raschida and fifteen-year-old Laura, both of whom were visually impaired, attended the same mainstream secondary school. Accounts from their peers described how they 'felt sorry' for Raschida and Laura, yet were afraid of offending them:

> Sometimes I don't like to, I'd feel as if I'd patronise her by saying 'here's a seat over here' but at the same time I'm trying to help her. I just don't know what to do sometimes . . . I'm afraid, afraid I'm doing that sometimes, but I don't mean to. I'm just trying to, like, go out my way to help her a wee bit.
>
> (Mainstream pupil)

The mainstream pupils' main tactic was to try to pretend all was normal, avoiding all reference to blindness or visual metaphors. Occasionally, however, they tripped themselves up and Raschida said their efforts reminded her of the *Fawlty Towers* sketch in which Basil is told not to mention 'the war' to a party of Germans, but ends up goose stepping before them.

Raschida and Laura, for their part, shunned all visual symbols of their impairment, refusing to undergo rehabilitation training on the school grounds, or 'losing' a long cane (and enjoying the wrath of the specialist teachers). Laura and Raschida knew their way around the school as well as any sighted person. The two girls appeared to have resisted successfully an identification as disabled in which they were incapable or deserving of pity. Yet, this process appeared to be highly uncertain and incomplete, placing them under constant scrutiny: 'What is interrogated is not simply the image of the person, but the discursive and disciplinary place from which questions of identity are strategically and institutionally posed' (Bhabha, 1994: 47).

In response, Raschida and Laura had acquired a high level of self-awareness, patrolling what Goffman calls the Umwelt, 'the region around a person from which the signs for alarm can come' (Goffman, 1971: 297). These signs might stem from their own transgressions (which threatened to reinforce disabled identities) or from the discourses of others (including the embarrassed silences). The girls had to be ready to repair such damage, which they often did with only partial success:

> There was one time when I went out for a meal with my mum and dad and my sister and instead of pouring vinegar on my chips I actually poured the water from the flower vase on my chips. I could hear everyone stop eating and they were all looking at me, thinking 'what a shame', I could tell. I just wanted to disappear. The only thing I could do was burst out laughing then everyone else did as well.
>
> (Laura)

Laura said she could 'feel' the looks which spoke to her of pity and embarrassment. She erased this by laughing aloud, which enabled others to join her. However, this erasure was incomplete. She left her parents and friends with an estimate of her as heroic, because of her ability to laugh at herself. As Shapiro (1993) notes, this construction of individuals as inspirational is just as oppressive or disabling as one depicting them as objects of pity.

This example is intended to offer a brief illustration of a Foucauldian analysis. It shifts from viewing individuals as having a fixed identity or of being included or excluded and explores instead the oscillations within the pupils' informal discourses. This disturbs the 'binarism', which is characteristic of accounts of special education (e.g. integration/segregation; ordinary/special) and which constructs disabled people as 'the undesirable half of a binary pair' (Marks, 1994: 730). It also allows for the possibility of individual agency or of 'technologies of the self' (Foucault, 1988: 18).

A Foucauldian perspective, then, allows for an exploration of 'the space between' these binary divisions, where there is both an attempt to subjectify children with special educational needs *and* a deliberate failure by the pupils to return the identificatory gaze. It posits the subject as 'both autonomous and disciplined, both actively self-forming and passively self-constructed' (Schrift, 1995: 34) and challenges those who have criticised Foucault on the grounds of pessimism (e.g. Rorty, 1990; Fairclough, 1992), since it offers scope for social change. The response, according to Foucault, is to 'give one's self the rules of law, the techniques of management, and also the ethics, the ethos, the practice of self, which would allow these games of power to be played with a minimum of domination' (Foucault, 1987: 129). Schrift reminds us, however, that we need to work 'to tilt the balance of power towards the forces of production rather than those of repression' (Schrift, 1995: 34).

Implications for research and practice

A Foucauldian perspective focuses on discourses at all levels within special education:

> If we want to politicise the concept of disability, that is to interrogate the norms for responsibility, authority and power embedded in the discourses that contain it, we must reflect on the ways that disability is constituted in utterances.
>
> (Shapiro, 1981: 86–7)

Above all, the voices of pupils with special educational needs and their mainstream peers are foregrounded. These are normally silenced by professional discourses and some effort is required to incite the pupils to speak. The researcher needs to find ways of distancing him-/herself from the professional discourses operating within the school without alienating teachers and others. At the same time, it is important to avoid essentialising the pupils' experiences, by treating them as if they have their own external reality. They are always embedded in the 'power/knowledge knot', which is not supposed to be unravelled (Simons, 1995: 27).

Policy statements are not read from a technical empiricist perspective, as expressions of intent (Codd, 1994). Rather, alternative narratives have to be constructed and techniques such as reversal (Simons, 1995) involve exploring the implications of a different set of outcomes to those claimed in official discourses. Policies are viewed in this context as instruments of power/knowledge relations through which the identities and experiences of children with special educational needs are constructed.

The kind of practice implied by a Foucauldian perspective is one which centres discourses, particularly those of the mainstream pupils, and allows them to explore the ambivalences and contradictions in their understanding of disability and their relationships with pupils with special educational needs. It acknowledges the important role of mainstream pupils in constructing the identities and experiences of pupils with special educational needs, but does not attempt to prescribe how they should behave towards them, since that would be futile. As far as the pupils with special educational needs are concerned, a Foucauldian perspective reveals them to be active, rather than passive, subjects, constructing their own identities and experiences. Discussions with the pupils which focused on this process as well as on issues of gender and sexuality could encourage positive forms of the 'technologies of the self' (Foucault, 1988: 18).

Conclusion

The limited success of social theoretical models of theorising in understanding the experiences of disabled people makes it vital that we explore new ways of theorising special education. As Shakespeare points out, however, 'this is not the same as offering researchers *carte blanche* to parasitise disabled people's experience and develop careers on the back of disabled people's lives' (Shakespeare, 1996: 118). It is particularly important for researchers to operate reflexively and to avoid practices which merely reinforce a sense among disabled people that they are merely objects of interest.

Researchers need to work hard to demonstrate that they are committed to improving the lives of disabled people. As Barton and Clough (1995) argue, they also need to use their knowledge, skills and positions of privilege to challenge the oppression experienced by disabled people. If they succeed, there may be no need to debate whether able-bodied researchers have any right to be involved in theorising special education; if they don't, they may well be shown the door.

4

FROM THEORY TO PRACTICE

Special education and the social relations of
academic production

Derrick Armstrong, Felicity Armstrong and Len Barton

Starting out: placing theory within the context of social and political struggles

The suggestion that a theory of special education is 'needed' should not strike us as all that surprising. If nothing else, it does give us academics some self-legiti-mating acts to indulge ourselves in. Of course, it might also be argued that there is a pressing need for a theory of special education, because in recent years the education system of the UK has changed dramatically. In addition, there is evidence that increasing numbers of children are being excluded from schools, either because of 'troublesome behaviour' (Bourne *et al.*, 1994; Hayden, 1996; Parsons *et al.*, 1995) or because they have been identified as having special educational needs and consequently 'in need' of specialised provision, often outside the mainstream sector (Norwich, 1994). In this context 'theory' may have some explanatory value, yet, as the editors of this volume acknowledge, it is far from clear what a theory of special education should look like, or why it should make any difference to anything if one was developed.

The central contention of our chapter, therefore, is that research is itself a form of social engagement, it involves the construction of experience and as such neces-sarily constitutes a form of theorising that is informed by a whole set of assumptions and experiences which contextualise the nature of its critique and therefore its stance in relation to political action. In our own work this has led us to challenge the atheoretical assumptions that characterise much of the research in special education which is loosely and perhaps misleadingly centred upon unexpli-cated and unproblematised humanitarian values such as 'care', 'equal opportunities', 'access', 'school improvement'. On the other hand, we have become increasingly aware of the institutional pressures academics work under and how these operate structurally to inhibit critique by separating researchers from the subjects of inquiry, which can lead to a separation of theory and research.

We have attempted to examine some of the issues about our own practice as researchers in order to understand more fully the nature and role of theory in our work. In doing so we have explored and tried to make explicit some of the values upon which our own social practice is based. We see theory as a part of social practice and it is therefore important to understand the relationships which inform that practice and the ways in which this practice is contested. This necessitates reflecting on our values and identities as revealed through an analysis of our own professional practice as teachers and researchers. We have begun this process through collaborating in the production of this chapter.

The social relations of academic production in theory and research: some personal reflections

A useful starting point for a discussion of the relationship between theory and research as social practice might be to look at our own experience in writing this chapter. To say that it has been challenging and difficult would be an understatement. It has certainly stimulated serious personal and collective reflection and critique. It has also provided an interesting, and sometimes idealised, backdrop to some of the more lively and contentious debates we have had about our working relationships and practices.

Although our backgrounds are very different we do have much in common both in respect of the interests and the values we bring to our work. Writing this chapter has provided an opportunity for us to explore collectively the role and significance of personal biography in our work. In writing this chapter we have encountered differences between us that we had not previously been aware of. It has also proved to be a welcome opportunity to consider the differences between us at a time when the climate of higher education is encouraging individualistic and instrumentalist competition rather than collaboration and collegiality whilst celebrating diversity. Many of the issues that have been raised in our own discussions are a long way from being resolved within our group. Yet one of the most important outcomes of this process for us has been the valuable discussions we have had and the commitment with which we have agreed to pursue them further.

We have all previously worked as members of collaborative research and teaching groups and experienced a wide variety of ways of working collaboratively. Collaboration is a difficult process. A common feature of our experience has been the way collaboration can generate conflict as well as provide challenge. Working together requires trust and respect for colleagues particularly with regard to the differences which can develop out of collaboration. However, collaboration can also raise difficult questions about, as well as conflicts over, the way power is exercised in relationships. In working together we have begun to question the ways in which power is exercised through the informal as well as the formal relationships between us. This has not been easy and there remain unresolved issues regarding ways in which unequal power relationships are perpetuated and become disabling within the group. Thus, collaboration has raised serious implications for us.

Sometimes together and sometimes separately in quite different ways we have attempted to challenge the individualistic assumptions characteristic of much academic work. On other occasions we have failed to confront these assumptions adequately and there have been times when they have actually been reinforced by our own actions and words. We believe that it is important to encourage and celebrate co-operation in our work and especially to encourage the qualities essential to an enabling environment – openness, a willingness to listen to others, and respect for differences. Yet, such sentiments do not necessarily place us in a better position to challenge similar individualistic and disabling assumptions that seem to us to underpin the institutional role of special education and within which dominant discourses of disability are located. What our reflections have done, however, is to force us to recognise that we do not stand outside of those disabling discourses as commentators; they arise and are contested in our own personal and professional lives as well as in the lives of those with whom we engage through our writing and research.

In talking together about the nature and development of theory in relation to systems of special education it is important to contextualise such a discussion by considering why we are asking the questions that we do. The reason why one set of questions rather than another are chosen for discussion itself raises important issues. What questions are put aside and why? What is it about the type of forum in which certain questions are raised that leads to the belief that they are appropriate and important questions? By asking 'Who is this for?' we are forced to address other questions; for instance: 'Who are the "we"?', 'Who does the notion of "we" exclude and what are the implications of that exclusion?' How are our lives as academics related to the lives of the people we are 'theorising' about and what does this relationship entail for both groups? To what extent, for instance, does theory, when divorced from the practical politics of resistance to disabling identities, reinforce those identities and operate as part of a system of control and social reproduction?

Mike Oliver has argued that 'The very idea that small groups of "experts" can get together and set a research agenda for disability is . . . fundamentally flawed' (Oliver, 1992a: 102). Yet:

> The social relations of research production provide the structure within which research is undertaken. These social relations are built upon a firm distinction between the researcher and the researched: upon a belief that it is the researchers who have specialist knowledge and skills: and that it is they who should decide what topics should be researched and be in control of the whole process of research production.
>
> (ibid.: 102)

In the same article he goes on to argue that

the major issue on the research agenda for the 1990s should be: do researchers wish to join with disabled people and use their expertise and skills in their struggle against oppression or do they wish to continue to use these skills and expertise in ways which disabled people find oppressive?

(ibid.: 112)

Although we agree with Oliver that the problem is fundamentally political and cannot be reduced to narrow methodological or technical issues, our own view is that a critique of the social relations of academic production must be directed not only against methodological individualism but must also address itself to the relations of commodity production within the institutions of higher education and the construction of alienation in the lived experience of those who work in these institutions.

It is important to us therefore that we take responsibility for identifying and challenging our own discriminatory and disabling practice in different roles, contexts and arenas. What assumptions do we convey through the language we use, the questions we ask, the interpretations we make and the institutional practices we do not challenge? For instance, we need to examine why, when we are writing about inclusion and discrimination, there are so few disabled people and black people working in our departments, so few women in positions of authority. Who do we include and exclude when we talk about 'disabled people' or about 'children with special educational needs'?

The growth of academic 'specialisms', together with the fragmentation of 'knowledge' that this entails, has important implications for the subjects of inquiry who are 'appropriated' by these disciplines. Not least, it raises issues about the relationship between our own discourses and social practices as researchers and the fragmentation of the experience of the subjects of our inquiry. The post-modern construction of difference may be as much about academic professionalism, and the interprofessional rivalries over ownership of clients that this gives rise to, as it is about anything else. Yet a consequence of this is that commonalities in the nature of oppression and the way it is experienced in people's lives are hidden under the cloak of an impenetrable individualisation of difference. The anti-intellectualism of a position that suggests an incommensurability between different experiences of the social world in particular raises serious issues about the possibilities for change. The question we must ask ourselves is: What are the implications of this fragmentation into specialist knowledges for the way in which the experiences and interests of groups of people are represented and internalised through the research process? The specific forms of these experiences may be very different but it is important to understand both how and why these differences are theorised in ways that either emphasise individual experiences of marginality and exclusion or emphasise the potential solidarities implicit between those with different experiences of marginality and exclusion.

35

Contesting power: the limits of a critique of methodological individualism

It is fairly commonplace to find researchers talking about the relationship between themselves and the subjects of their research as if the problems raised by this relationship are entirely methodological. For some, the primary concern is to minimise the extent of 'contamination' of the data by the researcher. The solutions proposed for dealing with the methodological problem of 'contamination' are often ones that seek to disembody the researcher from her or his own biography. Yet, as Goodley (1996) has argued in relation to researchers working with people with learning difficulties, 'contamination' of informants' stories is an inevitable part of the research process and is especially so when the researcher writes. Despite this, some accounts of the research process are written in ways that simply assume the concept of 'neutrality', to have meaning independently of the personal and social biographies of researchers and their relationship to the lives of the subjects of research. However, if there are grounds for believing contamination cannot be prevented and that the lived experience of informants is mediated through the biography of the researcher, then it becomes necessary to develop new theoretical understandings of the relationship between the researcher and those people who are the subjects of inquiry. In particular, how are research and its outcomes constituted both within and as social practice?

There are many academics, and indeed academic traditions such as phenomenology, that recognise the significance of personal biography in relation to the research process. For instance, ethnographers sometimes argue that the relationship of researcher to the subjects of inquiry must be seen in terms of the specific interactions and the negotiation of shared meanings within the research setting itself. Yet who writes about these 'shared' meanings and through whom is the lived experience of the subjects of research articulated? Where this story is told by the researcher, it is as much an exploration of the researcher's 'self' as of anything else (Clough and Barton, 1995). However, this has the contradictory outcome that in the elicitation of stories the researcher gives 'voice' to informants whilst at the same time becoming part of a process of disempowerment (Bhavnani, 1990). The story that is told is mediated through the personal values and experiences of the researcher and in this way becomes a story of the researcher's own life. The informant is alienated from his or her own biography to the extent that it is appropriated by the researcher.

How one should theorise the relationship of the researcher to the subjects of inquiry remains an important concern. As Jagger (1983) argues, every method entails at least an implicit commitment to a certain theoretical understanding of the social world. This, more than anything else, emphasises the importance of recognising and listening to the voices of children and adults who have experienced institutionalised discrimination. It is essential that researchers recognise the 'voice' of those who encounter and confront discriminatory practices in their lives and in so doing also acknowledge the ways in which people contribute to the development of ideas through their engagement in critical encounters with discriminatory and divisive social institutions. By looking at how institutionalised discrimination and oppression operate through these systems and through other social institutions, hopefully we can begin to confront the connectedness of the forms of oppression and exclusion which people experience in different aspects of their lives.

The issues that have been raised so far are important, but it is also crucial that we explore them in the institutional context of academic/research activity as well as in a moral and political context. Most importantly, there is more to this than methodology, even a methodology informed by a social and political consciousness. If this were merely a methodological issue, then the sort of research we do would be informed solely by the sort of moral and political choices that we make. However, this implies a form of methodological individualism in which attention is focused primarily upon the interpersonal negotiations between researcher and informant and the values that underpin those negotiations without regard to the power that is exercised in these negotiations, its purposes and outcomes. This focus is one that may inhibit consideration of the different ways in which participants in these negotiations are situated by roles that are contextually specific and structurally constructed. Exploration of these aspects of the activity of research raises questions about the operation of research as a professional activity within the context of institutionally defined goals and practices and about how professional identity is related to the social identities of disabled people.

Research and the social relations of academic production

It would be difficult for anyone working in British higher education today to be unaffected by the competitive climate which is so pervasive. The prevailing ideology of 'marketisation' is likely to undermine attempts at collaboration within and between different institutions. We would argue that it has also been at least partly responsible for raising even higher the barriers that stand between academics in the social sciences and the subjects of their inquiry. The instrumental character of this ideology has had a powerful influence over our daily lives as workers in education. In addition to increasing teaching and administrative loads we are constantly under pressure to produce publications and to obtain research funding. This has led to a growing commodification of knowledge in which academic products (on the one hand, students and on the other hand, research outcomes) are turned into exchange value in the market place.

The pressures we experience in our professional role as academics are both institutional and personal. At an institutional level our continued employment is often made dependent upon the achievement of identifiable 'worthwhile' outcomes. At a personal level we are increasingly struggling against the effects of operating within a regime of competitiveness which not only works to isolate us from colleagues in other institutions but also from colleagues in our own departments. Academic engagement with colleagues, particularly with those in other institutions, is often forced by these demands into channels which encourage 'contrived collegiality' (Hargreaves, A., 1994).

Working with people outside of these institutions, people who do not share and may even actively resist the institutional values and goals of higher education, is something that is not only difficult but actually demands some courage on the part of academics because it involves us in a practical critique of the goals towards which our working practices are framed institutionally. Such a critique can very easily bring us into conflict with our employers. It would certainly be a brave academic who declared her-/himself unwilling to seek research funding and unwilling to publish in academic journals on the ground that such work only panders to academic professionalism and does not serve the interests of disabled people. It is important for academics to examine the conditions under which such conflicts may be produced.

In modern societies groups who specialise in the production of knowledge become increasingly important, in part because of the expanding role which such knowledge production plays in industrial development but also because of the ways in which forms of knowledge contribute to the reproduction and control of social power in those societies (Weber, 1948). Power not only resides in these 'knowledge professions' in their own right but is mediated through the interests of those who control and benefit from the services provided (Johnson, 1972). In modern societies this has increasingly become the state and is evidenced, for instance, by the ideological and material centralisation of knowledge production under the control of the state through funding arrangements and mechanisms of accountability. Ironically, the marketisation of education alongside the centralisation of the school curriculum, enforced and maintained through the dominant role of particular social and political interests within the state apparatus, has probably had a far greater effect on the construction of intellectual orthodoxy than any other educational reform this century. This is not to suggest that the interests represented in the state are homogeneous, nor that institutions of the state simply reflect the interests of dominant social groups. The point is that the state is a site of conflict between different interest groups but it also represents the form taken by a consensus that is constantly being renegotiated. In so far as this consensus is one which sustains the power of dominant groups, it is a hegemonic consensus (Apple, 1982).

The 'professionalisation' of certain occupational groups is an essential feature of the construction of a hegemonic consensus in modern societies. In relation to higher education we see this professionalisation occurring in the transformation of the system from an elite into a mass system. The state becomes the principal client of academics, not because it is their ultimate paymaster but because the state now specifies through funding systems and quality assessment the nature of services to be provided by professionals. In addition, the state acts as a mediator between the professions and their clients, defining who those clients should be and how they should be helped. Through this process of mediation certain occupational groups are incorporated into the decision-making machinery of the state, which in turn brings about the dependence of these groups upon the state.

On the one hand, professionals, including academics, derive their power from their position within the bureaucracy of the state and in consequence professional interests are tied up with the interests of the state. On the other hand, these interests are constantly being contested both within the institutions of the state and between the state and those whose interests are unrepresented and therefore the nature of professional interests are continually being redefined by, and in relation to, the forms of social and political practice in which they are situated. This may lead to an increasing demarcation of professional areas of responsibility, authority, expertise and control (as, for instance, suggested by recent proposals discussed within the British Educational Research Association for a register of 'chartered' educational researchers (Deem, 1996)). It may also create conditions in which alliances can be built between professionals and social groups whose interests are unrepresented or opposed by the state.

Theorising special education

The exploration and critique of how the processes of academic research and writing are affected by the professional role of academics and by the production of knowledge as a commodity is something that we feel should be undertaken. It is important to understand the hegemonic character of both 'inclusion' and 'exclusion' in different contexts and how social practices based on these ideas are arrived at, in part at least, through the processes by which knowledge is produced as a commodity. This involves us asking not only how the subjects of research stand as commodities in relation to the process of social production, but also how researchers reproduce the social identities of their research subjects as commodities through the research process. This is not a simple matter of ethics, a question in Howard Becker's (1963) words of 'where do we stand?', but a matter of social and political analysis in which the point of departure lies in the social relations of production. Not only are the subjects of research alienated by the appropriation of their lives taking place through the research process, but researchers are themselves alienated to the extent that their professional role, and the relations of research production that frame this role, transform the outcomes of the research process into commodities separated from any social value.

For the academic interested in issues of disability and/or special education it is important to understand how the relations of academic production can operate to limit the effectiveness of any critique. The relations of academic production create constraints which encourage a separation of the researcher from the subjects of inquiry which in turn may lead to the exploitation and devaluation of the latter by the former. The academic is separated from working in collaboration with the subjects of inquiry towards mutually defined goals because academic products are turned into commodities in the markets of institutional and peer-group review. Moreover, the privileging of certain activities and outcomes over others by the academic institutions disguises the connectedness between the marginalisation many people within those institutions now feel and the marginalisation experienced by people whose lives are constrained and oppressed through the institutional control of 'special' systems of education and care. For these reasons, a critique of the social relations of academic production becomes the starting point from which issues of audience and the role of research in relation to inclusive and exclusionary social practices in the lives of disabled people, for instance, can be explored.

This critique can help us better to understand how theory can become a retreat from practice, a retreat from the social and political injustices that young people and adults with disabilities experience in their lives on a daily basis. To talk of 'theory' and 'theorising' can give the 'respectable' glow of radicalism to social practices that are most profoundly conservative. Following Foucault (1977b), there are good reasons for understanding the project of theorising to be at particular moments in history a strategy for the advancement of professional interests. Thus, Booth (in Chapter 9, this volume) suggests how concerns with theorising might become a distraction from real-life struggles over, for instance, inclusive schooling. However, we would argue that theory, rather than being a distraction from political struggle, is firmly located within that political struggle. Theory is important in developing those insights and generalisations of experience that can inform and advance political struggles against specific acts of injustice as well as against more global or structural forms of oppression (see, for instance, Slee, Chapter 11, this volume). On the other hand, theory does not necessarily centre upon emancipatory goals. Theorising can also operate at the level of legitimisation by disempowering social and political critique through the creation of a metaphysic of personal deficits or in the reification of theory as something available only to intellectuals in furtherance of their understanding of the experience of others. As C. Wright Mills (1959) argued in his book *The Sociological Imagination*, when abstracted from any grounding in the social and historical experience of what it is to live in a particular society, the ideological meaning of theory tends strongly to legitimate stable forms of domination. This is likely to be so even where such theory is ostensibly critical of domination. The point Wright Mills makes here is not that theory is irrelevant, quite the reverse. His argument is that theory is itself part of social action, a set of organising principles by which social practices are understood. This understanding may either legitimate or challenge particular social practices and because of this we need to look at theory in relation to its specific historical manifestations.

It follows from Wright Mills's argument that theorising is not the exclusive prerogative of a group of academics. Theorising takes place in many different contexts, taking on particular forms leading to particular outcomes that can only be understood by examining the point of intersection between biography and history in the lives of those who are involved in this activity. From this perspective, there is a clear political dimension to the activity of theorising. For instance, as a radical engagement with particular forms of social domination and oppression, theorising is a form of action that aims to provide a clearer purchase on identifying, understanding and challenging the oppression of disabled people (Abberley, 1993). In the context of the role of theory in exploring and struggling against oppression, the colonisation of theory by academics may itself be experienced as a form of oppression to the extent that social critique is obfuscated by forms of argument and expression that are excessively abstract, inaccessible, decontextualised and disabling.

For some academics, however, the activity of theorising is seen as an abstraction from practice *per se*. One response to this has been an attempt to bring theory 'to heel'. In other words, it is demanded of theory that it be 'relevant'. In its most extreme form adherents of this position suggest that there should be an abandonment of theory in favour of a focus upon real-life classroom concerns as expressed by teachers (Hargreaves, D., 1996). What this comes down to is the collapse of theory into a research agenda to be determined by the 'users' of education on the basis of criteria that they specify. We would suggest that Ainscow in Chapter 2, this volume, provides us with a good example of how 'relevance' is counterpoised to theory.

In Ainscow's chapter the close relationship between research and the world of schools, classrooms and teachers in terms of relevance and credibility is seen as that which gives credibility to the activity of theorising. Biographical positioning may lead to an interest in school improvement and an approach to research that places these concerns at the centre of an empirical project focused upon ascertaining the conditions of 'inclusive' schooling. However, where this is so, theorising may be described in terms of the different variables that are specified as possible indicators of effective 'inclusion'. What remains untheorised is the specific meaning and historical significance of 'inclusion' as a 'normalising' concept 'in use' within current educational and social discourses. In other words: who is being included, why and into what? On its own, empirical analysis adds nothing to an understanding of the processes of inclusion/exclusion because it can tell us nothing about the meaning and significance of these concepts as organising principles of social life. In the absence of any theorisation of the concept of inclusion in its particular social and historical contexts, appeals to credibility and to relevance merely legitimate at the level of practice those social forms and practices that at a more abstract level it is claimed are being critiqued: in this case the 'normalising' ideology of inclusion.

It is at this point that we find the real difference between our own view of the role of theory and that of Ainscow: while certainly not dismissing the importance of engaging with professionals, we would take a very different view about the nature of this engagement. We approach the topic from the position of a social model critique of exclusion as articulated by those, including disabled people, who experience social exclusion through particular constructions of difference and who challenge these forms of exclusion through political organisation. It is from this perspective, which emphasises the relationship of theory to political practice, contextualised by the historical location of personal biography as itself an aspect of this social and political engagement, that we begin in considering the organising questions raised by the editors of this volume in their introduction (Chapter 1).

Conclusions

In the light of our collaborative discussions it is appropriate that we conclude our contribution to this debate by re-examining the original questions posed by the editors of this volume. We have learnt much from working together to produce this chapter. We have learnt about each other and about our individual and collective engagements through our work. In consequence, the questions which we were asked to consider at the outset of our discussions now look different. We believe that they also involve a different form of response. This response focuses upon an analysis of the specific contexts in which theorising and research take place and how these contexts serve to construct the research process in the lives of people who are participants in that research. This analysis is one that requires us to examine the connectedness in our own lives of different experiences of oppression and resistance. We believe that it is necessary to emphasise the importance of theorising that connectedness in ways that acknowledge how our own practice connects with the lives of our subjects of study. From this perspective our work should be guided by values of collaboration aimed at developing an open debate and an effective opposition to discrimination and oppression.

When the question 'Who is this for?' is posed in the context of a critique of the social relations of academic production, it is a question that goes right to the heart of the problem for academics whose work is concerned with the categorical and exclusionary character of educational and other social institutions and processes. The relations of academic production often sever the links between researchers and the subjects of their inquiry by making the former accountable to systems of control within their institutions and within the academic peer group, and encouraging the representation of the latter as objects of study rather than as agents of change. The instrumentalism of academic engagement operates as a form of oppression for both academics and the subjects of study which devalues and undermines the broader social significance of that engagement. The institutionalised relations of academic production are closely connected to the ways in which relationships with our subjects of study are subsequently constructed. This raises issues going beyond the moral or political stance of individual researchers. It concerns the way in which knowledge is hegemonically constructed as a set of shared assumptions and the discriminatory and oppressive outcomes that follow from this for, amongst others, people labelled as having special needs.

Theory is therefore important in its documentation of the nature of discrimination and oppression. It gives us some purchase on the forms of discrimination and their relation to each other. It gives us a 'language' with which to describe and talk about them. This is valuable because it provides insights and understanding from which more effective opposition and political action can be mounted. Theory is also useful if it enables us to have purchase on the ways in which those who experience and challenge institutionalised discrimination, individually and collectively, generate alternative visions. The consequences of theory for ourselves, therefore, are dependent on the extent to which: it elucidates and informs in reflecting participant experiences; it arouses people to raise questions about their experience and social practice; it contributes to the overall development of demands for change.

In working together to write this chapter, we have become increasingly aware of how important it is to understand that we are all learners. The limitations of our own work are apparent. We have done no more than identify some of the issues and concerns that, for us, have arisen out of our work as researchers and 'theorisers'; to consider what it means, on the one hand, to be positioned by our professional role and, on the other, to position ourselves on the basis of a political and social critique. This chapter is not an end-point but rather a beginning. The story is unfinished, but if we could encourage one thing it would be the continuation of this type of collaborative engagement with the nature of critique and its contribution to an inclusive society.

5

MEDICAL AND PSYCHOLOGICAL MODELS IN SPECIAL NEEDS EDUCATION

Jeff Bailey

Recent developments in special education

It is an interesting time to be writing a chapter on models for special needs education because there are so many pressures for change being exerted in education in general. While this chapter seeks to explore the shortcomings and benefits of medical and psychological models in the provision of education to students with special educational and developmental needs, in order to place a consideration of these models in perspective, I will provide a setting by outlining two significant influences in special education over the last quarter of a century. The first is the behavioural revolution and the second is inclusive schooling.

Behaviourism

As a development of B. F. Skinner's enormously influential research of the 1950s, the late 1960s and 1970s saw a revolution in special education, particularly in the USA. A strong movement to behavioural models of educational instruction and programming became the battlegrounds for fierce debates. The notion that anything that was not 'observable, measurable and repeatable' was not relevant or testable in education became the catch cry of the behavioural movement. Behaviour modification, a technique of particular value in behaviour disorders classes and in schools for students with severe disabilities, became a most popular technique for classroom practice. Relying strongly on operant conditioning principles, this technology became a powerful influence in special education, extending into the realm of curriculum and instruction. The very popular DISTAR curriculum materials in maths, reading and language became common sights in special education classrooms everywhere, while direct instruction, a strongly behavioural approach to instruction, dominated classrooms and debates for a decade.

It is important to remember that the influence of behaviourism, now soft-ened to recognise the power of cognitive mediation, motivated special educators to examine carefully any approaches which relied on intuitive or projective models for child development, curriculum planning and instruction. Some of the models rejected by the behaviourist school included medical explanations for disability, educational planning based on presumed organising constructs, like categorical labels, and even instruction based on assumptions about cogni-tive processes and styles, for example, psycholinguistic training and aptitude–treatment–interaction models of teaching. More than any other trend in special education, the behaviourist influence was largely responsible for the rejection of the medical and psychological models of the day.

Inclusive schooling

These changes, together with what appears to be a fervent crusade promoting inclusive schooling, pose significant challenges to the field of special education. It is important that we understand what inclusive schooling is and from whence this very powerful movement derived. Inclusion can refer to any group of students who may, for whatever reason, have been identified as different and/or may have been discriminated against in terms of either access to educational opportunities or to equity of educational treatment and/or outcomes. Besides persons with disability, inclusive schooling may embrace people of different ethnic or religious grounds. The inclusive movement grew out of the pressures for more normal education and lifestyles for people with disabilities.

But what is inclusion and how important is it in considering current models of relevance to the education of students with special instructional needs? In trying to define inclusion, one has to consider the principles of normalisation, integration, mainstreaming and least restrictive alternative. All of these princi-ples suggest a movement along a number of dimensions (for example, social, instructional, educational, locational) from the most atypical, specialised, segre-gated setting to the more normal, general and integrated environment. At a lower level, it is also important to understand the concepts of non-categorical approaches to special needs education, parental involvement, individualised education plans and curriculum-based assessment (see Clark, Dyson and Millward, 1995a for a comprehensive treatment of school inclusion).

When considering the relatively recent inclusion phenomenon, I recall an article I read twenty years ago by Superintendent Henry Bertness of the Tacoma school district in Washington state, USA. Bertness (1976) then referred to his district's policy about handicapped students (the term more commonly used then), which promoted a policy of progressive inclusion, that is, the student was moved from the most segregated to the most normal setting on a progressive basis, suggesting regular review and consideration of the student's progress and needs. This was a surprisingly prophetic title and approach but it is one that recognises the importance of more specialised, even separate settings. This is a view not supported by full inclusionists who wish to see, as Fuchs and Fuchs suggest, either 'a complete dismantling of special education – no more special education placements, no more special education students, no more special education teachers' or a role for special educators providing 'services to disabled (and non-disabled) students, but only in regular classrooms' (Fuchs and Fuchs, 1994: 22).

There are two sides to every debate and inclusive schooling is no stranger to fierce debate. The arguments centre on two polemics: the presumed purpose and major benefit of people being included fully within a regular classroom, that is, social or academic outcomes; and the empirical support for or rejection of the efficacy of either segregated schooling or inclusive schooling. A recent issue of *Educational Leadership* (vol. 52, no. 4, 1994/95) was devoted entirely to 'The Inclusive School'. The 'full inclusionists' believe the evidence supports their position while the more cautious view taken by Jim Kauffman, Lynn Fuchs and Doug Fuchs, three well-known figures in special education, is that the most appropriate placement selected from a range of settings is the best way to proceed.

Special education as a service

Leaving aside the merits or demerits of inclusive schooling, I have introduced the debate and an overview of some of the issues and trends in special education to provide a more comprehensive backdrop to a review of which models suit or are most antithetical to the educational outcomes of students in special education. When I use the term 'special education', I must point out that there is growing resistance even to that expression. In the UK, the expression 'special needs' suggests an entirely different focus, that is, the emphasis should be on the needs of the children to be served, rather than on a special subset of education, which includes special teachers and special instructional skills. This approach is not reflected in the USA where there is still a strong orientation to funding and teacher certification on the basis of traditional special education categories. Australia sits somewhere between the two. In New South Wales, for example, the expressions 'special educator' and 'special education' are used without any self-consciousness. The groups for whom special education is provided are students with disabilities, learning difficulties or behaviour disorders.

Probably the major reason why special education is a term that some are fearful of using is that special education has meant a *place* in which the education of students with special instructional needs has taken place, typically in segregated settings. If we take special education to mean a *service* for students who need additional or specialised assistance, rather than a place in which this service occurs, we may avoid some of the rhetoric and heat. Special education, as a service, involves both direct and indirect assistance.

The direct services may occur in a range of places, for example, hospital wards, home placements, special schools and units either physically distant from regular schools or placed adjacent to regular schools, resource units within school used on a full-time or part-time basis, and learning support provided to students away from their classroom or in their classroom. Indirect services may include case management of included students, assistance with assessment, counselling students or parents, advising teachers, working collaboratively with teachers in any of the aspects which relate to the day-to-day instruction of any students, signing for children with hearing impairments in regular lessons, and preteaching, reteaching or co-teaching (see Bailey and Bailey, 1993).

For those cautious about full inclusive schooling, two problems of service delivery and repository of skills emerge. The first is that 'full' inclusion may mean a reduction in services to students with special needs militating against equity of outcome, a major purpose of inclusion, and, second, the range of specialist skills of many special educators will be lost to the educational system. Indeed, in the debate between Myra Sapon-Shevin and Jim Kauffman in the special edition of *Educational Leadership* referred to on p. 46, Sapon-Shevin acknowledges that one potential problem with inclusion is that it may be a way of reducing education costs. For this reason, I prefer to refer to the concept of supported inclusion, that is, placement in the regular class in the neighbourhood school but with the addition of whatever direct or indirect services are required in order for that child to have both equity of treatment and equity of outcomes.

Key principles in special education service delivery

There are several philosophical ideals enshrined in the inclusion movement. The first is that the use of diagnostic labels for students with disabilities is unacceptable. The assignment of labels has the potential to limit one's view of the student by a focus on the negativity of the disorder. It is akin to the problems confronted by health professionals in an advanced state of burnout when they try to depersonalise their patients by referring to a patient as, say, 'the kidney disorder in Ward 6' (Jackson et al., 1986). Referring to students as 'the LD kid' or 'the EMR class' is insulting, limiting and discriminatory.

The second ideal is similar to the labelling issue, that is, that a non-categorical approach is more considerate and equitable. The categories 'mental retardation' and 'cerebral palsy' have little functional value in the education of these students because, for example, the child's intellectual strengths, current levels of academic achievement, description of behaviour, indications of social skills, motivation or interests are not described by the category. In short, the diagnostic label does absolutely nothing to assist the child's education except, perhaps, to give a global indication of the *place* where the child should be educated – and this is a dangerous and limited approach to providing the least restrictive alternative.

A third ideal is that the assessment of a student should be as functional as possible, that is, the tools and content of the assessment should be directly connected with the programmes being provided by students. Curriculum-based assessment is receiving strong support from the field because the content against which the student is being appraised is the material which that child will be taught. Rather than test the student on an unrelated set of 'typical' intellectual behaviours, particularly those that are based on an hypothesised model of the intellect, teachers are urging assessors to use the material of the classroom to measure gains and levels of achievement. Besides the relevance of such an approach, teachers receiving this form of information are in a better position to understand the assessment and adapt the information to the development of their classroom programmes. Allied to this new view of assessment is the belief that students should be appraised regularly in normal, not clinical settings, and when the teachers want to. Many of the tools of direct instruction, particularly probes, lend themselves more readily to this world view. Having teachers undertake responsibility for assessment means no waiting lists or visits to clinics for what teachers see as less relevant forms of assessment.

Having given a backdrop to two significant influences in special education, I will now proceed to explore how the so-called medical and psychological models have been viewed in the past and how they should be viewed so that the expertise and insights from these fields can be used profitably to improve the opportunities and outcomes of students with disabilities and their parents and families.

The medical model

What is the medical model?

My current position is a joint appointment as Professor of Special Education at a university in Sydney and Director of the Children's Hospital Education Research Institute (CHERI) in Australia's leading paediatric hospital. At my first meeting of the Advisory Committee established to support my work in CHERI, the representative from the state department of education, a special educator, suggested that caution had to be observed in the mission and operation of CHERI that it did not lean too heavily on 'the medical model'. This admission surprised some of my medical colleagues and, subsequently, one of them, a professor of paediatrics, sent me a copy of an article he wrote on 'the medical model' (Oates, 1996). Oates quotes an earlier article written by Ray Helfer, MD, who was Editor-in-Chief of the journal *Child Abuse and Neglect*. I will quote some of Helfer's challenge to his readers to define the medical model because it is instructive to learn that the medical community is not as clear as non-medical professionals about the nature of the medical model:

> For almost ten years I have heard a variety of professionals, mostly social workers, refer to 'The Medical Model'. At first, I thought it was something one might find in a museum of medical history, easily

viewed and photographed. Later I realised it referred to something I
was doing and I was flattered. . . . Lately, I've come to think this has
something to do with process; not something I do or don't do, rather
how I do or don't do something. Maybe it's even related to how I think
and solve problems.

(Helfer, 1985: 299)

Helfer probably reflects the views of many of his medical colleagues about the
medical model because it is an expression used more by other professionals.
Indeed, when Helfer asked colleagues for a definition, one responded: 'I don't
know what it is, but I know it's bad!' (op. cit.).

What has been interesting to me as an academic who, in the 1970s and early
1980s, used the term repeatedly with graduate students, is that when one begins
to search the literature there is almost nothing of any substance which defines
the model, or outlines its strengths or weaknesses, or even tries to justify the
model in any way. In the nursing journals one finds quite a few references to
'the medical model' as a set of behaviours and attitudes which, in charting new
nursing programmes and approaches, one is advised to avoid – perhaps it is bad
after all.

I shall try to describe the general view which is held of the medical model to
provide a framework for the analysis of the strengths and weaknesses of the
model. In terms of medicine, the medical model appears to be a professional
orientation which is highly focused on pathology, not normalcy, on sickness,
not wellbeing, on the nature and aetiology of the presenting problem itself, not
on the individual who has the problem, on dealing with the specific pathology
in a centred way, not on the social or ecosystem which surrounds the problem,
that is, the patient, his or her family, social and financial circumstances, values
and attitudes.

Now this might sound like a pejorative definition but, in fact, it is not. The
job of a medical doctor is to find out what is wrong with people and fix them
up. If a person presents with severe chest pains, is short of breath, has shooting
pains up and down his arms, has a history of cardiac disease in his family, is
overweight and smokes, the doctor will examine the facts and information, will
make a diagnosis based on a suspected pathology and will implement interventions and procedures to deal with the problem. In the first instance, they will be
short-term interventions, that is, measures to prevent a heart attack or stroke.
In the longer term, the doctor may well investigate life-style issues, refer the
patient to a nutritionist, suggest the need for a fitness programme and advise the
patient to cease smoking.

If this is the medical model, and if I were the patient, I would be much more
impressed with having my life saved, and a stroke or heart attack prevented,
than if the doctor were to examine my family situation, provide counselling,
take me to a gymnasium, and so on. In other words, I have a pathology, I want
that pathology identified, I want immediate restorative or ameliorative action

to be effected and I want to resume a well state as quickly and as safely as possible. I am more than happy for that doctor to employ a diagnostic–prescriptive model of intervention focused on the immediate presenting problem. If medication is suggested, I am more than happy to take medication, recognising, of course, that in the long term I may have to accept further recommendations for a change in lifestyle. Naturally, in other circumstances, without a pathology of this seriousness, I would want the doctor to focus on wellness and measures to improve my wellness, for example, blood tests, blood pressure tests, and cholesterol measures – nothing specifically oriented to any detectable problem, but strategies which would promote my wellbeing and ensure my future.

A pejorative view of the medical model

My particular characterisation is an intuitive view of the medical model. However, I suspect that criticism of the medical model derives more from the manner in which medical practitioners have conducted themselves and the ambivalence people feel about medical personnel. The ambivalence derives from the amount of trust we place in these professionals and a resistance to what has often been characterised as a dominating and compelling style. The archetypal Sir Lancelot Spratt from the 'Doctor' film series springs to mind. However, to be more rigorous in exploring this 'model', I will turn to an analysis of doctor–patient communication in a book written by two UK medical practitioners (Pendleton and Hasler, 1983). They suggest that a 'tendency to be authoritarian characterises some doctors' consulting styles' (p. 10). The expectation of patient compliance is something that concerns many professionals who tend to take a less directive and positivistic approach to working with their clients.

Pendleton and Hasler also raise questions about the diagnostic–prescriptive methods employed by medical practitioners, in particular the 'medicalisation' of the process by 'the organisation of vague symptoms into categories then labelling these producing a disease that can be approached in the traditional medical manner' (ibid.: 80). Holden (1990) asserts a dehumanising approach in the medical use of diagnostic labels. The terms category and labelling ring immediate alarm bells for the special educator who adopts a functionalist, inclusive view of the world.

To provide a quick overview of how different professionals have described and evaluated 'the medical model', Table 5.1 describes the views and explains the reason for the views. Two points need to be made about the material in the table. The first is that most of the comments are quite negative about the medical model. These critiques appear to stem from resistance to the notion of professional-centred care and support for a more participatory model of health care management, a model in which the patient plays an active role. Second, I include only a few articles because it is extremely difficult to find publications describing the medical model. Indeed, a criticism of the selected papers is that the authors make the criticisms but provide no empirical evidence to support their positions.

Table 5.1 Summary comments from selected critiques of the medical model

Comments on the medical model	Rationale for the comments	Authors
The focus of the medical model appears to be narrow and reductionist; patients are seen in terms of their pathology; when care is described in physiology and disease, fragmentation can occur and psychological and sociological factors are overlooked	Research suggests that a more holistic approach to embrace psychological and sociological concerns improves health care	Reed and Watson (1994)
The medical model pays insufficient attention to the role of the client in medication management; clients are made to feel too receptive, passive and compliant	The role of clients in being responsible for and impacting positively on their own health improvement is cited as evidence for a change in the model; argues for a more participatory model	Chewning and Sleath (1996)
The dominant paradigm of scientific medicine violates patients' rights; the patient is viewed as having no subjective content; organs and tissues are the focus of attention; little notice is accorded of the abilities and potentials of the patients; human helplessness is promoted as power is stripped from the patient	Argues the case from a philosophical and human rights basis; draws upon the notions of objectivism, reductionism and mechanistic determinism to suggest that rights are violated and the dominant paradigm of the medical model is continually refurbished	Stambolovic (1996)
'Nursing and medical routines … confer privileges on nurses and physicians while objectifying and disempowering patients …'	The article posits a move from acute care to community-based health care to engage in community partnerships in health care, an approach not possible under the medical model	Schroeder (1994)
'Diagnosis is the core of the traditional "medical model"'; it is a process which is multifunctional and complex	Diagnosis has 4 purposes: description, classification and taxonomy; predicting prognosis; determining therapy; and pathological understanding	Eastman (1992)

The medical model in practice

The final paper by Eastman (1992) is the only article which highlights the complexity of the medical model. Eastman's position is akin to that of my colleague, Oates, whose definition of the medical model has five elements:

1 Studying the problem carefully to find causative factors. This includes good data collection to understand the epidemiology of the problem.
2 Experimentation to help determine the most effective form of treatment.
3 Intervention, which usually means some type of treatment of change in lifestyle.
4 Rigorous evaluation of the results of the experimentation and treatment.
5 Long-term follow-up of patients with the problem to review progress, to determine the effectiveness of the treatment, and to see if any harmful side effects have developed (Oates, 1996: 3).

What follows now is an attempt to draw from the preceding comments an outline of some of the concerns about the medical model in relation to teaching students with disabilities.

Lessons to be drawn from the medical model for special education

There are obvious lessons to be drawn from the criticisms of the medical model which allow one to sketch a view of how we should be dealing with the people with disabilities to whom we are professionally responsible.

Working together in multidisciplinary teams is an important part of providing informed and effective special education services. The notion of superordinate status of one professional over another, say a psychologist over a special educator, or a special educator over an occupational therapist, is unacceptable. There are constant hints in the medical model about the subordinate and less-valued status of nurses compared to doctors. Such hierarchical arrangements are to be avoided in special education where the focus must be on the target of the services, not on the professionals providing the services.

While I would not support a wholesale commitment to 'observable, measurable and repeatable' behaviours to the exclusion of a strong commitment to self-regulatory behaviour, for example, motivation, locus of control, attributions and self-empowerment, I would argue that the manner in which we describe our diagnostic statements must be based on functional attributes, must be positive and optimistic and must take into account the whole person. The notion of focusing on pathology and organicity is not acceptable in special education; equally unacceptable is the use of such diagnostic views of the world, expressed as labels and categories. Our role is to seek information on the strengths of our clients and to provide services which harness those strengths and make the person more adaptive and effective within their environment.

The refusal to be involved in 'narrow and reductionist' views of our clients must be endorsed wholeheartedly so that we see the whole person and so that our services will be: integrated, not fragmented; holistic, not atomistic; healthy, not pathological; and enabling, not disabling. In my own clinical work, I have taken a strong ecological approach. This perspective attempts to account for and understand the importance of the range of influences in the child's context, for example, familial, personal, intellectual, developmental and instructional influences. Students are a product of all the influences acting upon them. To assume that we can understand the complexity of instructional and developmental needs of a student with disability without attending to the complexity of the multiple contexts which influence their behaviour is limiting and unprofessional.

The dominant paradigm in special education must be to facilitate the development of our clients in ways which ensure they participate fully in their engagement in these services, which promote their rights and responsibilities, along with our own rights and responsibilities as people and as professionals, and which are ecologically valid and comprehensive, in a psychological and sociological sense. The lesson is to focus on the student as a client, not as a patient.

With regard to privilege and power, special educators will ensure that their professional model is characterised by mutual empowerment and personal growth. While the clients of our services have the right to be treated as 'whole' persons with efforts made to reduce disablement and eliminate models of disablement, special educators have the right to reciprocal respect, empowerment and personal growth. The notion of special education professionals being privileged to be permitted to 'serve' disabled people is as unacceptable as a model which denies clients' rights, forces them to be passive recipients of professionally determined services, and increases their handicap through the disablement process. Similarly, any efforts to patronise clients must be avoided.

By combining the views of Eastman (1992) and Oates (1996), the medical model suggests to us the scientist–practitioner model in diagnosis, prognosis, selection of interventions, and review of the efficacy of our professional programmes. Special educators, indeed all educators, must be effective diagnosticians, evaluating strengths and weaknesses, determining the reasons for a student's failure to thrive personally, intellectually or physically. We have to make informed decisions about the best type of intervention using our sound knowledge base and upgrading this information through careful reading of the research literature and regular and careful data collection in our professional practice.

We must test our interventions against ecologically valid measurement indices, that is, we should be sure that our approach embraces the personal view of the world of our clients, takes into account their attitudes, beliefs and values, and engages their total life space, including their family and home circumstances. We will have to be thorough in evaluating the effectiveness and relevance of our professional programmes. We will need to be outcome-oriented, not input-dominated, and we will need to take into account multiple information sources to ensure the most appropriate methods of evaluation (see, for example, Lewis *et al.*, 1994). We should be committed to continual review and we must take a long-term view of our planning, programming and programme implementation and development.

If we are to harness the strengths of the medical model and avoid the reported pitfalls of this model, we will do a great deal of good for our clients and ourselves. Let us now consider the assumptions underlying the psychological model and extract principles to guide our theoretical perspectives and professional practice in special education.

The psychological model

A *definition of the psychological model*

One of the first cautions to be drawn when discussing 'the psychological model' is that such discussion assumes there is *one* model and that psychologists represent a unified group in terms of training, interests, skills and orientation. Anyone familiar with the field of psychology will be aware of the great variety of classifications of psychology, for example, the American Psychological Association caters for the interests of over fifty types of psychology. These types range from those we in special education would know best, for example, educational, developmental and perhaps clinical psychology, to psychotherapy, forensic psychology and physiological psychology. The empirical framework, philosophy, tools for assessment and intervention, and research vary considerably across the areas of psychology.

The major worry about 'the psychological model' is in the assumptions underlying and the practice of intelligence testing and subsequent placement of students in special settings. Seymour Sarason once said: 'School psychology was born in the prison of a test, and although the cell has been enlarged somewhat, it is still a prison' (1977, cited in Cole and Siegel, 1990). This prison often sees the psychologist relying on a single test in a single testing situation to make very significant decisions in the life of a child. But there are other concerns as well.

To focus the criticism of the psychological model, I will describe six issues of specific concern to teachers about psychologists in their assessment role.

1   Many of the psychologists used were 'mental testers', people with training in test administration and psychology but virtually no training in child development, instruction or curriculum development and implementation. This immediately placed them at a disadvantage with teachers because teachers expect advice on a much broader scale than that provided by most intelligence tests and most psychologists.

2   Even those psychologists who had some background in education tended to be dominated by the psychometric domain, by the context, constructs and importance of the test. If you are unsure of what I mean by this, read a psychological report from a psychologist. The main descriptive framework is the construction of the test. Information is reported on such seemingly irrelevant activities as assembling blocks under time pressure or nominating the uses of a common object. The explanations are all about the performance on the actual items of the sub-test, with comments on what one could expect of students of a similar age. The conclusion implied is that if the child achieves at a percentile level of, say, 27 on a sub-test which manipulates three-dimensional objects to form a pattern as per the model provided that this will mean something to teachers. Will it explain the characteristic learning style of the child? Will it specify in what way the cognitive demands of that particular test might be replicated in classroom learning? Will it speak to instructional practices in a related area, say spatial geometry? In fact, what will this information mean for the classroom teacher? The answer is that almost nothing of any value is transmitted in those psychological reports which have as the beginning and end of their concerns a description of behaviour on sub-tests of an intelligence test.

3   What of those psychologists who add some practical assistance at the end of their report? Teachers are very busy, practical people. They want immediately translatable advice and information. They want advice which is manageable and implementable in a classroom of 28 or 30 very different students. They want to know some of the practical methods which might assist in their task. They want the information in language which they can understand. They do not want summative scores only, although most teachers appreciate these scores and use them as a frame of reference. They want help not mysticism. It is true that many psychologists have the knowledge, experience and interest to address teachers' needs. The reality, though, is that many either do not have this knowledge or fail to provide what teachers need. There are practical alternatives occurring in practice and in the literature (Sandy, 1986).

4   Another area which has caused teachers to be sceptical of psychologists has been in their traditional role of testing children's intelligence for placement in special education. In previous years, many school systems have relied almost exclusively on the results of a single assessment to place children in special settings. It is likely that in many cases, these tests have been conducted in one-on-one situations with no involvement by parents and little information sought from the teacher. We are all aware of the limitations of testing by strangers in artificial settings. We are all concerned that assessments, which have a very large influence on a child's life, be as comprehensive and grounded as possible. All parties involved in the decision should have equal access to the information. In the USA, informed consent and procedural safeguards institutionalised in PL94-142 guaranteed

this by law. This has not been the case in many other western countries. When psychologists act as gatekeepers for students with special needs, particularly when the prevailing *Zeitgeist* impels psychologists to place the child in a segregated setting, psychologists place themselves in a vulnerable position.

5   There are other limitations of psychological tests, particularly standardised tests, which have emerged over the years. For example, many of the tests use norms which are not representative of the population being tested (see Salvia and Ysseldyke, 1991). These tests have little to do with learning, they have limited predictive value, the end purpose is to categorise and label children, the tests are often unfair to minority groups, and the breadth of knowledge tested in the selected domain is very narrow (Worthen and Spandel, 1991). There are, of course, answers to each of these criticisms but the concern about psychological practices may well have caused special educators to respond emotionally rather than rationally.

6   The newly emerging interest in 'authentic assessment' and curriculum-based assessment (Choate *et al.*, 1995) has meant, in large measure, a rejection of clinically based, standardised, norm-referenced testing. Instead, what is sought is instructionally relevant assessment, based on the current curriculum content, in classes, using informal, teacher-made tests, administered by the teacher. Such assessment has a direct connection with the four major purposes of assessment: screening; programme planning; assessment of individual students' progress; and programme evaluation. The only purpose missing is placement, the major role of educational psychologists.

These are the primary concerns of special educators. These are the limitations of psychological practice which have caused special educators to be wary of, and sometimes very angry about, the 'psychological model'. In some ways, much of what I have said was how things used to be. I have no evidence, though, to suggest that any major changes have occurred. Some of the testing conducted on children is still extremely remote from everyday realities of classrooms. The problem would be ameliorated if the psychologist was not attempting to influence practices within the schools. Teachers are less concerned, for example, about a medical doctor prescribing Ventolin puffers for children with respiratory problems because that decision and prescription are clearly the domain of the medical specialist. However, when psychologists assess children, place them, report on them and attempt to work with teachers, the teacher's domain is entered and the teacher will expect significantly more of the professional entering that domain. Unfortunately, in too many cases, the psychologist has been found wanting in terms of useful, practical advice.

In fairness, I should say that many psychologists do not fit this stereotype, particularly in educational psychology. They often have an excellent teaching background with significant experience in curriculum development. They have added to their educational experience a much deeper knowledge of children's development and behaviour. They have also learned to be rigorous in assess-ment and testing. They have developed a broader view of the educational process. They have learned how to assist teachers in the teacher's domain without incurring rancour. They have also developed multidisciplinary, case-conferencing approaches to the all-important decisions about placing a child in a special class or school. They also provide practical, relevant, intelligible advice in long and useful reports. With psychologists who have these demon-strable skills, teachers would have little difficulty, and the psychological model would be respected – not scorned.

To be fair in another sense, psychologists have not always wanted the mental testing job which has been foisted on them. Indeed, there is sufficient evidence to suggest that school psychologists want much more varied roles (Huberty and Huebner, 1988). Cole and Siegel (1990) blame university training for constructing a role which is marginally relevant to educational psychology. Levinson (1990) suggests that psychologists feel that they spend far too much time on assessment and clerical activities.

In a paper outlining the contribution educational psychologists might make in schools, Gale's address at the 1991 UK Association of Educational Psychologists' Conference outlines the expertise that psychologists have:

> selection, assessment, training, observation, counselling, guidance, therapy, group work, organisational change, time management, resource management, stress management, decision-making, group and leadership behaviour, personal constructs, vocational guidance, ergonomics and safety, health education, behaviour change, attitude measurement and attitude change, social representation and social change processes, family process, family therapy, emotion, anxiety and depression, and very important also, research and evaluation . . .
>
> (Gale, 1991: 71)

Assessment figures as only one of a myriad of skills. Gale describes a better role for educational psychologists, based largely on increased staffing. He suggests that if psychologists 'want to make schools work, they have to work in schools' (ibid.: 72). He suggests that a team of six psychologists should be based in each comprehensive school. Their role would be, essentially, school renewal and development. Their focus would include organisational change and person development. They would accept greater responsibility for in-service training and induction of new teachers. Psychologists would have to develop a wider range of expertise to be able to provide such support. Their initial training would be much longer. Their influence would be much more pervasive and probably better accepted.

This is an interesting view of a new role for educational psychologists. As is often the case, though, it is predicated on an increase in resources to schools. The recommended case load of one psychologist to 200 students (ibid.: 73) is probably eight times the current case load, at least in Australia. One of the difficulties psychologists have had to confront is that they have had to work in four or five schools. They have been responsible for all the testing and placement, the major role for many years. If they had high schools in their case load, they also had to run vocational guidance programmes, and, if time permitted, they engaged in therapeutic counselling with students. This massive load permitted very little time for the type of educational and psychological consultancy that teachers wanted.

Lessons to be drawn from the psychological model for special education

I have constructed my argument that the major concern of special educators about the psychological model has been based on the use of intelligence tests for placements of students with special needs in segregated settings. A secondary concern is the notion that educational psychologists do not provide the type of advice that classroom teachers want. If these two points are valid, the lessons to be drawn are for educational psychologists, not for special or regular educators. Perhaps if I draw up a list of recommended improvements for the practice of educational psychology the debate can be put in perspective.

First, the process of assessing students for significant decisions about their schooling has to be reviewed carefully. The implications in the US Individuals with Disabilities Education Act (IDEA) (Choate *et al.*, 1995) need to be taken into account. These include: provision of assessment and instructional services which ensure an appropriate education for students with disabilities; clear guarantees of practices which honour the rights of the parents and the children; effective programme planning represented by individualised family service plans, individual education plans and individual transition plans; and assessment and evaluation to ensure adequate outcomes for these students. The role of educational psychologists could be broadened so that they act as consultants with special and regular educators to ensure these ideals are met.

This collaborative approach will also require special educators to be less territorial about their students. Psychologists have a range of skills that special educators do not have. Clearly, the reverse is also true. There is little point in these two groups of professionals reacting in defensive ways and limiting students' opportunities. There needs to be a merger of interests and a joint recognition of the roles, responsibilities and skills of each group. Effective interprofessional collaboration should be the major aim of any interaction between the two groups.

Teachers need to recognise that while the science of measurement of human behaviour is not an exact one, it is still a very sound science. There are valid uses for a range of psychological tests, particularly standardised tests. There is no need to adopt an 'either-or' approach to measuring and assessing the development of students in our care. Sometimes, learning probes conducted by the teacher based on classroom content will be the most valid and useful form of measurement. At other times, a broader frame of reference might be needed and norm-referenced measures of educational achievement will have their place. The issue is not which tests we should use – the issue is how well we use the measurement instruments at our disposal to ensure that our students receive the best possible education.

For many years I have advocated what I call 'first-line counselling'. Growing alarmed at the number of children I was seeing clinically with high levels of frustration and rage, and knowing that educational psychologists have huge case loads, I have been suggesting (Bailey, 1992) that teachers should be sensitive to and respond to the emotional problems their children are experiencing by entering into helping relationships. Such a relationship may reduce the stress and trauma that children experience. However, with an increase in the clinical severity of the student's conditions, teachers should call in qualified counsellors. This is where I see a profitable relationship occurring between the educator and the educational psychologist. The teacher provides initial help, and this may be sufficient or it may not be, and then enters into a collaborative relationship with the educational psychologist to see a resolution of the student's emotional problems.

Another valid role for educational psychologists is that of measurement and evaluation consultant (Bailey, 1997). I assert that many educational psychologists have excellent statistical and evaluation skills. They should use these skills to support teachers by implementing well-constructed useful evaluation systems. These systems may be for either programme planning or programme evaluation, or, at the classroom level, for appraisal of the progress of individuals, particularly those being included. While this is not a new vision, the importance of the approach is in teachers respecting the skills of the educational psychologist and the educational psychologist recognising the needs, priorities and skills of the teachers in terms of programming and instruction.

There are other possibilities for educational psychologists to alter the face of assessment in schools. One area of concern in schools is the over-reliance on pencil-and-paper measures of ability and achievement. The educational psychologist can assist in classroom-based measurement by providing a range of 'authentic performance' models of assessment, for example, building achievement criteria into practical demonstration of achievement and growth (see Choate et al., 1995: 17).

The major way of engaging the mutual efforts of teachers and psychologists is by consigning the pejorative view of the psychological model to the history books and by both groups of professionals entering into new collaborative contracts. The purpose of these contracts is to use the training, skills, insight and knowledge of each partner to effect better educational programmes and more equitable outcomes for all children, but particularly for children with special instructional and developmental needs.

Conclusion and recommendations

The conclusion is obvious: with good will on the part of medical, psychological and educational personnel, with an awareness of the importance of each group in the development and education of children, and with a clear commitment to collaborative engagements across the professions, the old tags and models will disappear. We owe it to our children to provide the most comprehensive and most effective professional guidance and interventions for all children. It is time to break down the territorial boundaries and interprofessional criticism and act as fully professional people in providing exemplary services to our clients.

6

MODELS OF COMPLEXITY

Theory-driven intervention practices

Phil Bayliss

Introduction

The Teacher Training Agency has recently introduced a profile of teaching competence that lists (under the rubric of professional development) the ability to identify *and* meet the special educational needs of *all* pupils as a necessary competence for all newly qualified teachers. This all-encompassing statement assumes that there exists a coherent view of what a 'special educational need' is, and that there exists a coherent set of procedures, or techniques which can be defined (and taught to newly qualified teachers) to meet such needs. The idea of a 'coherent view' assumes a theoretical perspective and it is the overall aim of the book to explore issues in what such a theory would look like and its implications for practice and research. In this chapter I would like to explore the idea that a 'coherent view' of special education requires us to move beyond simple linear causal models of 'children who have problems' towards an understanding of the complexities of how a school (or more generally, how an educational process) is constituted and its function in meeting 'needs'.

At the core of any understanding about special education is a notion of 'intervention'. If we address the idea of 'special', the multiple connotations of this word all contain a germ of change – there exists an educational context which is 'special' (out of the ordinary) which implies that practitioners (educators, special educators) must undertake some action to make the 'special' 'ordinary' (Dessent, 1987). Implicit in this underlying assumption, I would argue, is that 'special' equals 'bad' (a pathology) and the direction of change is from 'bad' to 'good' (remediating a pathology). An alternative view sees 'special' as 'different' which does not imply change at all but rather a celebration of that difference. The two positions have validity in the way that children (or more generally, learners, if we are examining educational practice) are viewed, in that both positions are represented by different constituencies in the special educational world. Crucially, however, whichever view is held by the practitioner will affect what is done in practice for any given individual learner. Do we intervene

61

and change, do we celebrate and stand back? How do we distinguish between these positions and how do we decide what we should do in any given case? A theory of special education ought to provide principled ways of making such decisions and as such it should provide a theory of intervention.

Towards a theory of intervention

Intervention can take place in schools, classrooms, communities or homes, or clinics, hospitals or institutions. As a practitioner, my experience of such places where educational intervention takes place is that the contexts of intervention are multifaceted, dynamic and complex. Children or adults change, grow, develop, act and react from moment to moment. As a teacher working with groups or individuals, the 'reality' of intervention is chaotic and messy. As a researcher attempting to understand such complex realities in order to improve or extend the range or efficiency of intervention practice, I am forced to adopt particular frameworks of analysis:

> Research demands that we make sense of the chaos of experience; what it has not yet allowed for is that this chaos is not a datum but is already organised by consciousness as the condition of the insight and the research finding is an identity arrested as a way of seeing, a way of putting it.
>
> (Clough, 1995: 141)

This 'chaotic view', as a 'way of seeing', which directs us as teachers and as researchers, is not something which can be divorced from the reality or a succession of realities constructed by individuals within a society (Berger and Luckmann, 1966). For the minority of people seen (either by themselves or by others) as being 'different', 'disordered', 'deficient', 'retarded' or 'abnormal', the outcomes of actions derived from 'chaotic views' have practical applications in driving programmes of intervention: they affect people's lives in fundamental ways.

Programmes of intervention can operate at macro-societal or legal–legislative levels (Bricker, 1978). Examples of such intervention programmes include: the introduction of the Code of Practice for the Identification and Assessment of Special Educational Needs (Department for Education, 1994); the Headstart Programme (Ziegler and Valentine, 1979); the establishment of antenatal screening programmes to detect genetic anomalies; providing school dinners to improve national levels of nutrition; the laws relating to the compulsory sterilisation of 'feeble-minded' women in Southern States of the USA (Gould, 1992); or as an extreme case, the 'final solution' of the Nazi programme.

They can also operate at the level of the individual: at psychological–educative, or biogenic micro-levels. For example, the use of 'gene-therapy' to remove genes which condition cystic fibrosis (Wilkie, 1993); the specific learning programme designed to support the individual learning needs of the child with 'dyslexia' (Hornsby and Shear, 1974); the prescription of 'Ritalin' for the child diagnosed as having 'attention deficit and hyperactivity disorder' (Hinshaw, 1994); the use of 'Circle time' to provide peer support for the child with significant disabilities in an inclusion programme (Forest and Pierpoint, 1991).

All of these interventions are driven by 'chaotic views' derived from theory or rather a range of theories, in that each of the above examples of interventions can be explained, justified and given credence by specific constituencies (mainly professionals) who have (or have had) power to establish a dominant view: 'He who has the bigger stick has the better chance of imposing his definitions of reality' (Berger and Luckmann, 1966: 127) and in some instances, 'reality may be enforced by the police' (ibid.: 137).

Dominant views of intervention bring with them their operating procedures which also support moral imperatives:

> the 'deviant' probably stands as a living insult to the Gods, who love one another in their heavens as do their devotees on earth . . . and . . . whose conduct challenges the societal reality as such, putting into questions its taken-for-granted cognitive and normative operating procedures. . . . Such deviance requires therapeutic practice grounded in therapeutic theory. There must be a theory of deviance (a pathology that is) that accounts for the . . . condition. There must be a body of diagnostic concepts (say, a symptomatology) which optimally not only permits precise specification of acute conditions, but also the detection of the deviant condition and the prompt adoption of preventative measures. Finally there must be a conceptualisation of the curative process itself , say, a catalogue of . . . techniques, each with an adequate theoretical foundation.
>
> (ibid.: 131)

The practice of intervention (the definition of symptomatology and conceptualisation of the curative process which leads to action) is guided by recourse to a set of implicit or explicit theories and the decision to act at all is underpinned by a set of culturally bound moral values. The particular action chosen in any given case is driven by conceptualisations of what constitutes 'the problem', the identity (in Clough's terms on p. 78) of the individual undertaking the action and the pressure of a moral imperative to intervene.

If defining the problem resides in a scientific conceptualisation of the 'child who is deviant', and this conceptualisation is seen as being objective truth, the 'strong' symptomatology of Berger and Luckmann adopted for intervention will be driven by a 'diagnostic–prescriptive' methodology (G. Thomas, 1995; Sandow, 1994). If a child has condition 'x', the diagnosis (derived from scientific understanding of condition 'x') leads to intervention practice 'y', described as a set of deductive rules (Berger and Luckmann's 'curative process').

The 'diagnostic–prescriptive' approach derives from ideological positions reflecting this process of 'scientific method' from which the 'adequate theoretical foundation' is derived and it has produced a powerful methodology for changing deviant individuals: the 'medical model' (Fulcher, 1989).

The medical model constructs the deviant ('special') individual as an 'object', i.e. the condition experienced by the child or adult has an intransitive objective reality, which exists outside of human interpretation. Historically, the medical model has reigned through the adoption of objective scientific realities which have delivered descriptive adequacy. Descriptive adequacy provides empirical justification for courses of action: therapies 'work' and can be shown to work through empirical justification. This circular approach to justification of action is essentially linguistic in the sense that the 'objective' paradigm can only be presented, validated and used for explanation through the presence of what Bhaskar (1986: 91) calls a 'mensurating, material object language' in which 'deictic, indexial and spatio-temporal expressions are strainlessly employed'. Here, the certainty of 'objective fact' is conveyed by the language of diagnosis (deictic, indexial and spatio-temporal expressions) and the objectification of deviance is established through the description of 'conditions' or 'syndromes', using the mensurating, material object language. Thus, condition 'x' (autism, dyslexia, Down's Syndrome, 'a learning difficulty') may be described as a set of characteristics which form a cluster (a 'syndrome' (Martin, 1980)). Individuals who experience the condition share few, some or all of the syndrome characteristics with other individuals and 'having "x"' becomes what Helmke (1989) calls an 'entry condition': deciding that an individual 'has "x"' is the starting point of a pseudo-algorithmic (Penrose, 1989) process of intervention, i.e. intervening becomes a process of following the intervention rules.

Deciding whether an individual 'has "x"' is subject to a variety of constraints. A range of theories are available to describe the individual. Thus, as a general example, an introductory textbook to psychology (Gross, 1990: 14) lists five major theoretical positions: psychoanalytic, behaviourist, humanist/existential, neurobiological (biogenic, genetic) and cognitive. Each of these theories describes conflicting views of the nature of human beings; the nature of psychological normality and development; causes of abnormal behaviour and preferred methods and goals of treatment.

Each of these theoretical positions also has 'preferred methods of study' (Gross, op. cit.) which use case-study and experimental approaches to derive the mensurating, material object language. In this sense, 'having "x"' can only be described in terms of that theory and is constructed by it. But 'having "x"' in one theoretical position is mutually exclusive with respect to other positions, the 'abnormality' or 'deviance' is constituted by a different underlying conceptualisation of normality and abnormality.

A 'behaviour difficulty', for example, could be construed as:

- a 'biogenic' failing (hyperactivity caused by a junkfood diet, or abnormal brain chemistry (attention deficit disorder));
- 'attention-seeking behaviour' created by the child's learning of maladaptive responses or the failure to learn adaptive ones in the first place;
- a psychodynamic view which sees the problem as 'caused' by emotional disturbance or neurosis caused by unresolved conflicts stemming from childhood.

If we ignore for the moment the fact that the above descriptions reify the notion of 'a behavioural difficulty' as something which exists independently of a child and his/her particular circumstances, we should be able to decide between the different theoretic positions empirically, i.e. whether in any given case the theoretical view achieves descriptive and explanatory adequacy (Chomsky, 1965).

Descriptive adequacy relates to the power of any given theoretical construct to define the 'problem', i.e. to what extent any particular psychological theory adequately characterises the object of study. In this sense, each of the psychological theories listed above is descriptively adequate. Each theoretical position 'works' within its own domain. Explanatory adequacy is achieved when we can derive universal statements which can distinguish *between* any of the given positions, i.e. in any given basis for intervention, which theory we can adopt to establish a more efficient intervention process. Is a biogenic approach more 'adequate' than a behavioural approach? Is a cognitive approach 'better' than a psychodynamic approach? Is there a new psychological theory waiting to be formulated which will better describe the problem? A theory of intervention should achieve explanatory adequacy if it is to form a consistent and universally coherent intervention practice.

Descriptive adequacy is relevant, whether we are focusing on 'within-child' or individualistic psychological models, or on 'environmentalism' (seen in its extreme form as strong behaviourism). In the latter, the theoretical positions underlying the explanation of the deviance derive from environmental/social models. In an educational context, this finds expression in models of differentiation ('if children cannot learn through the way we teach, can we teach in the way they learn? (Chasty, 1993; see also Moore, 1992)) or adaptive teaching methods (Wang, 1992).

Descriptive adequacy in intervention is outcomes dependent, i.e. if the intervention 'works' (effects change towards a positive outcome), the theory underpinning and the process of intervention may be said to be 'adequate'. If it fails, i.e. it does not result in positive outcomes, the difficulty arises as to attribution of the cause of failure.

Does the cause of failure lie:

- in the individual – the child did not 'have "x"', or 'the child has a specific form of "x"' (for example, in the case of dyslexia, some therapies may fail for some children and this attribution of failure is concomitant with a received orthodoxy that this therapy *will* 'work' for dyslexia)?;

- in the form of intervention, or its implementation? For example, a 'phonics' or 'phonological awareness' approach may be inappropriate for 'this kind of dyslexia' (Riddick, 1995);

- in the theory itself? It may be that seeing 'dyslexia' as a sickness-like condition is actually wrong (see Riddell, 1994). Could dyslexia be 'better' explained as a phenomenon of inappropriate curricula or the child's emotional responses to inappropriate curricula? Could it require a different psychological theory (for example, a cognitive approach to problem-solving or information-processing models)?

Again, deciding ought to be an empirical matter and the focus for research into special education, i.e. the search for a theory of special education ought to provide explanatory adequacy in our description of the deductive rules derived from such a theory so that we can provide the optimum intervention for any 'deviant' individual.

The matter is not, however, so straightforward. The process of intervention is not purely external to the object of that intervention (the child, or adult). How the child or adult themselves attribute 'deviance', or whether they even recognise that he or she is 'deviant', will also affect the process.

Brickman *et al.* (in Sugarman, 1986: 189) distinguish between attribution to the self or others of the responsibility for the problem, or the responsibility of the solution (see Table 7.1).

The four models: the moral, the enlightenment, the compensatory and the medical models construct the problem from different perspectives (and in a different way from psychological models) and deciding between *these* conflicting attributions of cause leads to a requirement of a further 'universal' or 'meta-theory' (grand narrative), which can provide explanatory adequacy to support an intervention. Here, the intervention process itself may require the individual to shift his or her attributions from one model to another, through a process of empowerment. The process of establishing 'meta-theoretical' statements lies outside of the theories themselves and is a property of what Bhaskar (1986) calls the 'transitive' aspects of science. If each theory maintains validity and reliability, choosing between them becomes a matter of professional choice or predilection and moves the process away from an objective view of theory towards more subjective approaches (a paradigm shift: Kuhn, 1970; and see Lewis, Chapter 8, this volume). Put another way, a positivist vision of the scientific method sees discovering 'objective truth' as a process of accumulating knowledge stage-by-stage without questioning:

the distinction between the (relatively) unchanging real objects which exist outside and perdue independently of the scientific process and the changing (and theoretically imbued) cognitive objects which are

Table 7.1

Attribution of self for responsibility for problem	Attribution to self of responsibility for solution	
	HIGH	LOW
HIGH	Moral Model	Enlightenment Model
Perception of self	Lazy	Guilty
Actions expected of self	Striving	Submission
Others beside self who must act	Peers	Authorities
Actions expected of others	Exhortation	Discipline
Implicit view of human nature	Strong	Bad
Potential pathology	Loneliness	Fanaticism
LOW	Compensatory Model	Medical Model
Perception of self	Deprived	Ill
Actions expected of self	Assertion	Acceptance
Others beside self who must act	Subordinates	Experts
Actions expected of others	Mobilisation	Treatment
Implicit view of human nature	Good	Weak
Potential pathology	Alienation	Weak dependency

produced as a function and result of its practice; that is between the intransitive and transitive objects of scientific knowledge and accordingly between the intransitive and transitive dimensions in the philosophy of science.

(Bhaskar, 1986: 51)

The cognitively imbued transitive objects of science, the 'subjective' view of objects, are constructed through experience (practice) and through a discourse ('mensurating material object language' – see also Fulcher, 1989; Corbett, 1994) which contains presuppositions and inferences about the nature of the objects to which they refer. Bhaskar argues that a 'theory constituting' language or discourse has three functions:

(The) language acts at once: a) as a common or garden a-theoretic intra-scientific auxiliary, in terms of which the conflicting implications of synchronically inclusive or widely meaning divergent theories can, in the last resort, be spelt out, in the event that the scientific communities or generations are not sufficiently bi-theoretically-lingual; b) as a medium for the expression of (always socialised but historically specific or transhistorically generic) human needs, wants and interests, in terms of which the explanatory power of modern natural science and the instrumental utility of science-based and/or characteristically capitalist technology can be motivated in comparison with alternative modes of cognition and appropriation of nature; and c) as a means of the initiation of the neophyte into the scientific mysteries and virtues, enabling agents everywhere to participate in its own esoteric rights and practices, including its apostasies, splits and schisms, under the sign of a supreme excellence: explanatory power.

(Bhaskar, 1986: 91)

Here, within the context of medical/social models, the language of 'diagnosis' as a strong indexial language establishes the object, defines a programme of intervention and evaluates its outcome (descriptive adequacy).

Even though the 'objective reality' of a child 'having "x"' is complex and dependent on interaction between a range of within-child and environmental factors, seen both synchronically and diachronically, the indexial function of the diagnostic language fixes the 'reality' for the purposes of (among others) to help professionals communicate: 'professionals must be able to communicate with each other, and for better or for worse, the diagnostic system is the way in which this communication occurs' (Bonder, 1991: Preface; cf. Bhaskar, op. cit.).

The use of 'diagnosis as communication' acts as a reification of knowledge:

In order to communicate the objectified understanding and to legitimate the social group that created it, knowledge becomes reified, fragmented and rationally ordered. In this way, the originally informal fluid and implicit understanding between people in a face-to-face situation becomes, formal, static, explicit and impersonal knowledge which can be culturally transmitted.

(Webb, 1989: 57)

'Having "x"' becomes a reified construct and deviance/abnormality attains the status of the objective reality as a disease-like condition which the individual child or adult 'has', 'experiences', 'suffers' or in the language of the People First Movement 'is with' ('the child with autism'). This has been ingrained in the professional and public psyche, compounded by what Berger and Luckmann (1966: 111) describe as the 'legitimisation of symbolic universes'. Legitimisation 'explains' the institutional order by ascribing cognitive validity to its objectivated meanings which are then transmitted to succeeding generations as unrecon-structed 'truth'. Here meanings become transhistorical and generic.

If the language of diagnosis ('the indexial language') is used to plan interven-tion for the deviant child, the problem arises in reconstructing the child (who is socialised and has an historically specific set of characteristics) from the reified indexial construct: can we reconstruct the child from the statements: 'the child with autism', 'he has autism', 'he suffers from autism'? Here, in the context of an intervention, can the practice of intervention be reconstructed from the concept 'autism'? Does knowing that a child 'has autism' lead us to develop a practical set of procedures (Berger and Luckmann's 'curative process')?

In this respect the term 'autism' acts as a compressed concept and as a computable 'essence' (Coveney and Highfield, 1995). The richness and complexity of a real-world system (in this sense, the child with autism) is reduced, or compressed to a set of descriptors, derived from analytic methods. The limits of 'compressibility' (taken as a measure of 'complexity') are those statements from which the original system can be reconstituted: 'the complexity of something is the size of the smallest programme which computes it or a complete description of it. Simpler things require smaller programmes' (ibid.: 37).

The converse of 'compressibility' is 'incompressibility':

> 'Boy meets girl. Family intervenes. Couple dies' is a compression that falls far short of Shakespeare's *Romeo and Juliet*. The only way to enjoy the play is to go and see it yourself, not read a review or a synopsis. [If Shakespeare or any 'real world system' is seen as chaotic] it is possible to achieve a degree of algorithmic compression for a chaotic system. This is a relief for any scientist daunted by the complexity of the real world: some very complex real world phenomena can be captured in a small set of deterministic equations. Chaotic systems are exquisitely sensitive to initial conditions and their future behaviour can only be reliably predicted over a short time period. Moreover, the more chaotic the system, the less compressible its algorithmic representation. Finally, if a property of the real world is algorithmically incompressible, the most compact way of simulating its behaviour is to observe the process itself.
>
> (ibid.: 39)

If we accept the view that *Romeo and Juliet* is an incompressible 'whole', it needs to be apprehended in its full, wonderful complexity. Why should not the child 'with autism' be experienced (observed, worked with, played with) in the same way?

The *word* 'autism' inhabits a symbolic universe (in the same way that Shakespeare inhabits a symbolic universe) that is constrained and constructed by factors operating outside of the immediate micro-level of intervention, i.e.

within wider societal, or social–historical processes (what Bronfenbrenner (1979) calls the exo- or meso-levels). The indexial construct 'autism' comes ready-made with a set of rules of procedure (derived from the word meanings associated with 'autism') implicit within the construct ('the programme to reconstitute the complexity') and it operates as a linear system: diagnosis, then prescription. In an educational context, teachers (or least teachers in so-called mainstream situations) generally do not possess access to the implicit meanings contained within the construct, and they must have recourse to experts who can provide rules of action, i.e. intervention procedures. This process is complicated by two factors:

- where diagnosis (compression) is effected by the expert, the non-expert is expected to implement the programme by following the 'expansion rules' which can be made explicit (by the expert);
- however, the non-expert also constructs the child, seen in terms of their own attribution systems, personal history, understandings and technical competence all subsumed under the rubric of 'attitudes' (Ward and Center, 1987). Attitudes also contain (implicitly or explicitly) attribution of value.

Even if this process is ideally construed, depressingly for many children or adults with disabilities, irrespective of the level of description of the problem, the *educational* intervention process appears to be identical:

In a review of language-intervention programmes, Siegel and Spradlin (1978) reasoned that differential diagnosis and the discovery of different underlying causes of language impairment would be important if it could be shown that these had significant consequences for the type of treatment and/or instructional programmes undertaken. They concluded somewhat pessimistically, however, that, given the present state of knowledge, the instructional task seemed to be identical regardless of whether the individual child was labelled autistic, brain-damaged, retarded or congenitally aphasic.
(Cromer, 1991: 192; see also DSM-III; Bonder, 1991 – for the range of intervention practices undertaken by practitioners in mental health)

Dynamic approaches: understanding 'needs'

In the preceding section, I have argued that the linear diagnostic–prescriptive approach will define its own 'object'. Here the 'diagnostic' needs (Stuffelbeam, 1977) which emerge from the diagnostic gaze will determine the nature and course of a programme of intervention. Such needs of a child are determined with respect to a reference group and implicitly reflect differential power relationships, construed as 'objective truth'.

A dynamic view sees the complexities of interaction between the child (individual characteristics) and his/her social environment as constructing an identity (the 'person', 'the disabled identity' (Abberley, 1993)). 'Person' here can be seen as an emergent property (Bronfenbrenner, 1979; Casti, 1994) or as an epi-genetic phenomenon (Piaget, 1971), which is phenomenological:

> Very few of the external influences significantly affecting human behaviour and development can be described solely in terms of objective physical conditions and events; the aspects of the environment that are most powerful in shaping the course of psychological growth are overwhelmingly those that have meaning to the person in a given situation.
>
> (Bronfenbrenner, 1979: 9)

This phenomenological experience of individuals is biographical in nature and underpins a moral view of 'being human'. One particular view argues that

> it is the richness and complexity of an individual life which is morally significant. [We must] distinguish the concept of 'being alive' (mere existence) from that of 'having a life' (in which the subject of that life experiences the world, acts within it and, so to speak, constructs a biography for himself or herself). Although biological life is a prerequisite for a biographical life, moral significance only attaches to biographical life.
>
> (Rachels in Wilkie, 1993: 177)

It is precisely because of this view of the requirement of 'having a biography' that the medical model holds sway in those specific areas of individual development where 'having a biography' becomes problematic. For those children deemed to be autistic, or to experience profound and multiple learning difficulties, or who experience deafness–blindness, and who do not interact with others generally, it is difficult to see how their difficulties are 'socially-constructed'. Gregory argues that

> disability is a social category which legitimates, or at least condones, the disempowerment of people with particular mental or physical attributes. The desirability of the norm has consequences for the expectations of disabled people and, thus, such social and cultural understandings of disability are fundamental to the ways in which people who are labelled disabled come to understand themselves and their own identity.
>
> (Gregory, 1996: 36)

Children or adults who experience gross impairments are excluded from the 'disability category' in that they are incapable of 'understanding themselves or their own identity' and it is here, for these specific children, that the 'social-constructionist' theoretical view starts to break down in that they are outside of the processes of socialisation deemed by Berger and Luckmann to be a prerequisite for inclusion as social beings, i.e. because they lack the ability (or opportunity?) to construct a biography for themselves, they do not attract moral significance (in Rachels's terms, op. cit.).

An opposing view, however, argues that although these children have extreme individual (ontogenetic) developmental anomalies, they are part of the human condition (they have phylogenetic characteristics), and as such are to be included within the moral framework of 'being human'. These 'phylogenetic' needs can be construed within a 'rights' framework (Garner and Sandow, 1995) and where we (i.e. society) confer human status on children, we assume that it is possible to be human without possessing a 'biography' in the sense that Rachels uses.

But 'special educational needs' are 'biographical' in the phenomenological sense of being meaningful for both the individual *and* for the group who form the social environment of the individual. This view presupposes that the individual grows and develops within a social environment as well as a material one, and meaning is an emergent property of the system. Such a system is based on interdependence between agents and agencies (Crossley, 1996). Biographies have synchronic and diachronic aspects: they have beginnings, middles and ends (Sugarman, 1986) and to see 'deviance' or 'difference' as being fixed in either organic (or genetic) *or* social bases, is to miss the richness of the biography metaphor.

Thus, some children or adults may have 'special educational needs' which arise through disadvantage arising from differences socially created through ethnic, gender or cultural arguments, rather than disability discourses. For such children or adults we cannot say that 'being female' or being 'Afro-Caribbean' (or being poor) are 'organic' deficits, but we can say that such personal characteristics may lead to disadvantage in particular social contexts (handicap in the WHO classifications (Wood, 1981)), and disadvantage/handicap can be seen as a 'special need'. We see both cultural disadvantage and organic impairment as constituting a 'special need', although the 'needs' arising from these two aspects are different. The position is further confused because certain constituencies are celebrating 'impairment' as 'difference' (Corbett, 1996; see also photographer Hevey, 1992; Lewis and Gilling, 1985). Celebrating 'impairment' in an educational context becomes problematic in that it would be a brave practitioner who refused to intervene in the case of a child diagnosed as dyslexic who viewed such a child as being 'different', rather than 'deficient' and who did not require the child to be subjected to a curriculum which required reading at its core.

If we accept 'difference' as a construct as opposed to 'deviant' or 'deficient', intervention becomes even more problematic, in that we are led to accept 'difference', rather than attempting to change the individual, where this process of change is seen as assimilation into the dominant culture (Csapo, 1982). Difference, as opposed to deficit or deviance, requires a democratic definition of 'needs' (Stuffelbeam, 1977) within a human rights discourse of empowerment (Riddell, 1994; Fulcher, 1989).

However, such a discourse, while offering a justification at a social/ethical level (Bricker, 1978), may fail to implement change, if this process, while supporting the concept of equality, does not address equity (Garner and Sandow, 1995).

> Equal opportunity implies the provision of facilities for a minority such as the disabled, where such facilities have been lacking, and the responsibility of the disabled to take advantage of them. Equity, on the other hand implies the restructuring of what is offered in such a way that final outcome is equally attainable. In one case, the responsibility is on the individual, in the other it is on the provider. For example, in the early days of educational integration, it was thought enough to include the child with Down's Syndrome in mainstream classroom, from which he or she had previously been excluded. The responsibility was his or hers to learn. When such children could no longer 'cope' they could be removed to the special school. Later it was realised that more than simple exposure was required if integration were to succeed.
>
> (ibid.: 5)

Here, unless the intervention process results in real change for the individual, any theoretical justification for understanding that failure is just that: a *post-hoc* rationalisation of failure. Unless a theory can provide directions for change, together with understanding of why such change is necessary (or its corollary, why change is *not* necessary), and is coherent across all cases (descriptive and explanatory adequacy), we are locked into short-term 'fixes' which have validity in restricted areas for certain children at certain times. Thus, Peters, writing within a cross-cultural perspective, argues that 'the social constructivist paradigm that (she) held so dear as the new axiom for study of disability began to fall apart under the cross-cultural analysis. Social constructivists have failed to effect change' (Peters, 1995: 70).

Towards a synthesis

The foregoing discussion has offered a view of what constitutes a 'special educational need'. This can be seen in deficit or diagnostic terms, it can also be seen as the outcome of a democratic definition of 'needs' within a rights discourse. Again, each of these positions achieves descriptive adequacy, but we still lack 'meta-statements' which will allow us to distinguish between the positions offered, and echoing the Audit Commission's (1992) report, it is clear that an understanding of what is meant by a 'special educational need' is of paramount importance.

A theory of special education will try to resolve the conflicts between these competing positions, but there is nothing in each specific theory underpinning each position to decide – and following on my argument above, even if one theory does predominate, the 'rules of intervention' generated by each position will not reconstruct the object in any kind of direct, algorithmic way. This 'linear mode' of reconstructing the object (the process of intervention) is insufficient. In an educational sense, practitioners do not see the world in linear or monochronic terms (Hargreaves, 1993), where simple problems have simple solutions. Instead they view the world in highly interactive, polychronic, ways which result from interactions in a complex world. Teachers adopt 'polyocular vision' (Cooper and Upton, 1991) to make sense of the 'chaotic views' (Clough, 1995), through the exercise of professional judgement. The exercise of professional judgement is a process based on both knowledge and experience and is what happens during the range of normal or ordinary practice. What happens in those special cases when our general professional procedures are no longer valid, or where the 'normal' rules of procedure do not work in specific cases (Brown, 1990)? When our rules of thumb do not apply, we as practitioners have recourse to other sources of knowledge and it is here that a theory of special education will inform the process of rational decision making in specific cases. Such a theory will not specify 'content' (in the way that, for example, a behavioural or psychodynamic theory will construct the object), but will rather specify process of deliberation: 'Aristotle's concept of "deliberation" (. . .) is an intellectual ability that we draw on when we must make decisions in cases where we cannot achieve certainty, but are not totally lacking in relevant information' (ibid.: 150). Deliberation requires us to evaluate evidence and to make decisions: the process is not divorced from action as a central aspect intervention.

If the judgement of the individual is constrained by the development of 'practical wisdom' (Aristotle – Nicomachean Ethics), or what Brown (1990) calls 'rational judgement', competing courses of actions (i.e. different interventions) will be analysed with respect to some wider understanding derived from theory. If classical rationality is concerned with deriving procedures for deciding between competing theories, we are left with an infinite regress: we need meta-theories to distinguish between 'lower-level' theories, and further theories to distinguish between the meta-theories (Popper, 1972; Kuhn, 1970). Thus, to decide whether to act according to behaviourist or psychodynamic approaches for intervention at the individual level, or to act according to normalisation or social oppression approaches at the social level, will be decided according to principles which lie outside of the domains of the particular theories. Here, following this argument, we would require a 'meta-theory' to distinguish between 'the medical model' and the 'social model' that underpins a particular course of intervention for people with 'special educational needs', and while one meta-theory may have explanatory adequacy, there may well be others which do just as well. This is the first step of a regression.

The competing social, social-constructivist or medical models each have merit within their limited domains. How can a rational model of special education be developed which allows the synthesis of these views to develop rational models of intervention?

A rational model will need to have clear understandings about 'special educational needs' as an emergent property of complex systems. This requires an analysis of how needs are determined and for us to be clear how this process is constituted. Here the process of needs definition must be problematised, and the subsequent intervention processes problematised in turn.

If we see individuals interacting within social and physical worlds and a 'special need' as an imbalance in the 'ecology' of individuals, then such a view requires a theory of intervention which sees 'specialness' as an emergent behaviour within chaotic or complex systems (Gregoire and Prigogine, 1989), which requires understanding of the dynamics of *both* the individual and his/her social and physical environment. It also requires an understanding of how these interact dynamically and over time – this is especially important where the crude 'moral imperative' contains hidden assumptions about 'normality' as opposed to 'diversity'. This understanding has two components (Brown, 1990): intralinguistic and extralinguistic aspects of the problem.

The first is rooted in discourse of special education: *how* do we define 'needs' (seen synchronically and diachronically) but also more importantly, *who* defines such needs; what makes such needs special; how do 'differences', i.e. those aspects of the individual which are accepted, become 'deficits' which are socially stigmatised?

The second is rooted in courses of practical action (intervention) which derive from the intralinguistic factors (the discourse of theory). An 'emergent' process of practical action is deliberative, i.e. based on feedback gained through the evaluative weighing of evidence of the effects of that practical action. It must be directed holistically and within reflective cycles and be subject to ecological validity:

> all actions must be considered in contexts, in relation to the actions with which they are combined (both spatially and temporally), and, more particularly, they must be considered from the point of view of the way in which they are used.
>
> (Crossley, 1996: 138)

Critical reflection on practice (Zeichner and Liston, 1987) which is dynamic and holistic will provide a synthesis of theory and practice (intra- and extralinguistic aspects) to allow the exercise of judgement.

If we are envisaging the learner(s) and the learning environment as a dynamic system (which also contains the educator or special educator as an integral and interacting component of that system), then the system can only be maintained through the exercise of feedback between individual components of the system. It is the requirement for feedback which allows the system (as a whole) to be responsive to change (Coveney and Highfield, 1995). Feedback, in the form of professional deliberation, can support dynamic systems and in Brown's (1990) view, professional judgement is developed through debate amongst peers. Within a 'priesthood' model (Berger and Luckmann, 1966) which sees special education as being the domain of experts, 'peers' here relate to other 'experts'. I have argued that there exist constituencies in the field of 'special education' and given this wider phenomenological view of how a biography of an individual child is constructed, the debate must be extended to include these other constituencies (see Wolfendale, 1992, in the area of parents, or Clough and Barton, 1995, who argue for the inclusion of people with disabilities into the research process).

More important, the process should include the focus of the intervention process itself: the child or adult within advocacy and self-advocacy models (Garner and Sandow, 1995) as ecological validity of intervention approaches must incorporate 'at least some knowledge of the subject's definition of the situation' (Bronfenbrenner, 1979: 30).

As such intervention must deal with the complexity of interaction, rather than simplistic ends–means theoretical positions (see, for example, Cooper and Upton, 1991), particularly where simplistic approaches fail and lead to misery. In the context of integration, Barton and Landman (1993: 47) note that maintaining mainstream provision for pupils with special educational needs has been concentrated on those pupils who are 'least difficult or objectionable and easiest to manage'. If we are to maintain appropriate interventions for all within inclusive educational practice and to meet 'needs' of all learners, we need to adopt reflective and dynamic approaches to intervention which can fulfil the outcomes of both 'deficit/diagnostic' and 'difference/democratic' models.

The reflective and dynamic deliberative process must problematise intervention across the following dimensions (Zeichner and Liston, 1987):

- technical: which practice derived from theory can be used in this context? Why and how can these be used? (Deficit/diagnostic needs.)
- situational: are there other interventions which can be undertaken in this situation? What are the characteristics of this situation that lead me/us to adopt this practice? (Analytic needs – Stuffelbeam, 1977.)
- social/moral ethical: what are the outcomes (seen historically) of this intervention process? Are they the desired outcomes? What should we change if we wish to achieve our desired ends (democratic needs)? Here the process of intervention may be directed at societal factors rather than individual ones.

Fundamental to all of these levels of reflection is the process of data gathering and the evaluation of the data with respect to wider knowledge gained phenomenologically which respects the 'we' in the intervention process. The 'we' in this process should reflect the constituencies within a partnership model and in context of the foregoing discussion, this is not something simply desirable, but is necessary to constitute the 'object' both in its objective and subjective characteristics (ecological validity). In this respect intervention becomes a process of historical inquiry where 'the teacher is seen as involved in the creative strategic responses to social and situational constraints, or as resolving ever present dilemmas through and with their interaction with pupils' (Ball and Goodson, 1985: 7–8).

If we are dealing with creativity and uncertainty within social and situational constraints, the symbolic universe of 'medial discourse' (Fulcher, 1989) as the more (most?) powerful paradigm for certain categories of problems ignores the transitive aspects of scientific understanding, which are socially and historically determined and which change in discontinuous ways. If we are to move beyond this objectification of the concept of deviance, we need to address the complex interrelationships of interactions between individuals, social groupings, systems and institutions, all of which have histories.

Here, Bronfenbrenner's (1979) distinctions between micro-, meso-, exo- and macro-systems, seen synchronically and diachronically, offer directions.

A theory of special education must offer a deliberative process which results in whole and inclusive societies. The logical extreme of the medical model is home tuition for the child excluded for a variety of reasons. Such an educational process can meet a very narrow definition of a deficit/diagnostic 'educational need', but fails to meet democratic/rights needs. The converse is the child with profound and multiple learning difficulties who is placed at the back of a mainstreamed class with an untrained assistant. Here 'democratic needs' are met, what about diagnostic/deficit needs?

A theory of special education (and future research to determine the nature and extent of such a theory) must provide a rationale for intervention which allows for all of our children to be educated together. Such a theory must also be constrained by ecological validity and explanatory adequacy. If we are concerned to develop meaningful interventions which are technically efficient, situationally effective and ethically sound for children or adults whose needs must be met through interactions in ordinary environments, we must address complexity.

Conclusion

To return to the Teacher Training Agency's request to train the next generation of teachers in the practice of special education, I have argued that a theory of special education should be concerned with processes of reflection and deliberation, rather than the delineation of technical 'fixes'. A process, by definition, is not finite and if we see the act of deliberation/reflection as a skill (Brown, 1990) this presupposes that the development of professional judgement is something which takes place over the span of a professional life. If we are dealing with complexity, we (as practitioners and researchers) must accept that change, mutability and non-predictability are natural parts of dynamic systems and that 'certainty' is only provided by an artificial view of the world. A theory of special education must provide practitioners with the confidence to accept that uncertainty.

7

THE POVERTY OF SPECIAL EDUCATION

Theories to the rescue?

Tony Booth

Introduction : what is wrong with special education?

In their brief to contributors, the editors of this book argued that there is some-thing wrong with the explanatory systems or theories, such as the medical model, which dominate thinking about special education, as well as those proposed to replace them. If theory not only provides 'a scheme of ideas to explain practice' (Williams, 1976), but also 'a framework to guide practice', then we have here a diagnosis of the ills of special education and a remedy. A barrier to progress in special education is to be removed with the generation of more adequate 'theories' about educational failure and improvement. This view of how progress might be made is a meta-theory to account for problems in a field of 'special education' and in this chapter I wish to contribute to the task of identifying and removing barriers to progress in special education by elaborating some elements of a meta-theory of my own.

I contend that the poverty of special education resides in much else besides the lack of adequate theories of student learning and school improvement. I have focused initially on three issues: a lack of the definition of the field; the submergence of conflict and critique; and the overproduction of 'knowledge'. I suggest that progress in these areas as in the use of theories of teaching and learning depends on a realignment of professional and political interests.

A lack of definition

There is an absence of agreement about what constitutes 'special education' though how the subject is defined is rarely specified. Some chapters in this book assume special education is primarily concerned with issues of *disability*, while others see it as about organisational and classroom responses to *diversity*. The absence of definition is a striking omission, for in taking for granted that

79

we all know what is meant by 'special education', a dominant view is permitted to hold sway which may undermine the position of those who wish to depart from it.

In order to take control of the study of special education we have to be clear about how we define it, for our definition determines what we describe, interpret and explain. There are two ways of approaching a definition. We can state how we use the term ourselves and provide a *prescription* for how we wish it to be used by others. Alternatively we can give a *description* of the variety of ways in which the term is used. A failure to distinguish between such approaches to definition may itself contribute to confusion. For example, it has been asserted that 'integration' or 'mainstreaming' means assimilation of students into an unchanged normality of curricula and school culture, whilst 'inclusive education' means schools adapting to diversity (Sebba and Ainscow, 1996). I regard this as a prescription, rather than a description, of how either term is used (see Booth, 1988).

There is a tendency to expect a definition of a complex and contested area of human activity to be accomplished in a few well-chosen words. It is generally far easier to do so if a dominant view is being offered, since the cultural penetration of such a view may lead to the presumption that a few words make unequivocal reference to a set of practices or processes. It is also easier to be brief if a prescription is offered rather than the range of ways in which a particular concept is used.

The term 'special education' is used less commonly than in the past, having been replaced by 'special needs education'. I avoid the latter term because I think that the use of the term 'children with special needs' implies a particular view of the nature of difficulties in learning which I reject. I regard the use of the term 'special needs' as an educational practice that requires explanation as part of a study of 'special education'. In placing the terms at different levels of analysis, I think of them as first-order and second-order concepts, respectively.

My discussion of definitions partly follows Patricia Potts's useful suggestion in Chapter 10, this volume, that special education can refer to an area of study, an approach to learners, a set of institutions and a set of policies. In mentioning institutions I presume she is referring to the practice of using 'special education' synonymously with 'special school education', a practice still common in some countries. This relates to a distinction between 'remedial' and 'special' education, officially out of vogue in the UK when used in these terms (Department of Education and Science, 1978) but officially required in effect through the statementing process and the staged assessments of the Code of Practice (Department for Education, 1994). In order to illustrate the range of views that comprise special education, I provide a selective trawl through differences in the way 'special education' is thought to encompass learners, approaches to teaching, policies and politics, and approaches to study.

Some learners or all learners?

Special education is commonly thought to be about students with 'special needs', 'learning difficulties', disabled students and perhaps students who are disaffected. Who is identified as having 'learning difficulties', 'special needs' or disabilities depends in turn on how these terms are defined. It has been the practice in the UK to define 'special needs' more broadly than disability although this is changing in particular through the broadening of the definition of disability in the 1995 Disability Discrimination Act. The word 'disabled' is often used in the USA, as well as in Australia and New Zealand, to refer to both physically disabled students and others who experience difficulties in learning, as in the phrase 'learning disability'. The amount of North American publication tends to lead to discussion on their terms.

Without careful specification of who is and is not included within the term 'disabled', and the reasons for extending or restricting its use, the control that is sought over the discourse of disability is lost. In Chapter 3, this volume (Julie Allan *et al.*), it appears there is an identification of the terms 'pupils with special educational needs' and 'disabled pupils' which legitimates the use of the first term, criticised by myself and others as derogatory and contributing to the exclusion and devaluation of large groups of students and preparing them for a tenuous relationship with the world of work (Tomlinson, 1982).

At the heart of the discussion of the meaning of disability is whether or not it implies *physical* impairment. If in addition to physically disabled students, we include as disabled all students categorised as having difficult behaviour, or as having low attainment, then we reinforce the medical model's resurgence in explanations of difficulties in schools and hinder the understanding and spread of 'a social model' of disability or learning difficulties.

We could interpret the idea of special education as a concern with all students who are vulnerable to exclusionary pressures in schools, rather than only those categorised as having 'special needs' or disabilities or as disaffected. The notion of special education as concerned with all 'vulnerable young people' is reflected in those historical concerns with overcoming barriers to learning and participation in education of disabled children and other groups such as children in poverty, for example, in aspects of the open-air school movement (McMillan, 1917).

This higher-order category of concern may be reflected in an interest in bullying in education, or children affected by HIV or AIDS, or the use of drugs by young people. Seeing notions of 'special need' or 'disability' or 'disaffection' as subsets within the category of 'students vulnerable to exclusion' might also help to avoid making a simple translation of educational priorities from the historical, cultural and economic circumstances in developed countries to those in poorer nations. When entirely different patterns of disease, school availability and attendance and literacy occur in two countries, what sense can it make to apply the same notions of 'special need' in both? When it was suggested that an international conference might adapt its agenda from a concern with categories of 'special need', to reflect some of the broader preoccupations of South World countries with access to education, a Professor of Special Education remarked revealingly: 'categories of special need are our bread and butter'. Yet, it can be argued, defining special education in terms of 'special need' and 'disability' obscured the class and economic basis of failure in, and exclusion from, schools in *both* developed and poor countries. It deflects us, too, from the action necessary to overcome failure and exclusion. Thus, it reflects particular economic as well as professional *interests*.

Like Patricia Potts (Chapter 10, this volume), I see special education as about overcoming barriers to learning for all students. I reject the ideological basis of the distinction between 'normal' learners and those with 'special needs'. I employ a social model of learning difficulties in which a difficulty in learning arises out of a relationship between students, curricula, teachers and other resources available to support learning. I find it interesting that authors who reject the medical model of disability continue to use the deficit view of learning difficulties as implied by the categorisation of children as 'having learning difficulties'.

Approaches to teaching

A view of which learners are subjects of special education may be related to particular views of teaching approaches and policies. The idea that special education is about identifying categories of special need and relating special curricula to them is prevalent. Despite official rhetoric in the 1978 Warnock Report that such categorisation obscured and misdirected the analysis of the difficulties in learning of children (Department of Education and Science, 1978) it remained a guiding principle for practice even within that report (Booth, 1985b). It has been given new overt encouragement within the Code of Practice (Department for Education, 1994) and fresh endorsement within the report by the 'consortium on special needs' on teacher education (Special Educational Needs Training Consortium, 1996).

The notion that special education is about responding to diversity has been used to counter the dominance of views which divide students into normal and less-than-normal learners. On this view, students who have relatively low attainment or are disabled are seen as aspects of a valued diversity of learners to which schools should respond. The recognition and valuing of diversity becomes part of the process of overcoming barriers to learning.

Policies and politics

Views of learners and teaching approaches can be seen as either contributing to a selective, or inclusive and comprehensive, view of education and special education. Although it is sometimes argued that the notion of special needs is about the *individualisation* of learning, the processes of identifying students as having special needs and assigning them to categories reinforces a *selective* view that there are student types who require different forms of education. Support for the existence of special schools is based on this view.

I see the increase in the inclusion and participation of students in the cultures, curricula and communities of mainstream neighbourhood schools and the reduction of their exclusion from them as providing a major part of the framework for understanding and studying special education. It is part of the process of developing comprehensive community education.

Discussion of rights is not common in writings on special education in the UK, though some do see special education as about the implementation of parental and student rights. The widespread acceptance of a view that special education policy is concerned with the recognition of the rights of children and young people and their parents rather than the making of decisions by professionals and administrators on their behalf, would make a considerable difference to education practice as well as the way it is studied.

Views about selection or inclusion, as well as rights and the relative power of people to make decisions in education, are clearly political notions. It is strange to think that there may still be people who think that education can be conceived without politics. However, some people give special education a more significant political role than others. For example, on one view it exists to preserve certain fundamental and progressive features of education and as a model for the rest of the education system to follow. According to Tom Skrtic it has this position because it is concerned with the failures produced by the contradictions inherent in mass education for individual learners or between 'the democratic ends and bureaucratic means of public education' (Skrtic, 1991a: v). An examination of special education thus provides for him 'the insights necessary to deconstruct and reconstruct 20th century public education for the emerging historical contingencies of the 21st century' (ibid.). While less grandiose claims may be made by others, the assertion that special education is 'real education' responding to individuals is not uncommon.

Equally, 'special education' has been seen to have the opposite function, to be about obscuring rather than revealing the contradictions in education. Thus, the creation of special education can be viewed as the means by which the failures of the system and the exclusionary pressures within it are transformed into the failings of students (Tomlinson, 1982). I have used the image that attributing 'special needs' to a student provides a screen onto which exclusionary processes can be projected and then hidden from view (Booth, 1996a).

Approaches to study?

The question 'How should special education be studied?' is one way of asking about the theories and their assumptions which help to make sense of the field. Medical, psychological and sociological models compete for influence in a way that remains to be fully exposed in terms of the interplay between the relative powers of explanation, ideology and interests that are involved. My own view is that these apparently separate disciplines cannot have a distinct object of study since people can only exist in the context of their bodies, cultures, societies and histories. Yet the removal of disciplinary boundaries meets with tremendous resistance. Archibald could argue against the boundary between psychology and sociology in 1976, after Robert Frost, that 'bad fences make bad neighbours', but his plea has been seldom heard or repeated (Archibald, 1976).

However much some people might wish it otherwise, a medical model still dominates the conceptualising of the problems students face in schools. Alan Dyson has argued that 'the last two decades have been characterised by a failure of the psycho-medical paradigm to defend itself against a barrage of criticism' (Dyson, 1994, personal communication prior to the symposium which preceded this book), and Tom Skrtic, writing in the USA, asked, 'What led 20th century special educators to believe in the theory of human pathology, an idea that seems so wrong today?' (Skrtic, 1991a: 82). I believe that these writers are mistaken in fact and assumption. The medical model is alive and flourishing, relentlessly and overtly pursued within departments of educational psychology and covertly pursued through the assumption of education by category in many departments of special education. It is part of the individual approach to educational difficulties, in which the failures of education are attributed to deficits in children and teachers, which have fuelled the rise in identification of dyslexia and attention deficit hyperactivity disorder (ADHD) and the exclusion of difficult students from school (Cooper and Ideus, 1995; Taylor, 1994). It creates and sustains the notion of 'special educational need' as I have argued, ad nauseum, elsewhere.

We may be tempted to think that we can exert greater freedom over our promotion of theoretical models than we think. While individual contributors to this book may define special education differently, we share a common history. We have inherited jobs which owe their existence to the concerns of our predecessors with 'abnormal psychology' in which the development of 'abnormal' individuals was singled out for particular study. However much I may reject it, this history not only generated my job, but also the audiences for the courses I produce and hence has created barriers to my attempts to redefine my field of study. Any transformation of special education has to sever the economic as well as conceptual connections with former perspectives.

The submergence of conflict and critique

I do not know whether the operation of the 'diplomatic imperative' is more prevalent in the areas in which I work than others, but it stands in the way of clear thought and the development of our knowledge. Disputes about facts and research approaches are defined or ignored in the interests of social harmony with some, though not necessarily others.

The position that disabled people occupy in the theory and practice of special education has an important bearing on the way the area is defined and has been insufficiently debated. As discussed too by Jeff Lewis (in Chapter 6, this volume), at times the study of special education as well as notions of integration and 'inclusive education' have been interpreted as requiring leadership by disabled people. This is a view held both by some disabled people (Oliver, 1992a, b) and those who wish to align themselves with the struggles of disabled people. I have no doubt that disabled people should have control over decisions about their own lives. They have a right of inclusion and participation in mainstream neighbourhood schools as well as the right to make the same choices as other students. But if special education or integration or inclusive education is concerned with all students rather than only disabled students, then disabled people cannot claim privileged status in understanding it.

I argue that the 'legendary public argument' referred to by Julie Allan *et al.*, in Chapter 3, this volume, in which Mike Oliver suggested that a debate about integration was masturbatory (Oliver, 1992b), had more to do with the macho politics of the locker room, professional self-interest and the termination of critique, than with the politics of disability (Booth, 1992a).

It may be seen as particularly important to avoid conflict with those in positions of power and hence there may be only muted criticism of official documents and policy. The fact that the Code of Practice on Special Educational Needs now contains four definitions of learning difficulty and has multiplied several-fold the confusion in the terms of the 1993 Education Act seems to have escaped most people's notice. Thus, in the code, a learning difficulty is a greater difficulty than the majority in unspecified areas, a disability, a learning difficulty defined as poor academic attainment relative to other students or a specific learning difficulty defined as poor attainment relative to other attainments of the same students. The 1995 Disability Discrimination Act has complicated the position further by redefining disability to include 'physical *and* mental impairments' which 'substantially' limit day-to-day activities. In writing their school policies on special education, teachers have to use this latter definition for some items and the 1993 Act definitions for others.

Of course there are real problems about the ownership and reporting of research and issues of diplomacy, or human decency, necessarily influence what is reported. In a piece of research in which I was involved the illness of the wife of one of the main protagonists had a major influence on events yet it was impossible to write about it. Yet there is little point writing about schools containing people that are diplomatic artefacts. As part of a personal Shakespeare recovery programme and in order to join in discussions about it with my daughter, I recently read *Hamlet*. In Rosencrantz and Guildenstern, Shakespeare portrayed functionaries who are a notable presence in some of the educational institutions I encounter . . . I finished it with a title echoing in my head: 'Rosencrantz and Guildenstern are alive and running an educational institution near you'.

In 1994 I attended a colloquium that led to the publication of the book *Towards Inclusive Schools* (Clark *et al.*, 1995a). Discussions were lively and informative, clarifications were sought and disagreements aired. However, at one point they took on an entirely different quality. There was a highly polarised reaction to the presentation of David Reynolds's paper on applying the insights of school effectiveness research to reach an understanding of inclusive education (Reynolds, 1995). Some of the people present disagreed fiercely with the assumptions, assertions and conclusions in the paper. Others felt that it paved the way forward for a science of 'inclusive education', which might, like the effective schools movement, develop its own journal and 'body of knowledge'. The Reynolds paper, then, seemed to act as a lightning conductor revealing fundamental differences of views held by members of the group that had previously been left in the air. For me this was a memorable event and the episode and its aftermath, an important piece of data about special education. Yet the dispute and the differences of perspective that lay behind it did not carry the same significance for the editors of *Towards Inclusive Schools?* (Clark *et al.*, 1995a).

Reynolds stated that his approach was 'positivistic in orientation and quantitative in method, working from the belief that it is possible to generate empirical truths about the world' (Reynolds, 1995: 126) and concluded that 'the most recent research evidence may cast doubt on the validity and practical value of the [inclusionist] enterprise' (ibid.: 121). This examination of research evidence presumes that the place of some students lies outside the mainstream until research tells us otherwise. Is it only disabled students and others in special schools whose exclusion is given legitimacy in this way or could it be applied to any group which is seen to lie outside a monocultural normality? It is not difficult to see why this would be rejected by those who think of mainstream education as a right for everyone.

Reynolds reported on some studies that showed that some schools did not have uniformly good social and academic outcomes. He argued that this evidence implied that they might have to choose between the two. Thus, the emphasis on social values required to include students who experienced difficulties might be at the expense of the academic output of the school. He appeared to employ a mechanical, hydraulic model, or theory, in which attempts to improve academic performance within a school would lead to poorer social outcomes and vice versa. Yet, while it is possible to see how the transfer of resources from science teaching into pastoral care, for example, might reduce both bullying and performance in science, it is hard to see why the reduction of bullying would lead to worse science results otherwise.

Reynolds's approach can be seen as a variant of the long-standing and persisting positivist approach to research on inclusion which compares performance on outcomes in integrated and segregated settings. I have listed elsewhere the conceptual problems with this approach, which compares schools on the basis of the labels on their name boards rather than the features of the educational experiences they offer (Booth, 1996b). Such research is never conclusive, and hence your starting assumptions can be defended indefinitely. Thus, it is possible for one person to ask in 1996, 'What evidence is available that educating children in segregated schools is either to their own or their peers' benefit?' (Sigston, 1996: 2) while another asserts in 1992 that 'there has been a lack of research evidence in support of the effectiveness of integration for children in ordinary schools' (Hornby, 1992: 138), while a third argues in 1988 that 'there appears no evidence that segregated schooling produces educational results superior to those achieved in integrated schools' (Biklen, 1988: 131).

Reynolds assumes that the natural place for an undefined and unquantified group of students, categorised as having special needs, is outside mainstream schools and then spins the research findings to support this presumption. David Hamilton regards 'the effective schools movement' as 'an ethnocentric pseudo-science that serves merely to mystify anxious administrators and marginalise classroom practitioners' (Hamilton, 1996: 56).

However, I suspect that the success of the 'effective schools' researchers in raising money for research and persuading others of its importance, depends on giving managers what they want. It is an outcome of a diplomatic alliance between researchers and the administrators of the education system, a point made effectively by Alisdair MacIntyre in his analysis of the misdirection of modern thought:

> What managerial expertise requires for its vindication is a justified conception of social science as providing a stock of law-like generalisations with strong predictive power. This account seems to entail – what is certainly not the case – that the social sciences are almost or perhaps completely devoid of achievement. For the salient fact about those sciences is the absence of the discovery of any law-like generalisations whatsoever.
>
> (MacIntyre, 1981: 84)

Research into effective schools which searches for a blueprint for their organisation is expensively misconceived. What might usefully be said in general about effective schools could be agreed in an afternoon by a group of experienced teachers pooling their ideas. Unless they had already given up independent thought in deference to the authority of published research, one would expect them to recognise the relativity of definitions of effectiveness and their political nature.

The overproduction of 'knowledge'

This book is part of a never-ending stream about special education. It has become impossible to keep up with the literature in anything but a very limited portion of the field. Communication with colleagues is therefore seldom conducted on the basis of shared texts. It is possible to read two articles on the same subject which have little overlap in references. While people continue to buy books and journals, they rarely read them. If they do, then they may skim rather than engage in any deep way with the text. If texts are referenced in a piece of writing they may only have been given a cursory reading by the author. People specialise in smaller and smaller areas of the literature and are hence oblivious to the connection of their ideas to the ideas of others. As more and more is published each year then the time band in which ideas are sampled narrows. Academic study is cut off from its history and the ideas of one decade are recycled in the decade after the next.

Yet in this crisis of overproduction, academics are pressurised into increasing their output further in the interests of the grading of their department and the research money that this brings from the Higher Education Funding Council. As output goes up, quality is reduced. People publish the same article, with minor variations in several places, safe in the knowledge that no-one will read more than one version or if they do, they will recognise a fellow professional.

So if I and others call for the removal of boundaries between subject areas or disciplines, even if our conceptual case is impeccable, what chance do we have of success? Susan Hart may have encapsulated part of the reason why the move away from a categorical and special approach to educational difficulties may be resisted, though there may be a hint of the diplomatic imperative in the final sentence:

> Once we have stopped thinking in terms of trying to diagnose difficulties or identifying unique, individual needs that require some sort of additional provision that other children do not require, it becomes much easier to recognise the relevance of the mainstream literature and pursue its possibilities more rigorously and systematically. There is for example a vast reservoir of untapped potential in the fields of social psychology, sociology, anthropology, feminist theory, linguistics, curriculum theory, learning theory, and developments in thinking and pedagogy in the subject disciplines.
>
> This is not to suggest that the existing 'specialist' literature ceases to have relevance . . .
>
> (Hart, 1996: 107)

I recently proposed, as a rule of thumb, to stem the growth in paper work in an institution, that any new administrative demand should identify a preferably longer piece of paper work that it replaced. In calling for an expansion of sources of inspiration, we need to identify ways of cutting the task overall.

David Hamilton drew attention to a further problem with the 'effective schools' researchers who 'aggregate results from different studies conducted at different times in different countries' (Hamilton, 1996: 56). The aggregation of studies is such a common feature of writing about special education that those who avoid it are the exception. If we give up the absurdly mistaken notion that we are trying to make globally valid generalisations about education, then we could avoid paying attention to a sizeable proportion of the studies in special education.

Rescuing special education

The editors have asked us to respond to a set of questions. Do we need a theory of special education? What might such a theory look like? What are the implications of such a theory for research and practice? In answer to the first question I argue that in trying to make sense of the practices and processes of education we all employ theories already. A major task is to make these theories explicit through careful analysis. In responding to the editors' questions, then, like Derrick Armstrong *et al.*, Chapter 4, this volume, I am suggesting that in addition to theorising about the processes of learning and teaching and barriers to learning and teaching, we need to reflect on what we are up to: to account for our own and each other's practice of the study of education. My account of why I find the study of 'special education' problematic leads me to advocate, as Jeff Lewis (Chapter 8, this volume) and as implied by Mel Ainscow (Chapter 2, this volume), a rigorous analysis, critique, pruning and redirection of the field.

However, while it is relatively easy to point out the direction in which I would like to see change occur, it is no easy matter to persuade others of my view. A lack of agreement about the nature of special education, its ills and remedies, will not disappear with more clarity in writing or more effective leadership of the field. It reflects fundamental differences and clashes of interest stemming both from deeply held political beliefs and from professional and personal identities. The replacement of dominant modes of thought is linked to far-reaching professional and political realignments.

8

EMBRACING THE HOLISTIC/CONSTRUCTIVIST PARADIGM AND SIDESTEPPING THE POST-MODERN CHALLENGE

Jeff Lewis

In a recent review of a book in the field of special education, the reviewer amusingly noted that the chapters were interesting in inverse proportion to the occurrence of the word 'paradigm' in the text. If that view is representative of potential readers of this volume then my task is indeed daunting. What I am attempting is a considered discussion of theorising in special education in terms of current debates about the emergence of a new paradigm, here typified as the holistic/constructivist paradigm. I am aware that the word has been used loosely, often as a suffix that adds nothing to what has gone before, or as a synonym for words that we already have, such as theory. I will attempt to sketch out the conditions under which the use of the notion of a paradigm is both helpful and productive. In so doing I will clarify what I understand the word paradigm to mean, suggest ways in which theorising in special education may be seen as an example of paradigmatic theorising, claim that there is available a new paradigm that would be helpful to theorists in special education, and examine some of the consequences of adopting the paradigm, especially in the face of the post-modern challenge to theorising of all kinds.

A productive point of entry for this discussion is the problem of attempting to describe a single theoretical basis for the study and practice of special education. Whilst it is clear that those engaged in theorising special education see themselves as engaged in a sufficiently distinct area of human enterprise, difficult questions arise about how far it is actually distinct. Research groups, delegations to conferences in the field and contributors to volumes of the present type seem to form in predictable and conventional ways, and do not often include practitioners from other forms of educational research, let alone non-educational exponents of theorising the human condition. This may be an artefact of the sociology of academia yet the protagonists still behave as if their concerns are in fact distinct in terms of epistemological rather than sociological categories. However, this position is challengeable. For instance, what makes this area of theorising distinct from other areas of educational theory, or indeed wider fields of theorising? and is it coherent to talk of a theory of special education at all, at least one that has its own distinct methods, content and areas of application?

An attempt to sidestep these difficulties is made when it is argued that special education is not a field of investigation, but merely an administrative category which expedites the targeting of funds in an underfunded system. This implies that if there were unlimited funds available for the wider project of education, then the notion of special education would be redundant, and would not need a theory. However, the argument fails on logical grounds. The category antedated the administrative problem and stands conceptually distinct from it. The administrative need to target funds only to those for whom they are intended presupposes that such a group exists, by virtue of their having unmet needs of a particular kind. The question then arises as to why their needs can be correctly described as special educational needs, usually in terms of a learning difficulty, rather than some other species of need.

It is precisely the pragmatic problem of targeting funds to those who 'really' belong within the category 'special educational needs' that requires the pre-existence of and a development of a theory of special education. That is, the administrative category marks the occasion for deployment rather than the genesis of a category that stands in need of theoretical explication.

The problems emanating from the use and abuse of categories within this field are not new, and this is not the place to review or attempt to resolve them. I will take it as an assumption that the practitioner depends on some form of categorical framework (being informed only that a child has special educational needs gives little clue to the source of the difficulty, nor of ways to proceed with the educational enterprise) but wishes to avoid unjustified discrimination. For a review of the arguments for a non-discriminatory categorical special education see Lieberman (1980). The point for us to consider is what type of theory would be adequate for the task. My claim is that the confusions and impasses that currently beset us are best understood when we see them as arising from the paradigmatic assumptions that have heretofore typified theorising in this field. I am claiming that these confusions and contradictions arise, and render theorising problematic, precisely because theorising in the field has been firmly located in a particular paradigm, that the assumptions of that paradigm are no longer tenable, and that if theorising in special education is to be adequate to the tasks facing it, then the adoption of a new paradigm is necessary and imperative.

So, what is a paradigm?

In order to substantiate the claims that I make in the preceding paragraph, I should define what I mean by a paradigm, and explain more fully how theorising in special education is an example of theorising within a paradigm. The first task is to stipulate a meaning for 'paradigm' that does not equate to other notions for which we already have words. By paradigm I mean an interconnecting set of assumptions, values and methodologies that are taken as axiomatic, and which cannot be further examined within the paradigm itself. This is not the same as an area of investigation, for instance 'The Paradigm of Special Education' or a theoretical orientation, such as 'The Behaviourist Paradigm'. These are both inaccurate uses of the word. A paradigm allows for the co-existence of a number of different, even conflicting, theoretical orientations, as long as they are all based on the same assumptions, which stand immune from examination, and which constitute a shared world view. This world view works at a level which more fundamental questions can be asked than is the case at the level of theory. Paradigms are what Lincoln and Guba call the 'ultimate benchmarks against which everything else is tested' (Lincoln and Guba, 1985: 15). Heshusius (1989) gives a fuller discussion of these points, including the claim that paradigms present a distillation of what we think about the world, but cannot prove, that they present a way of seeing that is also a way of not seeing, that they describe who we are in our epistemological make-up, and give us a way of understanding that we know how we know. She claims that within the field of learning disabilities (and almost certainly elsewhere), several authors have been renaming theories as paradigms, creating an illusion of fundamental change, when in fact only variations in theory (however important they may be) are discussed, while leaving the fundamental paradigmatic assumptions firmly in place. She concludes this section of her paper:

> Thus, it is argued here that the field of Special Education/Learning Disabilities does not contain paradigms within itself, nor does it constitute a preparadigmatic stage; rather it is *part of* a paradigm that has dominated the sciences and social sciences for several centuries.
>
> (Heshusius, 1989: 408)

The particular paradigm that she places special education within has been variously termed the Descartian/Newtonian, the Newtonian mechanistic, the positivist, the modern (hence the project of modernism) and the Enlightenment world view, or paradigm.

Much of the original thinking on the nature of paradigms and paradigm shift comes from Kuhn (1970) who took for his focus the natural sciences. He explained the process by which a paradigm emerges until its assumptions are fixed as the period of 'normal science'. During this period other contending paradigms are discounted and even persecuted as the hegemony of the dominant paradigm asserts itself. Findings which question the validity of the dominant assumptions are seen as puzzling exceptions that can in principle be understood within the paradigm, given more information, or rejected as bogus and relegated to fringe areas which are not given the status of authentic disciplines of inquiry. It is only when these puzzling findings aggregate to the extent that the assumptions of the paradigm are no longer competent to generate explanatory theories that the limitations of the old paradigm are fully realised, and a new set of assumptions must be agreed upon. This is the stage of revolutionary science. At this stage it is precisely the puzzling exceptions that assume great importance, and are brought in from the margins, as they now offer the fertile ground for searching for new paradigmatic assumptions that will resolve the puzzles. The revolutionary period does not discount what has gone before. Rather, it preserves what can still be seen to be valid under the old assumptions, and resolves the former contradictions by building more inclusive theories. An example of this would be our understanding of gravity. Newton's mechanistic assumptions were noted by Einstein not to account for some expected phenomena generated by his theory of relativity. His reformulation of ideas about gravity retained Newton's ideas, which explained how satellites were, and are, put into orbit, but showed that these understandings were only part of the picture, and extended his formulation to include, rather than see as impossible, phenomena that would previously have been considered to contradict the dominant world view.

The old paradigm and special education

As noted above, Heshusius suggests that the field of special education is part of a paradigm that has dominated the sciences and social sciences for several centuries. I would further claim that the field has allowed itself to become detached from wider theorising in education and the human sciences precisely because it has espoused a particularly unreconstructed, hard-edged version of the mechanistic paradigm. The old Newtonian/Mechanistic paradigm, as typified most accessibly by Ferguson (1981) and Capra (1975, 1982), sees the world in terms of a mechanical metaphor, that is totally explicable if only enough data become available. The basic drive to discover knowledge is the search for order, for generalisable theories, for more information about how each part of the machine works. The methodology is therefore reductionist, each field searching in isolation to understand how its own fragment of the universe works, tending to assume a pure or ideal discipline for its own investigations, and to minimise the importance of individual accounts (mere anecdote!) whilst searching for ever more objectivity.

This methodology assumes that the researcher can stand back from the investigation without in any way influencing outcomes, and can control the variables and select subjects so that objective knowledge is obtained which can be applied with confidence in other situations. We must be aware, as Kuhn reminds us, that these assumptions were themselves once considered to be revolutionary. They were the basis of an explosion of useful knowledge and the possibilities of further learning and discovery. The problem arises when the assumptions no longer offer explanatory theories to emerging phenomena which have come to be seen, through the process of investigation, as more complex than was allowed for. This is compounded when the methodologies of the paradigm have somehow become sanctified, when status in the academy is linked with 'pure' application of these methodologies, and competing methodologies committed to the trash can of bogus science. When this stage is reached, it becomes more difficult to question the very assumptions that have generated the contradictions which have puzzled us, and the enterprise sails on regardless of the fact that things are becoming increasingly problematic.

The common feature of the theoretical and methodological orientations arising from the old paradigm is that of reductionism, and much of what has been said and done in the field of special education can be described as a type of reductionism. A very thorough review of this feature of special education is provided by Poplin (1988a, b). She explains that the concept of paradigm is far more encompassing than that of theory, and that various theoretical orientations in special education all share features of the reductionist paradigm. She contrasts four theoretical models of learning disabilities which have been predominant in various eras. These she typifies as the Medical Model of the 1950s, the Psychological Process Model of the 1960s, the Behavioural Model of the 1970s and the Cognitive/Learning Strategies Model of the 1980s. She allows that these models all showed important variations, but were each tied to assumptions arising from the same paradigm.

She notes that each model shared the following reductionist commonalities:

1 Learning disabilities is seen as a discrete phenomenon rather than an explanation of a phenomenon.
2 Each model ultimately places the onus of responsibility for cause and/or the cure for learning disabilities directly on the student.
3 Each model proposes a diagnosis, the goal of which is to document specific deficits.
4 Each model attempts to segment learning into parts.
5 Teaching techniques proposed under each model assume that instruction is most effective when it is most tightly controlled, leaving the learner predominantly passive.
6 The proposed diagnosis for each model forms also the essence of the intervention.
7 Instruction in each model is deficit driven.
8 Teaching and learning are viewed in each model as unidirectional; that is, the teacher knows what is to be learned and the student is to learn it.
9 Each model assumes a right and wrong posture about the teaching and learning process.

10 Each model almost exclusively promotes school goals rather than life goals.

11 Each model supports the segregation of students into different categories.

12 Steps and sequences are valued within the delivery system itself.

These features are seen by Poplin to be examples of the reductionist fallacy. They are outlined by Angeles as:

1   erroneously believing:

    (a) that a complex whole is nothing but, or identical with, its parts and causes and/or

    (b) that a complex whole can be entirely explained in terms of the description of its parts and causes. Example: Mental states are caused by neural processes. Therefore Mental states are nothing but neural processes;

2   the error of explaining a phenomenon and regarding its explanation as being real rather than the phenomenon being explained.

(Angeles, 1981: 242)

This fallacy is also described in the context of learning theory by Gallagher and Reid (1981) and Poplin claims that all the major theoretical models reviewed, not just the behavioural model, have adopted the paradigm and its associated fallacies so that within the field of special education we are constantly, if unconsciously, reinventing assumptions that are fundamentally reductionist fallacies.

I would further claim that by adopting a particularly reductionist framework for theory and research, special education has allowed itself to be cast adrift from developments in other fields of educational theorising which have begun fruitfully to examine the possibilities and potentialities of a paradigm shift. As I have outlined elsewhere (Lewis, 1984), special education has remained largely unaffected by philosophical and sociological debates occurring elsewhere in the educational firmament, and relied on a far narrower set of scientised and psychologised perspectives. The balance, at the level of theory, has certainly broadened in the last decade to include critical sociological and philosophical perspectives, but the inheritance of the predominant reductionist paradigm remains with us. Sinha (1981) pointed out that the younger the child the more thoroughly 'psychologised' his/her education will become. If we extend 'youngness' into the field of developmental stages, then we can by analogy extend Sinha's classification into the field of special education.

This lack of a broader perspective has long been noted; Barton and Tomlinson concluded that the contributors to their edited volume were 'convinced that current debates and dilemmas in special education will be widened and clarified by the introduction of alternative, particularly sociological, perspectives' (Barton and Tomlinson, 1981: 13).

Tomlinson (1982) went on to suggest that the underdevelopment of curricula in special education was due to the concentration with the practical immediate, rather than thinking about wider goals. Aspin, attempting to open up the field to philosophical analysis, commented: ' . . . anyone who investigates the philosophical basis of special education meets with some difficulty. For there is so far, at any rate, little in the literature of special education that is rigorously philosophical' (Aspin, 1982: 114).

There are three possibilities as to why the situation as described by these commentators could have arisen:

1   Theorists in the wider fields did not become attracted to special education as a fertile area for their investigations.
2   Practitioners in the field found the narrower perspective adequate to their needs, and did not seek or commission wider theorising.
3   The special education establishment, with its ownership of journals, higher degrees and high-status posts within the academy, was fully committed to a particular perspective and did not encourage wider theorising.

My argument would be that possibility three is the overriding factor which made one and two more likely. There is much evidence for this assertion, but a particularly telling investigation is to trace the literature on the curriculum in special education. The Warnock Report (D.E.S. 1978) devoted only ten pages to wider aspects of curriculum development, and even here, materials and methods received most attention. As Tomlinson (1982) argued, the concentration on the practical 'what to do' questions at the expense of thinking about the wider goals of special education led to the underdevelopment of the curriculum. Crawford (1978) published a book about curriculum planning for the ESN(s) child, which was remarkable in that it contained no discussion at all of what should be taught and why, essential components of planning, but merely described how to break learning down into small chunks. The behavioural objectives approach, as advocated by Ainscow and Tweddle (1979), with its concentration on how rather than what to teach, was certainly in the ascendancy in the post-Warnock years, despite the fact that in mainstream education the arguments against behavioural objectives had been marshalled years previously (Stenhouse, 1975; Macdonald-Ross, 1973). It was not that alternative views did not exist, rather that they were not part of the orthodoxy. We have to go to a book not purportedly about special education, Blenkin and Kelly (1983), to find a devastating critique of the objectives approach in special education and a clear statement about an alternative process-based approach (Goddard, 1983).

Since the peri-Warnock debates, the advent of the National Curriculum, or rather National Syllabus, has provided a further temptation to lose sight of wider aims and to find ways of teaching pre-specified content in manageable chunks so that learning can be more easily assessed and schools will achieve good league-table results. The situation is ripe for change, however. The reductionist orthodoxy has been successfully challenged, notably by a series of courses and publications stemming from academics at the Open University (see for instance Booth, 1992a, b). Also the Professional Associations have re-aligned on a more holistic alliance, and the literature in the field is now represented by contributions from critical disciplines (see Barton, 1988a) and theorists in special education have been integrally involved in wider educational move-ments (see Ainscow, 1991a). These are the conditions that Kuhn would see as readiness for a paradigm shift. The contradictions stemming from the assump-tions of the old paradigm are now overwhelming, and newer ways of exploring can no longer be accommodated within it. If both the theory and practice of special education is not to develop yet another re-statement of the reductionist fallacy, then we must be clear about the kind of world view we wish to espouse. As Poplin concludes: 'Perhaps it is time to begin to shed the reductionist theory, measurement, instructional methodologies and organisational structures we have built upon our medical model origins, and to turn our sights toward a non-reductionist theory of learning, teaching and growth' (Poplin, 1988a: 398).

There have been a number of recent attempts, apart from those of Heshusius and Poplin, to recast special education theorising in terms of a new paradigm, for instance Skrtic (1995) and Skidmore (1996). In terms of the argument put forward here, however, these authors continue to discuss theoretical orienta-tions rather than paradigms. Skrtic suggests that there may be four paradigms of modern social scientific thought (to confuse matters he also refers to them as metatheories) that inform theory and practice in special education. These he typifies as radical humanist, radical structuralist, interpretivist and functionalist. It may well be true that these four theoretical orientations are all relatively modern, and that they are distinguishable from one another, but are they really representing four different paradigms? As Heshusius (1995) comments from within the same volume, Skrtic's systematisation does not see the distinction between reductionist and non-reductionist world views. To her, radical struc-turalist and functionalist views, be they ever so modern and radical, share reductionist assumptions, whilst the emergent holistic paradigm would incorpo-rate interpretivist and humanist perspectives, but could not be reduced to them.

Skidmore (1996), in his paper, suggests that there have been three dominant paradigms in special education. These he names as the psychomedical, the soci-ological and the organisational paradigms. He then claims that these three share reductionist assumptions. If they are indeed paradigms, then at what level do they share these reductionist assumptions? It would be necessary to invent a level beyond that of paradigm, perhaps a meta-paradigmatic level, which would be clumsy and would also obscure the nature of paradigmatic theorising. Surely it is simpler, and more accurate, to describe them as differing theoretical orien-tations within a single reductionist paradigm. Skidmore then goes on to suggest candidates for a non-reductionist integrated framework for research into special educational needs. The candidates are named, focusing on the interac-tive process of learning, the dilemmas of schooling and social construction of special education categories, and the dialectical analysis of organisations and organisational ambiguity. These candidate theories, it is claimed, share a number of common qualities, one of which is a radical anti-reductionism. It remains to be seen whether, as this framework develops, it does indeed constitute a paradigm, that is, whether it has principles of its own which do more than merely contrast it with reductionism, or whether, as Poplin (1988a) warns us, may replicate the past by reducing the present. Unless a set of procedural principles can be drawn up, it is possible that older assumptions are recycled and reinvented when a new candidate for a theoretical orientation comes up against the unresolved problematics that research in any area is confronted with.

The emergent paradigm and special education

As previously stated authors such as Capra and Ferguson have for some time argued that a new paradigm is available, they have described the assumptions that it holds and given examples of its application in various fields of inquiry, including education. Capra's most recent work (1996) is aimed at outlining a coherent, scientific theory that offers, for the first time, a united view of mind, matter and life. He claims that the theory will change the way we relate to each other and to our living natural environment as well as the way we deal with health, the way we perceive business organisations, educational systems and many other social and political institutions. It is this new way of looking that I will attempt to outline and suggest that, as regards special education, Poplin (1988b) and Heshusius (1989) be part of special education (Poplin, 1988b; Heshusius, 1989) typify this paradigm in terms of holistic/constructivist principles. Let us clarify what this term means and implies and then consider its application to theorising in special education.

The use of the word 'constructivism' suggests allegiance to the set of beliefs, usually associated with Piaget, Vygotsky and Bruner, which sees the learner as actively engaged in constructing their own learning. Such a set of beliefs stands in stark contrast to the beliefs that underpin much of the pedagogy of special education. A very full debate on the application of constructivist principles to the field of special education can be read in Harris and Graham (1994), in which several of the contributors counsel against a wholesale and unconsidered adoption of constructivist principles. They helpfully distinguish between three current versions of constructivism (endogenous, exogenous and dialectical) and warn that unless we are clear about what we are attempting to change when we adopt new labels, then faddishness and recriminatory professional in-fighting can easily be the result, rather than a healthy development of the field.

Poplin (1988b: 402) suggests that in common with other learning theories, constructivism taken on its own can be accused of taking too cognitive a stance, giving superficial credit to other non-cognitive variables related to learning, such as feelings, intuition, motivation and sociological variables. It is necessary therefore to locate constructivist understandings within holistic thought. Holism is concerned with the complete phenomenon, and therefore includes feeling, intuition and social context. The key distinction between holism and reductionism is that a holist view would claim that the whole is greater than the sum of the parts. It would not be possible to understand a phenomenon merely by understanding the various parts in detail and then aggregating these discrete parcels of knowledge. The ways in which the parts interrelate with each other, and with other phenomena, are important aspects of our understanding of the phenomenon. A holistic study would then be of necessity a systemic endeavour. The validity of any 'findings' arising from holistic investigations lies not in their claim to absolute truth, but in their fidelity to holistic principles. All knowledge claims are seen as provisional and partial. As in the old story of the six blind men inspecting different parts of an elephant's anatomy and coming to wildly differing conclusions as to the nature of the beast, it is seen that our knowledge of the whole is limited by our present perspective. Unlike the blind men, who are each convinced that their version is correct, the holist would always be open to new information, would see contradictions not as evidence that one side is wrong, but as an opportunity to look further for the whole that would make sense of both, or more, perceptions. A holist perspective is certainly principled; it is not the case that anything goes, which means that everything stays, nor is it a matter of my view being more whole than yours. Rather, there are principles of integrity and humility which seek to discover systemic connections rather than reductionist categories.

The adoption of holistic constructivism, then, allows the elucidation of a set of paradigmatic assumptions, values and methodologies that could characterise theorising, in this case in special education, in non-reductionist ways. What this would look like in practice is the subject of the last sections of this chapter, and other tentative ways of describing this are discussed by Stangvik (Chapter 12, this volume) and Bayliss (Chapter 6, this volume). The caution I noted above in discussing Skidmore's (1996) attempt to suggest an integrated theoretical framework will have to be applied to all of these attempts in order to move the field on.

Poplin tabulates principles derived from structuralist values, constructivist beliefs and holistic thought. The summary statement of the twelve principles, listed below, is that the whole is greater than the sum of the parts, urging us to move away from attempts to understand our field in reductionist ways.

Holistic/constructivist principles, after Poplin (1988b), are as follows:

1 The whole of the learned experience is greater than the sum of its parts.
2 The interaction of the learned experience transforms both the individual's spiral of learning (whole) and the single experience (part).
3 The learner's spiral of knowledge is self-regulating and self-preserving.
4 All people are learners, always actively searching for and constructing new meanings, always learning.
5 The best predictor of what and how someone will learn is what they already know.

6 The development of accurate forms follows the emergence of function and meaning.

7 Learning often proceeds from whole to part to whole.

8 Errors are critical to learning.

9 Learners learn best from experiences about which they are passionately interested and involved.

10 Learners learn best from people that they trust.

11 Experiences connected to the learner's present knowledge and experience are learned best.

12 Integrity is a primary characteristic of the human (learner's) mind.

Poplin gives an elaboration of these principles which space here forbids. The summary statement of these principles is, again, that the whole is greater than the sum of the parts so in order to understand an episode of learning one would need to attend to aspects of context referred to in all twelve principles. This would entail attention to details of background, intention and affective states that are seen as intruding variables in experimental research. The questions that a holistic/constructivist would be interested in could therefore never be answered by reductionist, experimental investigation.

In one major feature my contribution is now complete, as I am suggesting that the exploration of these twelve points will provide a very full agenda for theorists and researchers in the field of special education. Apart from providing a paradigmatic basis for investigating special education and its relationship to other areas of human experience, these principles provide the basis for undertaking a meta-investigation of their own validity, a matter that concerns theorising in all fields of human inquiry. Following Popper (1972), it is not now our task to attempt to prove the validity of our principles, but rather to examine them and search out their limitations. In the new paradigm, principles are to be seen as at best provisional, the hope being that as new evidence and knowledge is attained through the process of investigation this activity is regulated so that we do not find ourselves in the grip of assumptions that are no longer tenable.

I feel, however, that I must conclude by indicating some possible points for developing theory within the paradigm, and with the pressing question of the post-modern challenge to the notion of an all-embracing paradigmatic perspective. When the project of modernism was seen by many to run into the sand, three responses emerged. First, it could be claimed that the assumptions of the modern (reductionist) paradigm ought to remain intact, only methods would need to be refined. This idea is dismissed by Poplin (1988a) as doomed. Second, a new paradigm built on more holistic principles could be developed. The third option is to lose faith altogether in the possibility of an all-encompassing basis for theory and practice. It is this third option which represents what has come to be known as the post-modern condition. It is marked by an extreme scepticism about grand narratives or meta-narratives which are post-modern speak for paradigms. In this genre, ideas are interesting not in their construction but in their deconstruction, and a critical perspective is never held in check by allegiance, however temporary, to a provisional set of principles. This way of thinking leads to an infinite regress to confusion and chaos. In this climate anything goes, or at least everything has only the same (negligible) claims to authenticity. The result is a fragmentation of any field resulting in a myriad of competing interest groups.

I think it is a mistake to talk of 'postmodernism' (a single word denoting a view) rather we should talk about 'post-modernism' (a compound word denoting the temporal period after modernism). It is almost certainly true that we live in a world where learning in science and many other disciplines has brought us to a position where the modern view has been superseded; it does not follow, however, that we are now heirs to a period of confusion bereft of any guiding principles or regulatory ideals. The alternatives to Modernism may well be non-modern, rather than post-modern. That is to say that holistic alternatives are available many of which predated, and were ousted by, the project of modernism. Capra (1975) showed how findings at the cutting edge of science paralleled in many important respects the wisdom of the ancient Chinese. The renaissance of holistic, mystical traditions, as witnessed by what has come to be called the new age, need not be accompanied by intellectual Luddism. The time is surely ripe for a rapprochement between older holistic world views and the scope for exploration made possible by advances in western scholarship.

It is the formation of this new synthesis that Capra and the other leaders in the field endorse. By so doing, we sidestep the confusion and loss of faith that represents the post-modern challenge. By adopting a new paradigm that dissolves the contradictions of the old paradigm rather than retreating into extreme relativism we can seek out supportable, if provisional, principles to guide our theory and practice.

An example from the field of special education of the dangers of becoming enmeshed in the fractionalisation typical of the post-modern condition is the debate about who authentically can research in the field. In an oral contribution to a symposium on special education, two claims were made:

1   that academic research into disability served only the needs of the academics, and was therefore not supportive of the oppressed;
2   that members of the 'able bodied' community had no place in research on matters related to disablement, and that the disabled could be the only agents of their emancipation.

These two claims can only hold credence if we adopt a non-holistic view of humanity. These apparently discrete groups can only be seen to be discrete from the post-modern perspective that we all deconstruct and reconstruct ourselves without recourse to an overarching 'grand narrative', in this case, the indivisibility of humanity. If this is accepted, then we all have as good a case as anyone else to claim privileged positions with regard to our constructed positions, for instance, disabled academics who have the sole authentic right to pronounce on matters of disability. My opposition to such claims is based on the adoption of a holistic view which notices differences, sees them largely as social constructions, yet is more concerned with interconnections and points of contact. The two views cited above fail to notice first, as Corbett (1996) in her thought-provoking book reminds us, that we are all at best only temporarily able bodied, and that we cannot escape an interest in matters of disability; and second, that the radical emancipatory position begs the validity of the very categories from which emancipation is sought. That is, you cannot hold on the one hand that disablement is only an oppressive constructed category which should be deconstructed, whilst on the other hand state that there are people who authentically belong within it. Who decides where the line is drawn, using what criteria and in whose interests? Surely we should be mindful that no person is an island. We would not then have to ask for whom the bell tolls, who benefits from research, or who is emancipated when we all divest ourselves of the discriminatory categories produced by reductionist thinking. As Gramsci put it: 'The crisis consists precisely in the fact that the old is dying and the new cannot be born; in this interregnum a great variety of morbid symptoms appears' (Gramsci, 1971). The post-modern condition is just one such morbid symptom.

What, then, of the shape of theorising in special education should we embrace the holistic/constructivist paradigm? I only have the space here to outline some proposals, each one of which would demand a paper in its own right. First, we must analyse how far we are merely reinventing reductionist assumptions when we attempt to shift the focus of our theorising. When we adopt the notion of effective schools for all, for instance, how far are we moving towards a genuinely different perspective? How far are we embedding reductionist assumptions about what schools are for, what they are effective for, against which criteria and in whose interest? Until we can articulate a metaphysic of humanity, of the good life, of a holistic view of society in all its aspects, then our benchmarks of effectiveness could equally well be applied to the running of a concentration camp. When we talk of inclusion, then who are we assuming needs to be included, in what, and for what purpose? We really need to ally ourselves to wider streams of political, philosophical and scientific theorising in order to safeguard ourselves from dressing old practices as new by virtue of renaming our projects.

Special education, then, needs to be seen (theorised as) not a separate area of investigation entirely, but as part of the wider human, political, ethical project of securing the good life. As Carr and Hartnett (1996) have so skilfully shown, a curriculum is of necessity a political statement. In a democracy it is inescapably derived from what our view of a democracy is, and what part we wish the next generation to play in it. When considering a curriculum for special needs, we are not involved in an unproblematic technical decision, but are part of a wider debate that for too long theorising in special education has stood apart from. As Skrtic (1991a) has claimed, the problem with special education is not that it is atheoretical, but that it is acritical. A major plank of holistic theorising in special education should be to adopt a rigorously critical perspective.

In order to be seen as part of wider theorising, special education would benefit from the application of the findings and methodologies of wider theorising to its concerns. It is interesting that the natural sciences, once the paradigm case of reductionism, are now at the forefront of adopting new paradigm views (Prigogine and Stengers, 1984) and just as the human sciences once followed natural sciences down the road to reductionism, they are now adopting the holistic methods of the philosophers of science (Polkinghorne, 1983). Theorists in special education who attempt to offer less 'objective' accounts of the experience of special education in order to understand the ways in which learning is constructed within its ambit, but who wish to maintain epistemological and methodological integrity, would do well to adopt and extend the work of philosophers of science such as Popper (1972) on the limits of objective knowledge, Polanyi (1958) on personal knowledge, tacit knowledge and a defence of the ineffable, as well as Lakatos (1978) and Feyerabend (1975) on Methodology. New paradigm theorists such as Capra (1982) and Roszak (1978) place particular emphasis on systems theory and the ecosystemic approach, which is by nature holistic, and there have already been some successful applications of the ecosystemic approach to special education (see Molnar and Lindquist, 1989; Cooper, 1993; Jones, 1995).

A project of locating theorising in special education within the field outlined above would at least allow for it to be seen as an aspect of wider epistemological, political and practical theorising. In order to allow it to sit alongside current thought in the field of education we would also need to relate our specific theorising to certain areas of development well established in the study of education as a whole. Poplin (1988b) and Heshusius (1989) provide us with lists of current constructivist research in pedagogy that might be explored fruitfully in terms of their application to special education. The benefit of this project would be to determine whether educational principles based on holistic constructivism would benefit all learners, and make the idea of special methods redundant, confirming the intuitive belief of many support teachers that methods which benefit children with special needs benefit all, and in fact reduce the likelihood of the production of a group being seen as having special needs. Also the theoretical ideas of Rogers (Rogers and Freiberg, 1994) and Claxton (1990) which are avowedly holistic might also be applied in, or used instead of, special educational settings. The project for understanding educational phenomena in terms of social justice as described by Griffiths (1996; Griffiths and Davies 1995) would surely welcome theorists in special education as useful recruits.

Another newer allied field of theory that might also be of benefit is difference theory, applied to education, as outlined by Burbules (1996). Here, the assumption of sameness, against a standard of normality with the abnormal being viewed in terms of deficit, is replaced with a presumption of difference.

The burden of proof is shifted then to make this natural difference significant in some way. Burbules suggests that

> By shifting the burden of proof away from the presumption of sameness and toward an awareness of and sensitivity to difference, difference theory has created the possibility of rethinking education in a significantly new way. . . . The very purpose of examining the ways in which differences are made, I believe, is that it allows us then to consider this process against the background of categories of sameness and difference *alike*, to see these as equally open to reconsideration, and to open a conversation, together, of what we *want* them to mean, as we seek a way to live in this world together.
>
> (Burbules, 1996: 5)

This provides a very full agenda for theorising and research in special education, but has the virtue of placing it in the arena of more general educational theorising.

Finally, what the adoption of the new paradigm offers is the chance to adopt a more imaginative and creative stance towards the phenomenon of people finding learning, at least school learning, difficult. Rather than imagining that difficulty with learning is confined to a pathological minority (2 per cent? 20 per cent?) it enables us to reconstruct our view to suggest that in certain conditions (maybe just being in a classroom) we *all* experience difficulties. Even we bright ones found some aspects difficult (singing? drama? physical education? computers?) but had the carrot of some kind of certification and career opportunity to carry us through. Perhaps many more just gave up on the whole enterprise and, without causing too much trouble, achieved the air of acquired resignation to see them through to the day when they could have done with it for ever (Jackson, 1968). Such a strategy necessarily resulted in the construction of a discriminatory category for those who stubbornly persisted in the belief that education was a good thing. The category included teacher's pets, swots, boffins, girlies and trainspotters! A few, without the carrot or the ability to live with resignation, might have complained publicly, by behaving badly or by refusing to learn. These were described as having special needs, though more accurately they were the only honest and insightful ones, who dared to expose that the Emperor was wearing no clothes! The fact that they did this for the potential benefit of all their comrades who then deserted them and were recruited into the ranks of the Yahoos shouting 'divs, rems, spags, drongos or thickos' turns this particular fairy tale into a tragedy.

In order to develop such an imaginative approach to the phenomenon of special education, theorists would have to cast their nets far wider than those presently confined to the administrative category of those having special educational needs. Skrtic (1991a) discusses a strategy to make this possible; he suggests using critical pragmatism in order to reach a hermeneutical understanding. I would go beyond Skrtic's sources for dialogue and include other cultural groups such as persons with disabilities and their parents, so that in a holistic way all persons are involved in the enterprise of learning. The theoretical positions of Gadamer (1989) on hermeneutics, Habermas (see Young, 1989) on critical theory and ideal speech situations (Blake, 1995) would also be of use here. More practically the accounts of new paradigm research methods offered by Reason and Rowan (1981, 1988) and the application of more qualitative methods in the field of special education as described by Mertens and McLaughlin (1995) indicate that there is already a research base ready to be extended. Illuminative accounts of the lived experience of involvement in teaching and learning in the field exist in plenty (MacCracken, 1974, 1987; Lee, 1993) and it may well be one of our tasks to articulate a way in which autobiographical and fictionalised accounts may become 'theorised' in order to render useful, if not generalisable, insights. A highly instructive account of how teacher research may be developed along these lines is provided by Gallas (1994). It is interesting to note that elsewhere in the fields of philosophy and education fictionalised accounts are being accepted as sufficiently rigorous to be awarded higher degrees and to be published by the academic press (see Bell, 1993; Waterland, 1994).

To adopt, then, the holistic/constructivist paradigm as the basis for our theorising in special education would be to shift from 'a rationality of method to a human rationality' (Bernstein, 1983), or a shift from 'a natural science model to a human science model' (Iano, 1986). We would give up our investment in being rigorously disinterested and accept the challenge of being interested in a rigorous manner. Heshusius concluded her overview thus:

> Grasping complexity, guided by human rationality, will be far more difficult than inquiry informed by a machine metaphor of reality. But the effort will be more worthy of human beings, will result in more relevance, and is bound to be further reaching.
>
> (Heshusius, 1989: 413)

I conclude that if we were to join her in her project we may generate theories that may be less hard-edged, certainly softer, perhaps more feminine, and certainly more representative and inclusive of all aspects of humanity.

9

DECISION MAKING IN UNCERTAINTY

Sip Jan Pijl and Kees P. van den Bos

Introduction

In social sciences it is not uncommon that several, often conflicting, theories are applied to one particular subject. When special education is the subject, things are complicated because the term 'special education' is a fuzzy and all-encompassing term. It can be used to describe the instruction of students with special needs, the use of special methods and materials or the activities of special teachers. Sometimes it refers to special and separate school systems. Therefore, theories of special education can have very different aims. When thinking about special education theories it is necessary to specify the aim under consideration. What do we mean by special education and what is special education ultimately about?

In this chapter the focus will be on relationships between general theories of special education and theories of learning problems of pupils. We are interested in the paradigm shifts that have occurred in the past decades, and especially in the contributions of the various theories to meeting the special needs of pupils.

The object of special education

For decades the main aim of special education has been the education of the mentally, physically and/or sensory handicapped pupils. More or less in line with medical procedures, a thorough diagnosis and classification of the child's handicap(s) is seen as an important first step. Assessment focused on a classification of the kind of handicap in order to decide on the treatment of preference. The approach is characteristic of the psychomedical paradigm, in which a detailed diagnosis of the child's handicap(s) was both a necessary and sufficient condition to commence a treatment. Diagnosis and treatment were seen as two different, yet closely linked, activities. Each clinical picture had its own treatment, analogous to the medical diagnosis of 'a broken arm' which led to the treatment of 'putting the arm in splints'.

The different types of special schools which exist in a number of countries is a consequence of the psychomedical paradigm. Classifying pupils into categories is directly related to placement in a school which specialises in that handicap. The assumption behind such a referral system is that all pupils with, for example, physical handicap have the same needs, and that these needs can only be appropriately met in a school for the physically disabled. That some physically impaired pupils may well have similar special needs to pupils with other impairments is not considered. The focus is primarily on classification, assuming that the special needs of children with particular handicaps are comparable. Of course, thinking according to the psychomedical paradigm is not restricted to assessment, but extends itself to treatment and the instruction of pupils and to 'compartmentalised' approaches by specialists (Myers and Hammill, 1969). Examples can be found in traditional handbooks of learning disabilities:

> We have seen, therefore, the rise of remedial reading, language pathology, and educational therapy and the development of specialised training programs within non-educational disciplines such as optometry, occupational therapy, and school psychology. . . . As a result the optometrist has become a specialist in visual-motor problems and generally ignores the often critical influence of audition. On the other hand, the language pathologist may direct himself toward only the child's oral language to the detriment of perceptual-motor processes.
>
> (Myers and Hammill, 1969: vi)

In the late 1960s, the focus of general special education theories on the classification of handicaps lessened, and the aim of special education was reformulated in terms of the educational problems connected with a handicap or a developmental disorder. It was not the presence of a handicap which determined the need for special education but the question as to whether the handicap hindered the student's education (Vliegenthart, 1972; Bleidick, 1974). At this time assessment was still based on a description of the handicaps of the pupil, but it became more important to arrive at firm conclusions about the special educational needs that resulted from the handicap(s). In some countries, for example, the UK, this shift from classification to a description of special needs is embodied in educational legislation.

In more recent years, further elaboration of these theoretical and practical developments can be seen. Assessment in special education now involves consideration of the educational consequences of the students' special needs. In other words, the aim is to decide about the appropriate type of instruction for the pupil taking into account his/her needs. These needs are the basis for action by teachers, therapists and others involved in special needs education. The description of needs, then, leads to an educational programme for the pupil.

Summarising, in the past decades, criticisms of the psychomedical paradigm in special education have increased. In special education, classification into traditional categories of handicap is no longer seen as an appropriate way of meeting the special needs of pupils. Instead, the term 'special education' refers to the services which are required if problems arise in education (Ter Horst, 1980). Pupils' handicaps are no longer the central tenet of special education. Rather, the problems in education as experienced or expected by pupils, teachers, or parents are paramount. These problems generally result when pupils do not attain developmental, instructional or educational goals (Rispens, 1990). The existence of a problem can be detected by assessing the pupils' behaviour or performance.

The basic difference between this approach and the psychomedical paradigm is that a classification of the student in terms of a particular handicap has been abandoned. Assessment now focuses on the description of the problems a student has in the educational situation, and assessment is always linked with taking decisions about special support for the student. A central research question, then, focuses on the basis for our assessment and the resulting decisions about the education of pupils with special needs.

Theory as a basis for decisions

Quite a number of the decisions we take are based on theory. A theory comprises of a set of hypotheses to explain practice. A well-developed theory makes it possible to deduce predictions about concrete events. If the weather forecast, based on a meteorological theory, tells us to expect heavy showers, we decide to take an umbrella with us. Even without listening to the weather forecast we have expectations about how the weather might turn out. Our expectations may be based on taking a good look at the clouds and the sky or they may be based on yesterday's weather or even on a feeling of foreboding. The dark clouds, yesterday's rain or our hunch tell us that it is more than likely going to rain today and we prepare ourselves accordingly. In other words, we have our own theory about the link between two occurrences. So, many decisions we take are based on our own or others', limited or overall, scientific, common-sense or 'non-sense' theories. There are, of course, situations in which we have absolutely no idea what to do. If we are lost in the woods, we may not have a theory to help us find a way out and there may be no alternative than to guess. In this case we have to decide in complete uncertainty and just see what comes out of it.

The availability of a good theory makes it easier to make good decisions. This holds for decisions regarding the weather, and, of course, for decisions in education as well. Many decisions in special education are about children: decisions about placement in a certain school or in a group, about coping with behaviour disorders in the classroom, about educational goals, about instruction, about any special services needed. It would be very convenient to have an all-encompassing theory on which these decisions could be based. Such a theory would basically provide us with procedures to connect knowledge about current capacities, performance, and the special needs of students with appropriate ways forward in educational terms.

In Chapter 1, three leading questions were asked: (1) Do we need theories of special education? (2) What should a theory of special education look like? and (3) What implications should a theory of special education have for practice and research? In this chapter it has been argued that special education should involve theories which provide a basis for assessment and decision making. Theories in special education, or more specifically theories about meeting the special educational needs of pupils, should make it possible to utilise assessment to inform teaching. These theories of special education therefore basically look like 'if-then' statements. A useful theory allows reasoning that departs from 'if' statements (like: if a pupil has an impairment, has difficulty in performing specific tasks, shows a particular behaviour in certain situations) and includes 'then' statements about the content of individual educational programmes for pupils. Only theories that enable us to draw conclusions about practical ways forward will have a direct impact on practice.

The question now is whether there is such a theoretical basis for assessment and decision making in special education. The next section gives a brief analysis of the theories on learning problems that have been or still are in vogue.

Theories of learning disabilities and special education theories

The fields of learning difficulties and learning disability have a rich history in adopting and developing theories. However, are these theories suitable to base educational decisions on?

In the more traditional theories of learning disabilities particularly, a strong emphasis is placed on issues of classification, definition, aetiology and diagnosis. Similar emphases can also be found in very recent publications (see Adelman, 1992; Dumont, 1994). Important elements in these theories are criteria such as significant discrepancies between IQ and school task performance based on the hypothesis of psychoneurological deficits as underlying disorders of 'basic' learning processes. However, it should be noted that in their 1969 publication, Myers and Hammill did not consider their theories as examples of medical models:

> The medical orientation ultimately rests upon the assumption that something is wrong with the child. It emphasises his liabilities and short-comings, ignores his assets and strengths, and encourages grouping children on the basis of their disabilities. An alternative approach advocated by the authors, views the so-called brain-damaged child within a behavioural frame of reference. . . . A behavioural description of his learning style dictates the selection of appropriate instructional techniques and materials as no medical model can.
>
> (Myers and Hammill, 1969: v)

109

However, even a 'behavioural frame of reference' can be used as a basis for the medical model of diagnosis, treatment, prescription, evaluation and conclusion. This is what many traditional and modern learning disabilities models (including Myers and Hammill's composite language model, which combined Osgood's and Wepman's models) have in common. As we will see, more recent criticisms of 'medical-model analogies in special education' concern more the entities that are diagnosed and provided with treatments than the procedures of medical models. In traditional models of learning disabilities these entities are conceptualised as more-or-less specific abilities, for example, a child's articulation, motor speech, auditory discrimination, visual–perceptual functions, memory functions or selective attention. Models and theories which described these abilities and which prescribed remedial or 'educational' methods to 'treat' deficits in these abilities were called ability training models (ATMs) or specific abilities models (Reid, 1988). Again, in Myers and Hammill (1969) there are various examples of case studies in which educational recommendations are made based on these frameworks:

1   The superiority in visual decoding and the other visual areas, including memory and sequencing, indicated that M.S. would probably learn to read most easily by the 'look-and-say' method of teaching, i.e. an emphasis on the visual approach . . .
2   . . . The program should be organised to remediate his auditory deficits through utilising his visual abilities . . .
3   Articulation therapy was recommended to ameliorate the speech production problem . . .

(Myers and Hammill, 1969: 70)

In summary, the basic idea which underpins ability training is that problems in learning are caused by an insufficient or incorrect development of underlying abilities. Diagnosis is aimed at identifying these abilities in order to start remediation. It is presumed that the training of abilities will result in the disappearance of the problems and the backwardness. Another focus in ability training is not just to train the weak abilities, but to maintain and develop the strong ones as well – a distinction known as remediation versus compensation. For a long period of time the ability training approach has dominated thinking in special education in the western world.

Over the years, however, criticism of ability training has arisen (Arter and Jenkins, 1977; Ewing and Brecht, 1977; Torgesen, 1979; Ysseldyke, 1973). There is serious doubt about the assumed discreteness of the abilities, their relevance to learning, the reliable and valid measurement of the abilities and the consequences for learning. To overcome especially the last criticism, much research has been done on aptitude–treatment–interaction (ATI). Although some results are encouraging, the bulk of the ATI research has been disappointing (Torgesen, 1986).

Ability training is often compared to behaviouristic approaches such as task analysis, and attempts have been made to combine the two (Smead, 1977). In task analysis there is no direct interest in or attention to the causes of learning problems and backwardness. In task analysis a skill (like telling the time) is divided into smaller skills, such as being able to recognise the digits. These are presumed to be prerequisites for the main skill. Diagnosis is aimed at finding out which of the prerequisite skills are not yet mastered. Training of the not-yet-mastered skills is taken to be sufficient for mastering the main skill. Since task analysis is centred around skills that are important in education, the results are easier to translate into decisions about teaching. However, just as with the specific abilities model, several assumptions of these models have been criticised:

> there is no empirical evidence that most skills, such as reading comprehension, can be hierarchically ordered from simple subskills to more complex skills. . . . Furthermore, many skills, such as identification of the main idea of a passage, are neither present nor absent in children; instead, they are gradually refined over long periods of time. . . . Finally, there is no evidence that meeting criteria for mastery ensures that the skill considered to have been learned will be utilised in situations in which it is needed.
>
> (Reid, 1988: 36)

In the1980s, an important shift in learning disabilities research was made towards cognitive information processing (Brown and Campione, 1986; Wong, 1986). This is also called the cognitive developmental approach (Reid, 1988; Eding *et al.*, 1994). Rather than treating mental functioning as a collection of specific, independent or 'unitary' abilities or faculties that underlie learning, the interactive nature of knowledge sources or processes was acknowledged. Second, it was suggested that the activation and utilisation of these processes, rather than a structural or physical deficit, inhibited learning in most children (Reid, 1988). Third, learning processes were considered to be active, constructive and contextualised or domain-specific processes. Fourth, intellectual aspects of cognition (especially strategies) appeared to be closely tied to socio-emotional aspects of personal, motivational and social dimensions. The implications of these new perspectives for teacher education, educational programme design, and standardised testing have been described by Brown and Campione (1986) under the label 'support contexts for learning'. Reid expresses the implications as follows:

> We are arguing for a cognitive developmental approach to instruction that utilises direct, contextualised teaching in academic subjects, recognises that very important learning skills are self-directed and unobservable, focuses on student strengths, and advocates a single curriculum for all students. It is important to understand, however, that

by 'single curriculum' we do not mean that all children must complete the same work sheets or read the same books. What is important is that each child has the opportunity to build on strengths and be exposed to all different levels of knowledge.

(Reid, 1988: 37)

These notions can also be illustrated by the matrix in Table 9.1. This matrix combines Reid's (1988) and Pullis's (1988) schemes after Campione (1981) and Lovitt (1977). Table 9.1, to be read from left to right and top to bottom, has two dimensions: stages of learning and instruction; and learner needs and teacher actions.

As already indicated in this section, the education of children with learning problems has generated many theories. It is clear that these theories are based on different, sometimes conflicting approaches. Especially in the more traditional models, the link between students' needs and their education is based on the (dis)ability-oriented aspects of the psychomedical paradigm, and these do not help us much in making decisions about their education. Some of the more recent models and theories seem to be less focused on classification and (dis)ability, and therefore more able to accommodate a wide range of individual differences in learning, regardless of handicap. The traditional distinction between special and regular education has become blurred. The 'classic' special education expertise, in which assessment and treatment were thought to be linked, is increasingly criticised. Despite promising developments, there is no alternative yet. Decision making in (special) education still often lacks a solid base in theories on learning problems.

Professional decisions in education

The conclusion of the preceding section, that the theoretical basis to come to decisions about ways of overcoming the learning problems of students is weak, makes it clear that a lot of research and development has to be done to clarify pupils' learning problems and formulate an appropriate action plan to education. But pupils, parents and teachers in (special) education today cannot sit still and wait for the results from research studies. The education of pupils with special needs requires teachers to take decisions and to act. In the absence of a firm theoretical basis teachers have to decide in uncertainty.

The way professionals take decisions in education can be characterised by different process models. These models give a step-by-step description of the activities which are necessary for decision making. Two models will be presented here:

1   decision making as the application of a theory about, for example, learning problems; and
2   decision making as a regulatory cycle (Van Strien, 1975).

112

Table 9.1 A framework of teaching – based on models of Campione and Lovitt, adapted from Pullis (1988: 119) and Reid (1988: 63)

Learner Needs and Teacher Actions	Stages of Learning and Instruction			
	Initial Learning	*Supervised Practice*	*Advanced Learning*	*Proficiency*
Learner needs and levels of learning	Exposure to knowledge, strategies, and skills. Learner is not yet successful. Detailed instruction and encouragement are necessary. Contextual support.	Continued instructional focus and support. Learner learns under supervision.	Increasing independentness. Student is reinforced and rewarded for performance. Self-checking and 'product' checking operations are taught and monitored.	Students function independently and in a dedicated way. They have insights in the relevance of their efforts, and they know that successes (and failures) are due to own abilities and (lack of) efforts. The students master domain-specific as well as general study skills.
Interpersonal tactics (teacher approach)	Teacher creates positive expectations, provides feedback for effort, gives directions.	Feedback for effort *and* performance (reinforcement sandwich), slightly reduced direction.	Teacher reminds of previous success and demonstrates this again if necessary. The emphasis is on performance and internal attributions. Minimised directions.	Pride in accomplish-ment. Student has task-relevant attri-butions. Students and teacher can act as consultants. At initial stages of reciprocal-teaching settings, the student can be teacher supporter.
Grouping arrangements and responsi-bility for task performances	Large to smaller teacher-guided groups of students.	Small teacher-led groups with shared responsibility for learning and performance. Opportunity for individual practice and applications. Shift to working forms such as 'reciprocal teaching'		Small student-led independent groups of students.
Nature of instruction	Instruction involves: teacher model, demonstration and contextual support. Application of direct teaching methods.	Instruction is directed at reteaching. Practice under intensive supervision. Introduction of error analyses.	Instruction aims at gradual shift to self-responsible learning. Students get lessons in 'learning how to learn'; these skills are practised in domain-specific as well as in general learning contexts. Extended assignments and homework assignments. Introduction of reciprocal teaching contexts. Transfer of learned contents and skills to other students.	Instruction is focused on practising for maintenance. Applications for generalisation. Diverse assignments, challenge students to formulate proposals.

113

The application notion is based on the idea that decisions are in fact deductions from a well-developed, thoroughly validated theory. In the preceding section we have argued that the state of affairs in the development and testing of theories about learning problems does not currently allow this kind of deduction. With the often complex problems of pupils in learning, it is very hard to deduce an educational decision from theory. In many cases the decision maker, the teacher or the diagnostician, still has to base suggestions for instruction on their own experience and intuition. In doing this, the decision maker builds – over the years – his or her own practice-based theory which includes both explanation and action. A problem here is that mistakes and prejudices can hinder proper decision making. To overcome this, it is suggested that the decision maker should follow rigorous rules (Van Strien, 1975).

These are set out in the second model, and described as the regulatory cycle. Its phases are: the formulation of the pupils' problem in education, the advancement of a diagnosis, decision making about a plan, putting the plan into action and evaluating the effects. To do this it is necessary to make a detailed problem analysis, develop an $N = 1$ theory, use good instruments, carefully make reports, use theoretical knowledge to formulate the diagnosis and make decisions about the plan of action. The goal of the regulatory cycle is not to predict but to act. The evaluation of the action can be used to adjust or regulate the plan in order to attain the goal formulated in the problem analysis.

From this brief discussion it is clear that only the second model incorporates the construction and evaluation of a decision about a plan. At the same time it applies theory-based knowledge, intuition and experience in a justifiable way.

The conclusion is that if decisions in education cannot be based on deductions from a well-developed theory, the diagnostician, the teacher or the support team has to make a theory about the individual student. In making the $N=1$ theory and in carrying out the plan, rules must be followed. In practice this means that the decisions about education become part of a carefully conducted decision procedure.

The paradox of special education theory

If it is accepted that special education cannot be based on a classification of pupil handicap, we have dispensed with an apparently clear paradigm. A classification of pupil handicap does not provide a useful basis for educational decisions. The shift towards a description of the object of special education as having something to do with problems in education and with taking decisions about the special assistance for pupils with special needs poses a new challenge. What we need is a theory or a set of theories that help us to take decisions about the education of pupils with special needs.

As argued in the preceding sections, our theoretical framework to make such decisions is fairly weak. We have to take decisions in uncertainty using our experience, available knowledge, our intuition and our common sense. It is necessary to do that in a professional and scientific way following a disciplined procedure, a procedure in which reliable instruments are used, reports are carefully constructed and in which the evaluation of outcomes of the decisions is central. The basic philosophy which underpins this thinking is that incorrect decisions cannot always be avoided and have to be accepted. But it is unacceptable if wrong decisions are not corrected in time. That is why writing down goals, plans and evaluations of these educational decisions (preferably following a discussion with colleagues) is so crucial when decision making takes place in uncertainty.

The lack of theory on which to base our decisions makes it essential that we deal professionally with uncertainty. The psychomedical paradigm as a way of thinking and working is in fact being replaced by a way of working in which decision making in uncertainty is the norm. This sounds paradoxical. We are in fact suggesting that the quest for solid decision making based on special education theories results in handling uncertainty and that this is a new paradigm.

It must be clear that the proposed decision procedure to handle uncertainty is not in itself a new theory. Rather, it is a 'small' theory about an individual pupil, which is not a special education theory. It is at most a paradigm that replaces the psychomedical paradigm.

Theories to base decisions on in special education are still needed but that does not imply that we need special education theories. Most decisions in special education utilise more general educational or psychological theories. Special education does not need its 'own' theories. Special education with its often complex problems challenges professionals to give serious consideration to decisions about education. Special needs can only be met adequately if the professionals involved are aware that decisions often have to be made in uncertainty and if this uncertainty is handled in a responsible manner.

10

FROM MILTON KEYNES TO THE MIDDLE KINGDOM

Making sense of special education in the 1990s

Patricia Potts

Introduction

From our experience of here and now, we build up expectations about experience of there, then and times to come. From the particular detail of our own direct experience we construct overarching links of generalisation so that we do not have to start from scratch every morning. Making connections between experiences separated in space and time is fundamental to adaptive behaviour and social communication. If a definition of 'theory' includes 'making sense of', then we cannot live without it.

Theory has no life without experience. It is a set of related statements which offer an explanation for the characteristics of a defined phenomenon. As long as these understandings operate successfully and confirm the ways in which we recognise and refer to our experience, they influence us without demanding further conscious reflection. But when we are faced with situations which, because of novelty, scale, complexity or conflict, require us to go beyond our current understanding, then we have to extend our networks of connections and pay attention to a wider range of interpretations and the experiences from which they themselves are derived.

The epistemological status of a theory and the use that can be made of its explanatory concepts depends therefore upon what it is that requires understanding, which, itself, has to be identified. This may always be a problem, because of the mediation of language, but when the subject, as well as the process, of an inquiry is social, reaching an agreed definition of the subject to be explained may be especially hard. Social relationships and institutions cannot be extracted and manipulated in isolation from the contexts in which their meaning, for both the givers and receivers of information, has been constructed. So the sequence of questions, assumptions, demonstrations, analyses and conclusions that constitute the development of a theory cannot be

116

independent of the cultural, political and moral commitments of inquirers and subjects.

Theories which consist of explanations that are permanently and universally true are only found in situations in which the characteristics of the phenomena studied lend themselves to this kind of analytic control. The discovery of law-like explanations is not achieved by using a particular investigative paradigm, which therefore deserves top rating as a method of inquiry, but as a result of the interaction of subject and method. Of course, the more precise, thorough and systematic the approach to investigation, then whatever the subject of inquiry, the resulting understanding will have greater authority and force. But mismatching approach and subject, in the hopes of attaining, for example, universal statements about the meaning of social behaviour, can only result in misrepresentation, not in a closer approximation to an enduring truth. When we examine aspects of the social world we are looking at a moving target. We should not expect to be able to derive an explanatory theory that will last much beyond tomorrow. How far this is seen as a threat to the status of a theory in terms of its value as knowledge depends on what a theory is required to do and whether or not those demands are justified.

'Special education', the focus of our interest in this book, can be defined in various ways: as a set of institutions, a set of categories of learner or a firm body of expert knowledge; as a system of positive discrimination or as a system of social control. If 'special education' is seen as an activity in which the ostensible core task is to overcome barriers to learning, then the point of theory, which explains what is going on, is to inform the decision-making processes aimed at the removal of these barriers. But if the character and function of this activity are as hotly disputed as they are currently in the UK, then the framing of initial questions and the phrasing of possible answers are likely to reflect parallel and incompatible theoretical positions.

The editors of this volume have asked us to consider whether or not we need a theory of special education, and if so, what might such a theory look like and what are the implications for practice and research. I shall argue that we need to make sense of our present actions and to use these understandings to make future decisions. This necessitates explanation. However, explanations that facilitate our understanding of social situations, into which category I place relationships described as 'educational', are inevitably context-bound and therefore contingently, not universally true. Imitating the theoretical frameworks of natural science therefore obscures the problem of defining what we mean by 'special education' and denies the fundamental characteristics of social situations.

In order to elaborate on this point, in this chapter I shall present two examples of relationships between educational practice and theoretical understanding of which I have had direct experience. I shall discuss how teachers have set about making sense of their practice and the role theory has played in this process. I shall begin by describing work done on a UK Open University course and then go on to describe inservice work undertaken by teachers in China. The most striking contrast between the work seen in each of these contexts is that the UK teachers present a wealth of practical detail and personal experience which they find hard to analyse, whereas the Chinese teachers draw on shared theoretical frameworks to structure relatively sparse accounts of practice.

Investigating equality and diversity in education: experiences of student-practitioners in the UK

I belong to the 'special education' group at the Open University for which I designed a course of postgraduate project work to investigate equality and diversity in education. It was necessary to make available a range of material on current policy and practice and provide guidance on planning, carrying out and analysing student inquiries. The role of theory in the course was related to the stated aims of the project work as well as to the diversity of perspectives students bring to its subject matter. For example, we have included the perspective of disabled researchers, who define 'disability' in terms of social oppression and require that research outcomes be utilised to inform committed policy making (see Barnes,1995; Brock,1995; Morris,1992; Oliver,1992a). We have also included the perspective of a parent, who makes sense of the behaviour of the professionals she deals with by seeing it as derived from a definition of 'disability' as disaster. This is how she explains the otherwise contradiction of, on the one hand, a stated aim of strengthening family relationships whilst, at the same time, organising respite care on a regular basis (see S. Thomas, 1995).

Students on the course are required to undertake three 10-week projects, one on pupil perspectives on learning, one on curriculum analysis and development and one on decision making, policy and power. The aims of the course include enabling students to develop an active role within the education system: enabling them to reflect critically on their own experience and that of others, to make appropriate use of relevant literature in discussions and writing and to develop confidence in designing their own research inquiries.

The students, who are teachers, parents, nursery nurses, learning support assistants and other professional workers, bring a wide variety of perspectives and purposes to their project-work. For example, one nursery nurse came with a set of practical questions about the transfer from pre-school to mainstream reception class of a boy with difficulty in seeing. Close observation of Michael led her to interpret what others had described as 'aggressive' behaviour as 'inquiring' and consequently to outline an approach to future support that would reduce his boredom and confusion, rather than focus on social control and safety.

In the literature, this student found a number of arguments about the detrimental effect that reduced sight has on mobility and learning but she was able to use this to make some positive and practical recommendations, including repainting playground furniture to contrast with, rather than blend in with, the colours of nature, as they did at the nursery school. She also found a useful explanation of Michael's apparent lack of understanding of object constancy, which was influenced by the fact that he thought that there was no point in searching for something that you could not find. Michael was not functioning below the level that might be expected therefore, but rather with his own logic and relationship to the world, which was based on an assumption of the normality rather than the abnormality of his own experiences.

For another student, the central task was to work out ways to communicate with two young people who used little or no speech in order to develop an appropriate curriculum for transition from school to an adult setting. She employed visual and non-verbal approaches, such as signing and the deliberate use of body language. She also did some structured observation of the young people and explored her own ability to use the communication systems that meant something to her pupils.

She discovered that it made hardly any difference to the teenagers whether the classroom was well furnished with stimulating equipment or left relatively bare. One of the teenagers spent more time watching others when the environment was 'enriched', but the other teenager only participated when they went out of school. The student therefore included in her recommendations that teachers should pay more attention to non-verbal communication systems in order to discover as much as possible about what their pupils are attempting to communicate. She also recommended that they should continue to work outside school to stimulate learning. She concluded that the students' difficulties in learning were exacerbated by the tension between the demands of the National Curriculum and the particular requirements for independence skills. Thus, she advocated that teachers should resist the pressure to deliver the National Curriculum by what is becoming accepted practice, and instead, use strategies and approaches which are more appropriate for these young people.

For the nursery nurse in a pre-school setting and the teacher in a special school, understanding was enhanced by the detail of their project work, which gave them increased confidence to make specific recommendations for the development of practice during the next phase of their lives. Implicit rather than explicit in these projects was a commitment to the rights of each student to an appropriately differentiated and supported curriculum and a belief that teachers and other pupils should accommodate to the diversity of their requirements. Reference was also made to conflicts of interest and power relationships. Neither student, however, identified a specific research tradition or disciplinary position as representing their view of the system nor did they reflect consciously on the theoretical implications of their work.

In designing a course based around students' own questions, we tried not to impose a hero's conceptual scheme in which student contributions might well be peripheral. Instead, we hoped to enable students to develop an autonomous critical voice and make their own decisions about what approach to theory was useful. However, not only is this analytic task very difficult, the opportunity to explore pressing practical concerns is taken up with such a rush of energy by some of our students that the necessary relationship between theory and practice can be ignored.

An example of this is a redefinition of the task as one of evaluation. One student asked whether using drama in primary classrooms can help to reduce difficulties with literacy and numeracy. She did not focus on reading, writing or counting nor on any one group for whom these skills were particularly difficult. She set out to measure the reduction of barriers to learning in terms of increased communication and social integration, an approach which derived directly from her understanding of why learning was difficult for her pupils. Apart from the sequence of drama sessions carried out for the project, this student interviewed colleagues, before and after the project, and invited her headteacher to act as an observer in her own classroom to give an independent assessment of her work. She saw the positive outcomes of the activities she set up for the project as evidence that areas of the curriculum which develop social confidence should be seen as central and highly valued foundations to those which are officially listed as core learning activities. This student concluded that progress in what are seen as basic skills is facilitated by a whole range of social experiences and, therefore, that the priorities of the National Curriculum should be revised. The implicit critical position, here, is based on a link between co-operation, self-esteem and learning. This project therefore challenged the official value system by demonstrating the effectiveness of an alternative (see Haycock, 1995).

The belief that very little relevant work exists on which to base a critical discussion is the reason given by another student for ignoring the link between theory and practice. Given that there is an infinity of possible research topics for investigation by students on our course, this might appear to be justified. However, it also happens that students do not look for theoretical support because they do not set out with a question to which they do not already know the answer. This is true of some project work which merely displays current practice for approval. One student proudly stated that his project was entirely based on his own experience. I found, on the contrary, that his own experience was entirely missing from the project, as there was no reflection on the values and decisions behind the work he described. His high estimation of his own practice appeared to have resulted in an unwillingness to consider why he had done what he had done and whether there might be different ways to do it.

Not all insiders are as arrogant as this. While there are students who do not take the opportunity to make inquiries that might extend and change their practice, there are others who are prevented from doing so. For example, the status of one student as a non-teacher affected her access to the sources of information that she had identified as relevant to her research question. She came to construe her inquiries negatively. She referred to her research as 'digging', partly because of her unwillingness to cause discomfort to the subjects of her inquiries, but mainly because of the hostile response she received to her questioning. It therefore became necessary for her to understand and try to overcome the barrier to her own learning resulting from her gender and professional status, before she could go on to explore her initial research question. Tony Booth in Chapter 7, this volume, discusses the relationship between power and intolerance of challenges to that power, particularly evident when questioning alternative perspectives is suggested.

It seems that a research project on however small a scale represents an act of assertion that may be outside the students' previous professional experience. Anxieties about tackling theoretical issues are connected with student attitudes. If they are concerned about their right to do such a thing, it is likely that this will influence their beliefs about the inherent difficulty of doing it. I consider it to be part of the tutor's role to help students to become autonomous inquirers. This depends on their willingness to understand social situations through reflexivity. It also involves them in becoming aware that sources of information can be clouded by inequalities in the modes of communication.

Most students recognise that their inquiries are complex and that there are real difficulties in the interpretation of findings. However, what seems to happen is that, in their struggle to make sense of their findings, some students lose their critical voice in a cringe of apology for not being able to reach a conclusion in terms which they know would be quite inappropriate for their subject. This self-undermining reversion to the framework of 'scientific' knowledge, tautologous rock in a shifting social sea, is connected with a desire for certainty which is personal and political. The status in question is not just that of the students' findings, but also theirs, as people and practitioners in the UK in the late 1990s.

Responding to difficulties in learning: experiences of teachers in China

The opportunity for practitioners in China to make their own inquiries has opened up during the past ten years or so as teacher education has become a national priority. The overall context for this is the drive to implement a policy of nine years' universal compulsory schooling. The inclusion of disabled children and young people and those who experience difficulties in learning within the rhetoric of reform seems to be the result both of participation in international debates since the 1980 International Year of the Child and the 1981 International Year of Disabled People, and also the national organisation of disabled adults, led by Deng Pufang (son of Deng XiaoPing), who was disabled in the late 1960s.

The closure of educational institutions during the Cultural Revolution is one reason for the current chronic shortage of qualified teachers. There is an urgent requirement, not only for initial teacher training, but also for the upgrading and updating of in-service professional education. However, there has been almost no provision for practising teachers in university departments of education. Teacher education is related to the student population they are teaching: special school teachers should have completed junior middle school; elementary school teachers should have completed senior middle school; and middle school teachers should have an undergraduate degree. Only university research students and staff have engaged in postgraduate work.

In early 1994, the government legislated for a graduate secondary school profession, though this, too, is a target that has yet to be reached. The more advanced the level of qualification of teachers, the less likely it is that there will be direct contact with schools. Consequently, many teachers have been trained by people with a minimum of teaching experience, whose research interests would probably not entail the production of detailed case studies of practice.

The function of training has been seen as providing a framework for subsequent practice. This routine separation of theory and practice is by no means peculiar to China and can be found in countries more accustomed to diversity within educational institutions. Although there is regular, informal contact between academics and school teachers in China, the segregation of 'theoreticians' and 'practitioners' into separate institutions remains one of the obstacles to the formal entry of practitioners into higher education.

Another obstacle, despite the increasing cost to individual students of higher education in China (see Yin and White, 1994), is that part-time study by mature students is not accepted as the basis for the award of recognised qualifications. Though many universities have large departments of 'adult education', the accreditation of courses is restricted. Also, if part-time studies were to be recognised, this would then put pressure on the authorities to raise the salaries of those involved to match their upgraded qualifications. And if the level obtained could be seen as irrelevant to the age or attainment of the pupils to be taught, the likelihood of recognition or recompense would be further reduced. Implementing urgently required reform is hampered by funding difficulties and by a more strongly held view of education in which a teacher's role is seen to be more demanding as their students get older.

Nevertheless, there are Chinese teachers who are actively involved in programmes of professional development, organised by municipal teachers' centres, by institutes of educational research (which are outside the university system) or by peer groups in local consortia of schools. I am going to describe projects involving special school teachers in Hangzhou in Zhejiang Province. The dominant theoretical perspective informing the development of practice is behaviourist, derived from assumptions about the effect on learning and teaching of patterns of rewards and punishments.

Hangzhou

In Hangzhou, support for the special school teachers comes from the Child Development Centre in the university's Psychology Department. One of the handbooks in the centre's new Special Education Series is: 'Behaviour modification for children'. I wanted to visit the centre because I was curious to find out how far western theories of child development had influenced Chinese thinking since overseas books and journals have been available and travel has been possible through the 'Open Door'. I found that the centre ran courses on Piaget for psychologists, but that practice in schools was governed by approaches which were more obviously linked to quantified levels of educational attainment. Intelligence testing is routinely used to determine school placement.

Behaviour modification is a feature of mainstream education across China and I have seen star charts for good work and conduct in many classrooms. The education of children and young people seen to be 'mentally retarded' presents Chinese educators with a number of challenges. Special schools are seen as primary schools, in which the common core subjects of Chinese, maths, PE, music, art and natural science are taught. As well as these 'cultural' subjects, the additional areas of social and self-help skills and vocational training are seen as necessary. Early intervention for pre-school children is also receiving more attention. Assessing the requirements of students and identifying appropriate methods and equipment are priorities in these newer areas and, therefore, the focus of in-service work, which is supported by books, papers, checklists and test manuals published by Hangzhou Child Development Centre.

I visited two special schools in Hangzhou. One of them was running an in-service course for local, mainstream teachers who had students in their classes identified as 'mildly mentally retarded'. I was told that they wanted these children to go to special school but that parents wanted them to stay in the mainstream. The practical work of the course was directed towards the individualisation of teaching plans and the introduction of small-group work in the mainstream schools. University psychologists contributed advice on, for example, setting up systems of rewards and tailoring questions to the interests and abilities of each student. Behavioural approaches to classroom management offered the mainstream teachers a structure for responding to individual differences in the absence of differentiation in the curriculum. Informal in-service education provided a collaborative forum for investigating new techniques.

Teachers, as well as pupils, are rewarded for their good work and the second special school I visited in Hangzhou had become involved in joint projects with the university because it was seen by the local authority as doing well. This was a school which had once been an elementary school. Here, this meant that the teachers' qualifications were exceptionally high for a special school. However, they were similarly anxious about the current relevance of their previous professional experience. Their list of priorities for in-service education included: management, assessment, teaching methods, medical issues and early intervention.

A group of teachers from this school have written up a report entitled 'Experiment report of the first period of preschool ability reinforcement training of mentally retarded (MR) children' (their translation). They undertook a six-month collaborative project to see how far they could maximise the abilities of six 7-year-olds. This included training in visual perception, language and communication, self-help skills and social behaviour. Methods included:

presenting tasks in graded sequences; frequent repetition; presenting tasks as games; and keeping detailed records and assessments. Results were calculated according to specific behavioural measures in each of the four areas and marked progress was indicated for nearly all the children. The teachers describe their approach as compensatory and practical as opposed to one that includes the transmission of knowledge, a preparation for 'normal' educational activities and an independent life. Because they take into account individual differences, they see this as being different from customary practice in special schools and kindergartens.

It could be argued that this kind of behavioural approach is, in fact, theory-free, in the sense of not being concerned with explanations of why the children were experiencing difficulty or with the interrogation of the range of meanings behind educational classification systems. As a strategy for organising the work of experienced practitioners in an area new to them, however, it has enabled them to take an optimistic view of their work and to raise their expectations of pupils. Like the drama teacher in the UK, this project functioned both as an evaluation and a demonstration of the effectiveness of one approach.

As far as underlying theory is concerned, a medical model of educational difficulty prevails in China in which children and young people are identified and classified for schooling. The context is a canonical view of culture which shapes the definition of education and determines the scope of curriculum reform. The energy I have seen teachers put into their in-service education reveals a strong desire to make sense of their practice, which, in special education, is changing rapidly, despite the pressure of these cultural continuities. The framework taught in courses of initial training needs revising and teachers are searching for new ideas and understandings. That the task is one of reconnecting theory and practice is increasingly being recognised and it is already being accomplished on a small scale: the status of practitioners, here mainly women, is rising as they become involved in research projects; these projects arise from, are carried out within and are fed back into their practice; adult peer groups consisting of academics and teachers work together on locally designed courses.

Conclusion

One of the most striking differences between the inquiries made by the students at the Open University and the Chinese special school teachers on their in-service courses is that, whereas the Chinese teachers appear to share one basic framework for the interpretation of their findings, the UK group, which includes many non-teachers, do not. Another difference is that the approach to research amongst the UK students was generally qualitative, whereas in China, it was usually quantitative. However, there are also similarities. For example, both groups were keen to solve practical problems, particularly by undertaking more classroom observational work which Mel Ainscow also advocates in Chapter 2, this volume.

The kinds of questions asked and results obtained in each setting, however, relate to wider cultural and political contexts, as well as to immediate concerns. The perspective of a single discipline, which itself will have cultural and political significance, cannot reflect this complexity. It seems to me that explanations that are relevant to practitioners are those which both work for now and which preserve within them the uncertainties inherent in the situation which requires understanding. I agree with Sip Jan Pijl and Kees van den Bos when they argue in Chapter 9, this volume, that uncertainty is an integral feature of educational/social relationships. It does not benefit the status of our shared area of inquiry to deny this.

To advocate a multicultural, dynamic and reflexive approach to theory implies diminished validity across times and space, which, in turn, diminishes the possibility of order. It may be that, because of this threat, we have a deep-rooted need not to make as much sense of social phenomena as we could. This is perhaps the basis for a theory of the contradictory nature of theory. Our desire for order and fear of chaos is so strong that we avoid making as much sense of complex social situations as we might because of the risk of having to acknowledge that chaos might ensue. So the kind of theory we desire is a comfortable classificatory sham that can be projected, inadequately, onto future problems.

In China, theory and practice have been separated formally, as if to keep order and chaos apart. In the UK, the density of practical–theoretical intermingling forces people more actively to identify the strands that resonate with their own experience and professional purposes, though, as Tony Booth and Gunnar Stangvik illustrate in Chapters 7 and 12, this volume, the dominance of scientific, political and professional traditions endures. The tolerance of a range of perspectives depends on the interests of those in power.

Reducing the barriers to learning experienced by children, young people and adults in educational settings is a task that requires an understanding of what goes on at the moment and why. Yes, we need theory. However, definitions of what, exactly, any particular social situation consists of and what, exactly, may constitute a problem within it are bound to vary. There cannot be a single, adequate theoretical perspective – first, because, as Gunnar Stangvik and Tony Booth argue, an interdisciplinary approach to educational inquiries is the sensible way to reflect and respond to their in-built complexity and second, because the multidimensional approaches of some people may not be consistent with those of others.

Mel Ainscow argues in Chapter 2, this volume, for a practice-based educational research tradition. Similarly, the implication for research and practice implied by my own approach is that they should not be seen as distinct, neither in fact nor in value. If we use the ordinary language of 'inquiry' for the activities of students, teachers and researchers, then the commonality between these groups can be revealed and status differentials potentially weakened. This would represent a more inclusive approach to understanding and reducing barriers to learning.

11

THE POLITICS OF THEORISING SPECIAL EDUCATION

Roger Slee

Introduction

The practice of special education has proven extremely resilient since its beginnings in the nineteenth century with Johann Jakob Guggenbuhl's refinement of the work of Itard and Seguin (Kanner, 1959; Lewis, 1989) until its present and many manifestations. It would not be an overstatement to suggest that special education has reinvented itself to stake its claim in the so-called era of inclusion. The linguistic adjustments that have recently taken place to describe and legitimate the expansion of special educational interest and practice do not, however, constitute a comprehensive 'retheorising' of special education. In fact, at the risk of being provocative, I would assert that the failure to apply theoretical analysis has been detrimental to the project of inclusion. What has transpired is, as Bernstein (1996) demonstrates, better described as the 'submersion' of special educational interest within the distractive discursive noises (Ball, 1988) of integration and, latterly, inclusion. To be sure there have been some beneficiaries, but they remain those with an interest in traditional special educational practice, an unreconstructed school system and the bureaucratic and political imperatives of education policy makers.

The analysis of a theory of special education must be pursued with reference to its relation to a theory of schooling and coterminous changing theories of disability. In other words, few writers in the tradition of special education problematise school failure beyond defective individual pathologies in need of special provision to support their own specific educational needs and delimit the disruption such children cause to their own academic and social progress and that of their 'non-defective' peers. Highly complex sets of political relations articulated through the forms of educational provision are reduced in a 'spurious biology' or set of 'biological metaphors' (Bernstein, 1996: 11). Theorising special education is thus not an academic indulgence, a retreat from the 'real-world' problems of responding to difficulties in the everyday life of schools and classrooms: it represents a chance to throw into sharp relief the anti-democratic

126

policies of special education (Skrtic, 1991a) submerged in normalising disclosures and dividing practices which produce hierarchies of 'scholastic identities' (Ball, 1990). The largely unacknowledged obstruction of the educational requirements of democracy (Pearl, 1988; Bernstein, 1996) by discourses of special educational needs rests in the latter's 'closed local vocabularies' (Rorty, 1989: 77). 'Individual Educational Programmes', 'most appropriate setting', 'least restrictive environment', 'special educational needs', and other such 'clauses of conditionality' (Slee, 1996a), carry a self-evident authority which simultaneously privileges professional judgement and submerges and silences discordant voices.

Central to this problem of theory in special education have been the widely ignored questions:

1   Who produces theory? and, inextricably,
2   To what ends are theories manufactured and deployed?

This is captured by a disabled researcher, Colin Barnes, who speaks more generally of the politics of theory making:

> Since the politicisation of disability by the international disabled people's movement . . . a growing number of academics, many of whom are disabled people themselves, have reconceptualised disability as a complex and sophisticated form of social oppression (Oliver, 1986) or institutional discrimination on a par with sexism, heterosexism and racism . . . theoretical analysis has shifted from individuals and their impairments to disabling environments and hostile social attitudes . . .
> (Barnes, 1996: 43)

Such concern to expose and apply critical scrutiny to traditional theories of 'special educational needs and practices' was raised some time ago by researchers such as Booth (1981), Tomlinson (1982) and Barton and Tomlinson (1981) pursuant to the development of a 'sociology of special education'. This tradition of inquiry into the production of and responses to disablement in education (Oliver, 1990b, 1996) provides the intellectual base for this brief discussion which proceeds from two organising questions:

1   Why is it important to theorise special education? and
2   What might such theorising offer education in general?

While Clark et al. (1995a) warn against 'imported theories' applied to educational problems as incomplete, this chapter will seek to demonstrate that these imported theories represent a work in progress and, providing that they do not advocate intellectual foreclosure, there is considerable potential for addressing the 'under-theorised' state of special educational practice.

Why theorise special education?

In their paper tabled at a symposium bearing the same title as this book, Clark *et al.* (1995b: 1) interrupt ' . . . the long tradition of writing on special education which presents itself as atheoretical' to suggest two problems endemic to special educational practice: the application of unexplicated theory and imported theory. Both, they argue, are reductionist: the former in its failure to acknowledge its theoretical roots in psychological theories of pathological, cognitive and behavioural deficiency in children; the latter in its assumption that sociological theory enjoys easy transposition to problems of educational practice. While willingly adding my voice to the first plank of their thesis, I believe that the second has only been considered partially and too quickly dismissed.

In a recent and helpful attempt to impose order over the competing perspectives on disability Sheila Riddell (1996: 84–92) suggests five organising, but now always clearly separated, groups. This represents a reconfiguration of earlier work by Fulcher (1989), who depicted the following discourses on disability: medical discourse; lay discourse; charity discourse; rights discourse; and an emergent management discourse. To précis Riddell's adaptation:[1]

- *Essentialist perspectives* are those which locate disability in the pathological impairments or deficiencies of individuals. This perspective has established its dominance over the taken-for-granted assumptions of special educational theory, which proceeds from diagnosis of individual defect as the baseline for intervention and remediation. The aim is to minimise difference within the project of normalisation (Nirje, 1970). As Clark *et al.* (1995a) point out, there exists no room for problematising this perspective to suggest interactionist antecedents in the epidemiology of disability. The regular educational provision is accepted and special education assists in the identification and treatment of those whose pathologies 'naturally' exclude them from regular academic and social entitlements. Theory, accordingly, is unacknowledged. Proponents of essentialism are merely responding to practical problems presented by the individual differences of children. I will return to essentialism in its appropriation of inclusiveness later in this chapter.
- *Social constructionist perspectives* present disability as an oppressive and normative construct deployed against minorities enforcing social marginalisation. This perspective is apparent in the work of Goffman (1961, 1963) and implicitly lingers in the World Health Organisation construction of disability, impairment and handicap.
- *Materialist perspectives* are clearly enunciated by Abberley (1987) who eschews the reductionist urge to locate disability within individual pathology or dominant social attitudes. According to proponents of this view, impairment can be identified as both historically and culturally specific mediated through the organisation of labour and the processes of

material reproduction (Abberley, 1987; Oliver, 1990b). Stories are then produced to explain disability as personal tragedy or a medical problem to be managed within the health system in order to locate and keep disabled people out of the labour market as dependent consumers. In purer expressions of this perspective, their destiny is leashed to momentum of class struggle.

- *Post-modernist perspectives* cast doubt over the limitations of class struggle and capitalist production narratives as an explanation of the complex and fragmented experiences of disability across a range of identities. Post-modernist analyses provided space for other voices and expressions in describing and analysing disability. Consequently, feminist accounts (Morris, 1991, 1992) inserted women's voices of their particular and diverse experiences and struggles. Corbett (1996), following Branson and Miller (1989), Fulcher (1989) and Shakespeare (1994), deconstructs the disabling language to reveal the politics of identity and difference.

- *Disability movement perspectives* devote less attention to the production of a coherent theoretical explication of disability in their eclectic quest for social change and the incorporation of disability rights in the mainstream political agenda.

Riddell's schemata provide a way of taking up, and demonstrating the shortcomings of, the challenge for sociology of education offered by Clark and her colleagues. It will be argued that rather than attenuating practice in special needs teaching, sociological investigations, as they continue to push aside theoretical borders, have the capacity to offer broader options for learners' and teachers' 'enhancement' and 'confidence' consistent with Bernstein's 'announced' preconditions for democracy (1996: 6–7). This is where much of the current crop of special needs theorising comes adrift. There is a failure to recognise that imported sociological theorising of disability and education is not a quest to force theoretical closure to eliminate doubt. It is essentially a political project demanding ever-clearer explanations of complex realities in order that we know 'what's going on, why and how we change it' (Troyna, 1994). In this respect it is what Troyna (1995) referred to as partisan research, akin to the development of a theory of anti-racist education. The relationship between emerging discourses of disability and integration/inclusion resembles the struggle between multicultural and anti-racist schooling.

The assertion that 'multicultural education is synonymous with good practices in education' . . . soon became the clarion call of those who championed this educational orthodoxy. But it was not long before the allegedly emancipatory powers of this programme of reform came under heavy fire from those committed to anti-racist perspectives . . . in contrast to multiculturalism, anti-racism . . . rejects the view which sees racism as primarily an individual problem. Nor do anti-racists endorse the voyeuristic imperatives of multiculturalism in which 'they' rather than 'us' become the subject of scrutiny. The iconography of multiculturalism is the three Ss: saris, samosas and steel bands. . . . Its imperative is to ensure that people understand each other's culture; its conviction, that in a context of cultural understanding racial conflict would be unnecessary and would wither away . . .

(Troyna, 1993: 26)

In other words, special education proceeds from a theoretical position – from a particular way of seeing the world and the place of schooling and those who are seen to be disabled within that world. As Clark *et al.* (1995a) observe, that theory often remains unexplicated and therefore there is a tacit acceptance of the disinterested professional going about an unquestionably necessary set of tasks. The preceding discussion lays bare the centrality of theoretical perspectives and contests in the practice of special education. Having acknowledged theoretical divisions, I want to consider the suggestion that imported theory collapses in a reductionist heap when applied to special needs education.

Inclusion – a new language for functionalism?

The 'essentialist' position is intrinsically functionalist. Defect is located in the individual who becomes subject to classification, regulation and treatment. The school is not placed into the diagnostic frame by such a normalising gaze. The project for the special education professional is the management of difference. Formerly, this was effected through separation from the regular school and segregated educational provision. Latterly, the call has been for inclusion in the regular classroom. Inclusion, however, masks a range of theoretical positions with regard to the relationship between those targeted for inclusion and the nature of regular educational provision.

For some, inclusion, like integration, fails to progress beyond assimilation. The assimilationist's hope is that difference will be welcomed and tolerated and differentiated learning programmes will proceed in the regular classroom. Children with special educational needs are to be managed in the regular school. Their presence evokes the competing interests of delimiting their disruption to their peers, whose tenure is unquestionable, while trying to provide an educational programme suited to their particular needs (Elkins, 1990). This is indeed a complex and delicate area of management which the Code of Practice (Department for Education, 1994) aims to choreograph (Fish and Evans, 1995). Attempts have been made to deploy effective schooling research as a way of collapsing the special educational needs conundrum into the general mission of school improvement (Reynolds and Ramasut, 1993; Slee, 1991; Ainscow, 1991b). Such approaches accept the general framework of schooling and seek to resolve issues of fit: how do we enable these different students within the present arrangement of schooling? Inclusion is reduced to a technical problem of resourcing, management, social groupings and instruc-tional design within this scenario.

Herein, inclusion implicitly acknowledges and accepts the value of the regular schooling provision. Or, more accurately, it may reflect a painful compromise for those who have been locked out of the mainstream. If we were to put the question: 'Effective for whom?', we may then adjust our position and want to argue for education's reconstruction as the only avenue for inclusion. To demonstrate the reductionism of special educational theory, we need to deconstruct the language of inclusion against the policies and practices it connotes and enlist an historical perspective. A sociology of identity, difference and education exposes the reductionism and lays out greater possibilities for policy makers and educators (Yeatman, 1994).

Theorising special education is an important device for exposing intent. Discourse analysis provides the tools for us to expose the social relations of disablement as articulated through the forms of educational provision. From that point it is then possible to interrogate the meaning of inclusion. Is it a statement of location or value?

Reduced to inclusion?

For many, inclusion connotes a linguistic adjustment to present a politically correct façade to a changing world. In other words, vocabularies and practices undergo changes at the margins to effect a posture of sympathy to the plight of disabled students and their carers and advocates. The essentialist theory is constant. Accordingly, inclusion represents a technical problem of resource management. Inclusion will be achieved if the requisite resources, material and human, are located alongside the student in the new environment. The arrangements of the host classroom and school may undergo changes to accom-modate the differences of the special needs pupils. Teaching strategies may require greater flexibility. These are the technical issues confronting inclusion. Where compromises cannot occur, industrial stand-offs arise and legislation is invoked to prove institutional hardship. Such cosmetic surgery fails to excise the deep culture of exclusion.

Previously I have scrutinised the conceptual slippage inherent in such approaches and in the ways in which inclusion is described by special and regular educators alike (Slee, 1996b). Terms such as 'special educational needs', 'integration', 'normalisation', 'mainstreaming', 'exceptional learners' and 'inclu-sion' (this list is not exhaustive) merge into a loose vocabulary variously applied to manage the issue of disability as it collides with the regular education system. Some time ago now Barton (1988b) suggested that special educational need was a euphemism for school failure. In other words, those who, for a variety of reasons arising from the interaction between the school and the child, were at risk of failure could be absorbed into a catch-all category of special educational needs. This was a bureaucratic device for dealing with the complications arising from clashes between narrow, waspish curricula and disabled students. As the curriculum has narrowed further through the marketisation of schooling (Gewirtz *et al.*, 1996), and increasing numbers of students are being forced to stay on at school with nowhere to go (Polk and Tait, 1990; Marginson, 1993), the categories within the special educational net broaden to manage this expanding clientele (Tomlinson, 1993). This serves the interest of the school in holding pedagogy, curriculum, organisation and culture as constants and demanding conformity [*sic.* normality] from the students targeted for assimilation.

This process of adjusting special educational categorisation (Norwich, 1990) as social regulation (Rose, 1989) finds recent and dramatic expression in the escalating rates of exclusion and the proliferation of categories of behavioural disorders (Slee, 1995a). Media reportage (e.g. *The Times*, 28 May 1996, p. 11) documents an increasing volume of school exclusions extending down into greater levels of younger suspended and excluded students. These data confirm earlier (Slee, 1992) and recent (Edwards, 1996) claims elsewhere. Nigel de Gruchy, general secretary of the National Association of Schoolmasters and Union of Women Teachers, is not coy in identifying attribution for the outbreak of trouble in schools: 'Educating these pupils in ordinary schools can be disastrous for them. We need to reopen special schools and build more referral units' (*The Times*, 28 May 1996, p. 1).

Returning to our earlier discussion of prevailing perspectives on, or theories of, special education, de Gruchy adheres to an essentialist view. Increasing exclusions is reflexive to the movement of greater numbers of defective students from segregated special educational provision into a system of schooling intended for non-defective students. Employment of sociological theorising of this phenomenon, placing regular education in the analytical frame, tells a different story. A story that, I will argue, provides greater possibilities for teachers and these 'defective' students. Prior to doing so, let me complicate the story by introducing another layer of essentialist thinking. My aim is to uncover the intent of theory making and address our earlier question about the beneficiaries of special educational theory and practice.

It is not just a matter of opening up more special schools for these suspended behaviour-disordered students following their collision with the disciplinary apparatus of state education. There is also a surge to identify them prior to serious disruptive events. Australia, following the American precedent as it is wont to do, is now experiencing localised epidemic outbreaks of ADHD (attention deficit disorder with hyperactivity) syndrome. My intention here is not to deny the existence of severely problematic behaviour in relatively small numbers of children. It is to make a little more problematic the administrative windfall of an insidious device for regulation and surveillance of increasing numbers of students.

A relative newcomer to the educational landscape, ADHD provides a useful analytical platform for deconstructing special educational discourse and practice. While I have discussed the syndrome at length elsewhere (Slee, 1995b), I wish to make four observations in the context of this discussion:

First, ADHD transforms pupil disruption to pupil dysfunction. Thereby we return to an essentialist frame where the impaired pathology of the child is the problem to be managed. Disruption is no longer a complex problem in an inter-active matrix of the multiple identities of the child, youth culture, pedagogy, curriculum, school culture and organisation, race, gender and class. It is not about, according to this theoretical fix, political economy. It is individual pathology which becomes the site for chemical intervention.

Second, the relationship between child and school, parent and school, and parent and child is simultaneously transformed. Bad children bring hostile scrutiny to parenting skills. Bad children attract authoritarian interest from all quarters. The consequential conflict sets child against school, parent against school, parent against child. Impaired children attract sympathy and intense professional interest and intervention. There has been a proliferation of support groups for ADHD. The Foucauldian scholar will be fascinated by the trend to self-regulatory practices amongst parents and their children as schools seek to manage increasing rates of disruption. Parents volunteer their children for diagnosis and treatment.

Third, the incidence of ADHD in Australia is demographically perplexing. Differential rates of diagnosis between states and regions suggest that there may well be some degree of diagnostic predisposition connected with the incidence of the syndrome.

Fourth, though I cannot substantiate my claim with data at this stage, anecdotal evidence suggests a gender agenda in the onset and spread of ADHD. Boys are particularly susceptible to attention disorders. Theorising masculinity may offer other readings of boys' behaviour and sedentary academic activity.

Whose interests are served by the escalating exclusion and segregation of disruptive students? Whose interests are served by the discovery and spread of ADHD? Once again theory frames our responses. Some would argue that students have opportunity to receive special educational interventions from a range of professionals who will attend to their special educational needs (Bailey, forthcoming). I would pause to interrupt this professionally driven narrative. The immediate beneficiaries of exclusion and chemical treatment are students whose participation in regular academic schooling has been disturbed by this growing number of problem students. So too, teachers, who receive respite through the removal or sedation of these less-than-docile bodies. The special educational workers benefit from an expanding client base (Slee, 1996b). Some parents benefit from the chemical calm and the attendant relief from disturbed students.

The benefit to the excluded child is not so apparent. Edwards (1996) has tracked suspended students in Victoria through their high school years to demonstrate that:

- suspension places students' academic careers and post-school options at risk;
- multiple suspensions inexorably exclude students from final year certification; and
- the involvement of students in remedial support in the school disproportionately corresponds with suspension.

Previously Bodna (1987) acknowledged the coincidence of participation in segregated special education and adult incarceration. Mongon (1988) has reflected upon the dubious claim to student benefit from participation in behaviour units.

Particular forms of schooling promote greater levels of exclusion. The current surge in suspension and exclusion in the UK accompanies the press for selection, back to basics, market competition, league tables, inspection and national standardised testing. Within this educational policy context, conservative special educational theory has a glove-like relationship with the hand of exclusive schooling. Essentialists' views of disability are celebrated and derive benefit. Hence, the need to employ sociological theory to argue for inclusive education, which explicitly demands radical changes to the present culture of schooling.

An imported view of schooling

Returning to Riddell's discussion of theories of disablement, we can extract some important lessons for education which, in their application, generate opportunities for multiple identities in schooling and inclusive educational cultures. Following Oliver's argument that disablement speaks to political rather than individual pathologies, I would insist that consistent with the struggle to expose and dismantle racist and patriarchal schooling, an enabling education demands acknowledgement that disability describes unequal relationships of power and access to privilege. That this is the case is manifest in the disproportionate referral of minority group children to special educational services (Gilborn, 1995). Functionalist special educational theory serves imperatives of racism, class and disablement. It is not a technical issue of diagnosis and resource deployment. It is about exclusive and inclusive cultures which are mediated through the academic content and forms of delivery, and the structure and processes of schooling. Inclusion therefore demands that educators problematise their theories of disability and schooling. Imported structural and post-structural theories are prerequisite tools in this enterprise.

Shakespeare and Watson (1995) have argued that while the social model of disability (Abberley, 1987; Oliver, 1990b) was germane to the development of the disability rights movement, post-structural analysis needs to be employed to amplify the many and disparate disabled voices and identities. First, there is the necessity to acknowledge the diversity of identities which have hitherto been

134

collapsed into special educational categories to fit professional and bureaucratic imperatives and also into materialist narratives of disablement. Following Morris (1991), Shakespeare and Watson (1995) demand 'a re-examination of the role of physical difference [and its lived experience] in the disability equation'. Pursuant to this end they employ a range of theoretical tools, including post-modernist and feminist analyses. This is consistent with Ball's impatience with the parsimony and inadequacy of single-theory explanations for complex social relations articulated in schools (Ball, 1987, 1994). Rather than attenuating teaching methodology and educational development and delivery, this provides greater scope for inclusion of students into the project of education by building cultures according to the multiple identities of school users.

Such an imported theorising of special education and, axiomatically, regular education lends clarity to educational policy analysis through its resistance to reductionism. Conservative education agendas which collapse into the cultural singularity of league tables and a narrowly defined national curriculum are exposed as ineluctably exclusive for increasing numbers of students. Special education, like the unskilled labour market in days past, acts as a safety valve for the failure of schools to include all comers. Prescriptions for raising standards such as those announced by Tony Blair at Didcot Girls' school (Carvel, J. 'Blair rejects mixed ability teaching', Guardian, 8 June 1996, p. 7) or set out by Mandelson and Liddle (1996) in their prescription for 'new Labour's economic and social agenda' are thrown into sharp relief against the polycultural nature of educational inclusion.

The practical implications for schools and teachers can then be considered in relation to the various components of the educational, organisational and cultural life of schools. This theoretical reorientation presses us to consider how we celebrate and support difference through a range of resourcing arrangements, pedagogies and curriculum initiatives to expand options for all students rather than fuel a bifurcated educational system.

I will attempt to make practical sense of this by importing an example. Two schools I was invited to conduct research in provide an alternative view of students' disablement by traditional academic schooling. The difference is that neither are special educational settings. Rather they are schools which, responding to the needs of a range of student differences, sought to reinvent themselves to expand students' options and engender success. One of the schools, a technical school in Victoria, was presented with the opportunity of making greater claims on integrating funding because it had received a steady stream of students who had been ascertained as having a range of behavioural and emotional disorders while attending more academic schools in the area. Eschewing the integration funding track, the school entered into a long-term agenda of curriculum and organisational reform. This necessitated the development of new subjects and teaching approaches to host academic skill acquisition. The school was able to demonstrate that students who had been excluded from neighbouring schools and referred to them with special educational needs were, after working within a significantly reconstructed school, entering higher education, training and work in greater numbers than were students from the surrounding academic schools. This experience was replicated by another reconstructed secondary school in Queensland (Warner, 1991). Both schools were less apprehensive about disability because of their comprehensive educational programmes and inclusive cultures.

Special educational theory, osmosis and inclusion

This brief discussion is deliberately provocative. Political theorising demands no less. Inclusion as a cultural goal speaks to a reconsideration of the structure of power and social relations and their mediation through the ethos and activity of education. The symbiotic relationship between regular and special education constrains theory making. Special educational theorising will not of itself challenge its central canons to effect a reconstruction of schooling. The challenge has to be imported. This process has commenced with the unfolding sociologies of education in general and special education in particular.

Note

1   What follows is a summary of Riddell's ordering of perspectives on disability with some insertions of work characteristic of the perspective. It is a crude summary which does not, I hope, misrepresent her work in my usage of it.

12

CONFLICTING PERSPECTIVES ON LEARNING DISABILITIES

Gunnar Stangvik

Introduction

There is growing discomfort with the state of the art of special education. This book clearly shows that many workers in the field critically examine, or even deconstruct, concepts and assumptions and work to reconstruct the field of practice. In Norway, present reforms, which purport to dismantle special schools and institutions for the intellectually disabled, have made these needs paramount. In the wake of the reforms the state has launched an implementation project titled 'Restructuring special education' (Ormstrukturering av spesialundervisningen), and the Norwegian Council for Research has launched a parallel programme for special education research. This has brought special education issues to the forefront. Questions asked in this chapter are:

1   What is valid knowledge in special education?
2   Is there conflict between knowledge traditions?
3   What are the theoretical and practical consequences of different traditions?
4   What is the relationship between the field of practice and its knowledge traditions?
5   What is the relationship of special education to other sciences?
6   What future developments are necessary?

The concept of disability is the heart of the matter in special education. This concept is examined in the first part of the chapter. In the second part, transactional dimensions of disabilities are underscored and some practical implications of this line of thought are explored.

The relevance of perspectives

The necessity to scrutinise the assumptions that underpin current perspectives on learning disabilities is vigorously asserted by Reid and Hresko when they claim 'Until one examines the diverse orientations from which learning disabilities have arisen, the field appears to be in a state of chaos' (Reid and Hresko, 1981: 13). My point of departure assumes that the perspective, on which research and theorising are based, regulates and structures the research process. It may define what is regarded as the basic unit of data collection and analysis in research projects – i.e. the individual; social relationships; the system; society; or maybe some combination; which types of theory are thought to offer the best explanation of relationships; the relationship to other sciences and disciplines; and so on. The different designs encountered in the so-called efficacy research in special education may serve as an example. This research progressed from a stage where effects were interpreted within an additive model as results of a combination of individual characteristics and school variables (i.e. integrated or segregated school settings) to a stage where effects of special education are interpreted in terms of internalisation of social roles (i.e. labelling and stigmatisation). This development evidently implied a change of focus from psychology to sociology. Disabilities cannot be understood independently of social contexts, and should rather be thought of as processes which take place when a person with a specific set of characteristics meets a particular setting. Generally speaking, they are social constructs which are generated in the course of social processes. As such, disabilities may resist our attempts of simple operational reification. According to Poplin, the term has become a household word in the USA. She quotes a phrase from a Broadway play: 'I'm just an average American male; I have a two storey house in the suburbs, a wife, a cat, a dog, two cars and three children, one with learning disabilities' (Poplin, 1985: 37). Disabilities are complex phenomena. And consequently research is in need of a multiplicity of perspectives. However, as Callewaert (1992) points out, in a study of Bourdieu, research has its own practice which may restrict both observations and interpretations in a particular field of study. Hence, reflections are needed, not only in the area of disabilities, but also as regards research methods, models and theories.

Beyond functionalist special education

In an attempt to locate the special education knowledge tradition within general scientific thought, Skrtic writes:

> Given the assumptions and values of functionalist education, we can understand special education as a more extreme version of functionalist education, more extreme both in an objectivist and microscopic sense. As such, the field's guiding theories of human pathology and organised rationality yield an approach to diagnosis and instruction premised on diagnostic–prescriptive teaching and behavioristic theory.
>
> (Skrtic, 1991a: 105)

Too often special education is characterised by a pragmatic knowledge interest. Descriptive concepts, e.g. 'need', 'category of disability' and 'special education form', mostly appear (or are presented) as elements of professional and legal–administrative discourses about what practices are 'best for the child'. This approach tends to overlook the fact that special education practices and the types of knowledge on which they are based are also parts of a 'regime' for managing deviant and devalued people, which has its historical and cultural antecedents. In a wider sense this 'regime' with its theoretical language, its practices and its consquences for the individual may also be thought of as ways of 'objectification'. This aspect of social practice is dealt with by Foucault when he comments on what he considers to be the general goal of his work:

> My objective has been to create a history of the different modes by which, in our culture, human beings are made subjects. My work has dealt with three modes of objectification which transform human beings into subjects. . . . The first is the modes of inquiry which try to give themselves the status of sciences; for example objectivising the speaking subject in grammaire générale, philology and linguistics. . . . In the second part of my work, I have studied objectivising of the subject in what I shall call 'dividing' practices. The subject is either divided in himself or divided from others. . . . Finally I have sought to study – in my current work – the way a human being turns him- or herself into a subject.
>
> (Foucault, 1982: 298)

To analyse scientific language, dividing practices and the ways persons are turned into subjects seems to me to be extremely relevant for special education and may represent important cornerstones for furthering critical analysis of concepts, models and practices of special education. Such a project broadens the knowledge base by opening special education to other fields of knowledge (i.e. history, anthropology, sociology, etc.) and may thereby initiate a critical analysis of adopted paradigms in the field of special education. As Skrtic points out, 'A crisis in knowledge is a necessary prelude to growth of knowledge' (Skrtic, 1991a: 28). Hopefully this may lead to a better understanding of the implications of special education practices on a personal as well as on a cultural and societal level.

Frames of meaning

Figure 12.1 describes different modes of objectification of disabilities and deviance. How this process may take place through the description of disability 'syndromes' is outlined by Bayliss in this book. My objective is to distinguish some of the media and tools of this knowledge construction. Objectifications are socially negotiated and the construction of meaning takes place at different interrelated levels and within different frames.

First, there is a 'general discourse', which may be subdivided in several discourses (cf. Fulcher, 1989). Such discourses are frequently loaded with political and professional interests, making it rather easy to distinguish the social basis of objectification. The basis of each discourse is a particular perspective with a common set of value assumptions which serve to filter incoming information. Later in this text I refer to the 'client perspective' and the 'transactional perspective'. Perspectives are particular ways of looking at the world. Patton discusses difficulties in distinguishing between the observer's point of view, i.e. the personal perspective, and the datum: 'In effect the observer is here construed as one moment of the datum and as such the fabric of his thought is inextricably woven into the datum as he is assumed to be constitute of its meaning' (Patton, 1980: 191). This serves to underscore the intimate relationship between the social world of the subject and meaning construction. Second, there is the mode of scientific inquiry which is mediated through paradigms, models, theory and metatheory. Paradigms are not made explicit. Submerged in the language of scientific communities they may be difficult to distinguish. According to Giddens, 'The notion of "paradigm" refers to taken-for-granted, unexamined assumptions shared by communities of scientists, who confine their attentions to small-scale puzzle-solving within the bounds of those assumptions' (Giddens, 1993: 149). Paradigms are 'frames of meaning' shaping and reshaping scientific discoveries by adding to these discoveries the taken-for-

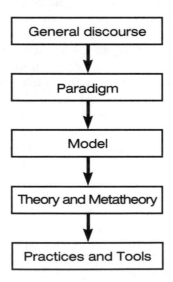

Figure 12.1 Frames of meaning

granted world of common sense. They may be more or less explicit. Kobi puts it this way:

> The paradigm can hold good either as a 'natural' self-evident truth (whoever places himself outside this notion is in the realm of the absurd) or it has the trait of an explicit, unspoken 'convention' for any so-called 'scientific community'.
>
> (Kobi, 1977: 11, editor's translation)

These notions of paradigm are very much in accordance with what Lewis in this book defines as 'an interconnecting set of assumptions, values and methodologies that are taken as axiomatic, and which cannot be further examined within the paradigm itself'. Through processes of generalisation, paradigms serve to define which problems and methods are counted as valid in a particular area of research. The term 'model' denotes specific ways of organising knowledge and practice within a dominant paradigm, i.e. within what Kuhn describes as 'normal science', giving priority to some types of knowledge and practices at the cost of others. It may be a set of rather asbstract and general concepts which are ordered in specific ways to explain causal relations between empirical facts, or it may be theoretical as in the case of ideal types used for comparing particular social phenomena (e.g. Weber's model of a bureaucracy). Theory refers to higher levels of knowledge construction and verification. Theories may be generated from logical deduction from *a priori* assumptions, or they may be based on inductive strategies (e.g. grounded theory). Metatheory directs attention to the value decisions which are always part of theory construction. The last level in the diagram refers to that mode of objectification which Foucault denoted as 'dividing' practices. By means of a particular set of practices and tools, the person with a disability is contextualised and ascribed a specific meaning. According to this view, social sciences construct the subject by transmitting views about the learner, about disability, etc.

Marshall discusses the role of science in the construction of the subject:

> . . . and in the normalising procedures of examination and 'confession' people are classified and objectified as the 'truth' about themselves is 'revealed' to themselves. In constituting the subject in these ways, in constructing the very identity of individuals, modern power procedures govern individuals through technologies of individualisation and normalisation.
>
> (Marshall, 1996: 108)

Marshall (1996: 115–17) also tries to show how 'normalised judgements' based on the developments within the disciplines serve to objectify and to subjectify the person and how they are passed on through:

- Organisation of space and time, that is, people are allocated to spaces in which they may be surveyed at any time.
- Placing of activities according to timetables prescribed by the disciplines and establishing a set of rhythm for these activities.
- Breaking activities into stages to be performed in particular sequences.

Current orientations to disabilities

There is no time here for the study of epistemology. It is necessary, however, to underscore that which is accepted as a valid construction of knowledge – also in the field of learning disabilities – is based on the acceptance of certain assumptions. First, these may have to do with general orientations to knowledge – resulting in different criteria of knowledge construction. A well-known example is Habermas's division between positivistic, hermeneutic and critical science. Such differences in scientific outlook may be denoted by the German words 'erklären' (i.e. explaining) and 'verstehen' (i.e. understanding). Another relevant distinction in orientations to knowledge would be between a theoretical and a pragmatic orientation.

Adherence to different criteria in different scientific communities has often resulted in methodological controversies and disputes as regards what constitutes valid knowledge. Second, using a term adopted from Thomas Kuhn, there is something which may be called 'normal science' – a commonly accepted cosmology defining the borders of the dominating scientific community in a specific period of time. Famous examples from the history of science are the judicial and religious persecutions used against the proponents of the heliocentric picture of the world and of the Darwinistic conception of the origin of species by means of natural selection. These are the dramatic examples. There are, of course, less visible demarcation lines within scientific communities between what is considered normal, and non-normal science. Paradigms, or 'frames of meaning', ought to be tested continually in order that one paradigm may constructively mediate another (Giddens, 1993). There is an abundant literature on perspectives and research approaches to learning disabilities which try to describe different general orientations to the concept. Perspectives and approaches may be described in terms of paradigms or models. 'Paradigm' is the more general term and refers to the metatheoretical assumptions on which the models, theories, assumptions and practices are based. Skrtic uses the more general term and makes a distinction between four 'paradigms of modern social scientific thought' (Skrtic, 1991a: 13): radical humanist, radical structuralist, interpretivist and functionalist. The term 'model' is used at a lower level of generality.

In American literature one finds the medical model; the psychological process model; the behavioural model and the cognitive or learning strategy model (Poplin, 1985). Reid and Hresko (1981) use the term 'threads' in order to describe perspectives and trends in the field of learning disabilities: the oral thread, the written language thread or the perceptual-motor thread. In German literature 'das caritative Modell'; 'das exorzistische Modell'; 'das Rehabilitations-Modell' (Kobi, 1977). Each model, or thread, offers a different explanation of learning disabilities and draws attention to different strategies of remediation. Such analyses clearly show the changing base of knowledge in the history of learning disabilities.

Some German writers in the field (Bleidick and von Ferber quoted in Stangvik, 1979: 170–4) have distinguished between paradigms in terms of their basic unit of analysis whether the main focus is the individual, the interaction, the system, or society. They are classified as:

- The individual–theoretical paradigm (i.e. 'disability as a medical category').
- The interaction–theoretical paradigm (i.e. 'disability as a label').
- The system–theoretical paradigm (i.e. 'disability as a system result').
- The society–theoretical paradigm (i.e. 'disability as a product of society').

The individual–theoretical paradigm is the basis of most learning disability models, the knowledge basis of which is found in medicine and biology. In other words, disability is treated as a medical category. As a result of this approach inadequate social interactions and deficient systems are easily overlooked because the 'blame' is placed on the individual as victim. Poplin (1985) characterises this as a 'reductive fallacy'. Categorisation is an important process related to this fallacy by which a particular syndrome (e.g. Down's Syndrome) is used to define a person instead of a condition. This application of medical labels has been called the 'clinical perspective' on handicap. Booth points out that: 'reduction of a person to a clinical entity in this way emphasises the similarities between members of the category and may obscure knowledge of their differences' (Booth, 1985a: 14).

The relationship of special education to other sciences

This above line of reasoning raises questions as regards the basis of knowledge in general in special education and knowledge about the subject in particular. Developmental psychology is of particular interest. Morss (1996: 4–7) distinguishes between four approaches to developmental psychology:

- Traditional psychology of development in which experimental research, carried out under controlled conditions, represents the preferred form. This line of argument is a functional one; that is, it treats the activity of the child (or adults) as a kind of adaptation to a stable environment. This approach to psychology favours normative definitions of disability, that is, disability is defined in terms of development norms of perception, reading, adaptive behaviour, etc.

- The social context approach; that is, attempts are made by traditional psychology to incorporate knowledge about influences from the social context. Interest in the ideas of Vygotsky and Bronfenbrenner arises naturally from this perspective. This approach underscores the impact of cultural and social settings and expectancies and defines disabilities in terms of the meeting between the person and society.

- The social construction approach; that is, attention is paid to interpersonal processes, like language and other symbolic systems, through which humans create the reality they experience. G. H. Mead's theory of the development of self and identity through communication with significant symbols may exemplify this approach. It underscores the impact of 'lived experience' on the subjective definition of disability.

- Critical psychology of development; that is, psychology itself is located as a science in a larger historical area of economic interests, and it is asserted that psychology, in fact, is created by those processes and assists in maintaining a particular political context. This line of thought is clearly expressed in Foucault. According to this, definitions of disability are political discourses relevant to different powerful groups in society (e.g. professional groups).

(Morss, 1996: 4–7)

Morss's argument signifies an increasingly critical attitude towards human sciences in western thought and underscores the impossibility of treating psychology as a separate sphere of knowledge. Construction is paralleled by deconstruction. The concept of disability may probably be deconstructed in the wake of the deconstruction of psychology, or, at best, decomposed into a number of specific and operational meanings, as in its present dominant form it seems mainly to be based on the theories and methods of 'traditional psychology of development'.

Evidently, each paradigm attracts attention to different sources in the construction of social reality, drawing upon different types of knowledge. In Figure 12.2 I have tried to sketch some relevant orientations to the construction of the concept of disability.

The distinction 'micro–macro' refers to the unit, or level of analysis of a specific phenomenon. There is also a difference between analysing disability in terms of processes related to social class reproduction, defined by processes at a societal level, or defining it in terms of processes mainly related to individual impairment. However, this difference certainly affects the relation of special education to other sciences as the two approaches rely on different bases of knowledge. Figure 12.2 suggests that this relationship may be characterised as

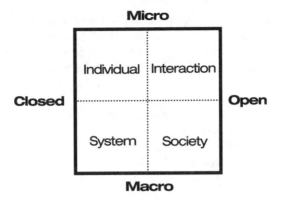

Figure12.2 Orientations to disability

'closed' or 'open'. There is abundant evidence that often developments in other sciences have vast implications for special education: the critique of mental testing, categorisation and special class placement as a result of developments in sociology; the adoption of new categories due to new developments in medicine and drug treatment, etc. Such developments serve to draw attention to other aspects of knowledge construction, for example, the social interest and the question of power.

Some implications for practice and research

Some writers in the field have also tried to outline practical implications of the above line of thought by showing how different perspectives form models of intervention by defining the primary task, by defining the focus of attention, by defining the goal group as well as determining ways in which problems are formulated (Nissen and Tylén, 1981). However, paradigms are cultural products, too. Based on a study of children and youth at risk, Stangvik (1993) has shown that the problem-solving strategies of different agencies are expressions of cultural processes. Through them, organisations develop what is termed 'restricted rationality'. They seldom try to reach a maximum achievement of goals. Their goal-oriented behaviour is strongly tempered by corporate cultures of the agencies. They determine which problems they focus on, the timing of intervention, their selection of locations for intervention, selection of content, who participates in interventions, as well as criteria of effects and ways of evaluating effects. These cultures seem to create professional identities and preferences which serve to rationalise even ineffective strategies and to make them legitimate. Hence, problem-solving processes may be terminated when a commonly accepted criterion of satisfaction is achieved – even if the problem has not been solved. This also applies to typical special education strategies which are allowed to persist without demonstrable effects. This indicates a necessity of paradigmatic analysis of special education practices. From this point of view, learning disability researchers have to consider a number of questions. Some of them are:

- What is the unit of analysis? Or, for what purpose are data going to be used? Which are the questions to be answered?
- What is the data unit? Or, put in another way, what types of data should be collected in order to answer those questions? This cannot be decided rationally without a thorough analysis of the phenomenon to be studied in which all relevant causes and consequences relevant to the research questions are discussed. Ultimately, this analysis would be dependent upon which knowledge paradigm one thinks gives the best meaning to a complex fabric of theories and observations in learning disability research.
- Are the data which have been collected compatible with the questions being asked? Or, is the research drawing upon a number of implicit and maybe unverified assumptions as regards relationships between the units of data collection and the units of analysis? There are many risks in this process. One of them, 'the reductive fallacy', has been mentioned.
- What kind of theory is most relevant for the research? This question is, of course, also dependent upon how causes, relationships and consequences are understood. Drawing upon my own research on the self-concept (Stangvik, 1979) I would say that there is a significant difference between seeing the self as a collection of individual traits, or seeing it as a part of subjective narrative. Theoretical insights into the dynamics of subjective biography would have to be based on the self as a relational construct.
- Which methods of data collection are compatible with the actual unit of data analysis and the purpose of the research? It is a fact that tradition and general scientific outlook may often be more important factors in this collection process than the nature of the phenomenon itself. The routine research of what is denoted as 'normal science' is always the closest available possibility.

It seems to me that the answers to these questions are dependent upon how disability is basically understood, i.e., which paradigm one prefers, or, sometimes, uncritically accepts.

Special education research is abundant with examples of 'ecological fallacies', i.e. research in which data on one level are used to draw conclusions on another level. As pointed out earlier, this fallacy has often been 'reductionistic', i.e. data on the individual level are predominantly used in order to describe or predict problems on other levels. I have previously explained how the effects of special education have been explained within an individual-oriented model without taking into account the social context – overlooking the self-concept as a mediating construct between the individual and the social setting. Historically, special education has been based on individual-oriented sciences – psychology and medicine. These sciences formed the general outlook and assumptions and research methods. One example from reading disability research is the use of discrepant individual test scores in order to predict learning disabilities, overlooking parameters which may be defined by interactions and transactions on other levels. This is not to say that such methods should be removed from the tool box of research, but that the assumptions on which they are based ought to be vigorously reflected upon. Allstaedt's (1977) comparison of the historical development of the special class system in Germany and Sweden may serve as an example of how a broader outlook on special education may be fostered by the application of a society-theoretical paradigm in a research project. Based on a Marxist theory of production–reproduction, she relates the thirty years' difference as regards the onset of the special class system in two countries to differences in the level of development of the means of production, creating an early need of a low-educated and well-disciplined workforce in Germany. According to this study, the special class system served that purpose.

Transactional approaches to disability

Evidently there is a paradigmatic conflict in special education between deficiency models and transactional models. Deficiency models treat social interactions as a 'black box'. Disability is explained by a lack of inherent capabilities and described with reference to some established norms. Training is ordinarily directed towards these deficiencies, or attempting to adapt learning environments to them. Accepting the risk of oversimplification I would say that there are two general approaches to disability:

- *Disability as deficiency*, i.e. the person is perceived as being located on the left tail of a normal distribution of some sort, or lacks ability to complete certain expected social functions. The focus here is the traits and characteristics of the individual. Ability is conceived of as something which can be studied relatively independently of the social setting. This conception is signified by the letters 'dis/de' as in deficiency, disability and defect.
- *Disability as 'negotiated social practice'*, i.e. the problems of the person are regarded as socially constructed and dependent upon dynamics of social interaction. There is no denial of the significance of individual dysfunctions, but the focus is on the social and subjective consequences of these dysfunctions in a particular social setting. Such consequences may be related to quality of life and described as isolation, deprivation, devaluation and repression. Or, dysfunctions may be related directly to psychological and social processes in terms of attribution, dissonance, labelling, social roles, and so on.

In my opinion this distinction is a fundamental one. It defines two very different ways of looking at causes of disabilities. Sarason and Doris (1979: 20–3) denote them as the 'continuum of reproductive causality' and the 'continuum of caretaking causality'. The key term in the last paradigm is 'transaction'. In the course of the transaction with the social and physical environment, the learning disability is vested with meaning. This is a two-way process in which the person is both constructed and constructing, and transactions are both interactional and interpretative, i.e. the disability is constructed both at the social and subjective levels, both as social roles and as subjective identities. This transactional perspective has had a very important impact on our understanding of learning disabilities, and it certainly also draws attention to the 'politics of disability' and raises a number of questions. Some of the policy-related questions are: How should learning disability be defined and resources allocated? To what degree does individual definition and assessment of disability for the purpose of resource allocation compare to a definition of disability as 'negotiated social practice'? Why are these practices not taken into account when disabilities are defined and resources allocated? How do definitions of needs and targets compare to processes that generate and define those needs and targets? There is some strong evidence that both needs and targets for special education for many students may actually be defined by the school system itself. Persson (1995) found in an interview study in Sweden that the need for special education was explained by teachers and principals in three ways: needs for special education were most predominantly explained in terms of individual symptoms. However, deficiencies in the school organisation as well as access to special teachers were regarded as creating needs for special education. The research showed that the perception of pupil needs was influenced by a parallel perception of needs by teachers to remove students from their classes, and, in addition, that the practical definition of special education was strongly influenced by the preferences of special education teachers. This type of professionalism may restrict democratic decision making. The study supports the assertion that special education may become part of a vicious circle in which schools both create their problems and decide methods for solving them. Hence, the problems of disability cannot be handled successfully by a special education system externalised conceptually, symbolically and practically from the routines of ordinary schooling. Still, this is precisely what is going on. The adoption of a comprehensive school system in Scandinavian countries contained an integration-oriented policy. Paradoxically, the process of adopting such an integration-oriented and comprehensive concept of schooling was paralleled by a steep rise in the number of hours spent on special education. Vislie (1995), discussing the Norwegian situation, asserted that this integration policy was based on an individualistic and compensatory concept of special education. It is reasonable to assume that this concept of special education served to make legitimate the separation of goals from means. It produced an education which was 'special' and at the same time prevented those who occupied the lower tail of the distribution from disrupting classrooms and from disturbing the reformers, at least for a while.

I do not intend to examine more fully a transactional perspective here. There are certainly writers other than those mentioned here who have made significant contributions to theory in the field of special education. It is sufficient to name the contributions of Goffman (the dermaturgical model), Mead (symbolic interaction) and Schütz (typification processes). The sociology of deviance is also of importance showing the impact of social sanctions and control on disability, so brilliantly applied to special education some twenty years ago in a study by Jane Mercer of labelling by means of testing. Many years later two Finnish researchers wrote: 'Deviation does not exist independently of the community of experts who make the diagnosis and carry out the special measures' (Kivinen and Kivirauma, 1988: 203). These researchers, and many others, created new concepts and explanatory models. They laid the ground for transactional approaches to disability which paid attention to social interaction and social control in the objective and subjective construction of disability. As regards social control, this perspective was 'macrofied' by Marxist theories of production and reproduction and by the French School. They contributed with paradigms which more than before directed attention both to political and symbolic power in the construction process, and further indicated that the distribution of disabilities and deviance in a particular society has its social parameters. There are indications that the gross national product of a particular society might be a rather good predictor of which categories of handicap are focused on by that society, and what models of special education are preferred. Highly developed societies tend to give attention to a great diversity of disabilities, to stick to a low number of categories, and to adopt an integration policy. This clearly underscores the necessity of a macro-social orientation in disability research.

Special education as discursive and divisive practices

There are a number of questions to be asked in respect of this issue. How do we explain the dominance of an 'individual gaze' (Fulcher, 1989) in special education? What is the basis for this seemingly taken-for-granted assumption shared by this community of special educators? Is it based on a 'purely' scientific discourse, or does it create an order of things in this particular system – a way of looking at them which makes decisions legitimate and rational? And, of course, there is always the question of power. There are several conflicting discourses going on which represent different experiences, ideologies and practices, and therefore interpreting differently the orders of things. However, these discourses seldom have an equal power base. The parental discourse may just appear as a silent murmur – a background noise for the more powerful discourses. Ballard (1994) gives voice to parents' stories. These stories often show that conflict between a professional and a parental perspective are an important constitutive element in the social interpretation of disability. Brown describes differences between schools and parents in this way:

> Parents emphasised the need for a good classroom teacher. Many principals and advisors claimed that the child needed 'resources' – the one-to-one teacher aide time, ramps, sluices, and teacher time. Thus, as parents worked to take the 'special' out of special education, some professionals worked equally hard to cement it back in . . .
>
> (Brown, 1994: 236)

Language plays an important role in the construction of social sciences and in the construction of disability. The concepts of 'discourse' and 'metaphor' are used to explain how language controls the development of theory and practice. The impact of metaphors on research particularly relevant to special education has been shown by Linzey (1991) in a study of metaphors used in Piaget's, Skinner's and Bronfenbrenner's works. They are important cornerstones in 'making real', or 'reifying', processes and relationships. Analogy is one important form of metaphor. By utilisation of analogies from the biological sciences Piaget reified a specific understanding of development, while at the same time overlooking other ways of understanding. He also shows that the scientific outlook serves as a lamp to light some places and to leave other places in the shadows. Metaphors become component parts of the scientific discourse. Foucault (1967) shows how the way language is used influences sciences. His example is that the structure of language in psychiatry is characterised by words like doctor, patient, diagnosis, therapy, etc. In fact, this was the language that was adopted to describe learning disabilities by the growing discipline of special education in the late nineteenth century (Alltstaedt, 1977).

Olssen states:

> . . . Foucault was interested in discerning how cultural formations were made to appear rational and unified, how particular discourses came to be formed, and what rules lay behind the process of formation. In doing so he sought to produce an account of how it constituted legitimacy and shaped the thinking of a particular period. Thus, in the case of the nineteenth century psychiatry and psychopathology, Foucault shows how the term 'madness' came to be applied to certain types of behaviour, and how, in its very designation by what it wasn't, it helped to establish our conceptions of the 'rational' and 'the sane'.
>
> (Olssen, 1995: 12)

When applied to normal special education practices and their results, the term 'special' has become a euphemism. The word describes more truthfully 'separate' educational activities and persons who are 'different'. But, it still serves as a money-bearing logo in resource-allocation processes, which are made to appear fair and legitimate through assessment procedures controlled by an 'individual gaze'. To ascribe the prefix 'special' to the child serves several purposes. It diverts attention from how schools may produce learning difficulties. It serves to postpone the need for changes, and to make the increasing demand for resources legitimate. In a certain power perspective, individualising learning disabilities is extremely functional. But there is more to it. As pointed out by Ballard, the effect is 'that people are labelled as damaged or inadequate and are subsequently viewed almost exclusively in terms of their "problems" or "deficits"' (Ballard, 1994: 18), and in need of 'special' provisions. This functional construction of 'otherness' may also be regarded as what Foucault denotes as 'divisive practices' which contribute to processes of 'objectification' (Dreyfus and Rabinow, 1983: 157–67). According to him, the practice of 'normalising judgements' was an important part of these practices. They are expressed through examinations, corrections, punishment and surveillance. Facilitated by the secluded setting of institutions, they serve both to reinforce cultural notions of what is 'normal' in a particular period in a particular setting, and to inculcate perceptions of 'otherness'. Such practices have their parallels in special education. Stangvik (1979) found that segregated special education settings had particular consequences for the development of identity of disabled children, and launched the concept 'segregation syndrome' in order to explain relationships between them. This syndrome contains both educational practices, social relationships and motivational orientations. However, such 'divisive discourses' have their specific historical, cultural, social and economic antecedents and construct theoretical and symbolic images of disability which penetrate theories, outlook, practices and tools (cf. Skrtic, 1991a). In other words, they indicate world views which are not easily changed. According to Foucault (1967) the way 'deviance' has been understood in different periods of time is an expression of the episteme, or mode of reasoning, of the epoch. Special education in a particular period may, from this point of view, be regarded as a way of managing deviance based on its dominant episteme.

A holistic orientation

Transactional approaches to disability do not define disability as something *per se*, but as a social construct, i.e. the social meaning of the concept arises from the interaction between individuals and society. In order to make this approach practical, the whole social life space of the person has to be taken into account in the process of defining special needs. This can only happen when needs are interpreted subjectively by educators and translated into forms of everyday practice, i.e. into goals and objectives, curricula, and methods of work. This internalisation is crucial if transactional approaches are to become operational.

Special education practitioners often select narrow targets of education which do not compare well to the actual needs of their students. The 'watered-down curriculum' delivered in 'ecological niches' in the school environment often is the only answer to complex needs. At the organisational level, transactional approaches have to be translated into interagency models, which make it possible to solve special educational needs throughout the social life space of the individual. Stangvik (1994) describes a model for this type of interagency problem solving. It is based on the model which Pijl and van den Bos in Chapter 9, this volume, call 'the regulatory cycle'. This model is, however, not a panacea. The somewhat tragic history of the 'individual teaching plans' under-scores the difficulties in trying to implement an individual-oriented transactional focus in fragmented education settings. Individual planning easily becomes a 'ghost in the machine' – an extra-curricular activity for teachers which they see as being something alien to their 'real work'. Hence, a holistic model cannot be built by the mere summation of defective parts, but demands re-education, reorganisation and value change. The main objective of this is to broaden and to transform the concept of disability into a concept of social and educational intervention. In order to do this, the social consequences of disabil-ities have to be focused more strongly. Norwegian definitions underscore transactional aspects by drawing attention to functional implications of disabili-ties. 'Funksjonshemmet' (i.e. handicapped) is a person who – due to some kind of disability – is unable to master the demands of the social and/or physical setting. The distinction between impairment, disability and handicap in the World Health Organisation definition points in the same direction. Hence, disability is regarded as relative to the setting, and the interactional and inter-pretative consequences of the relation between the disability and the setting come into focus. This calls for a new approach to intervention in which intera-gency networks are related to informal networks in the life space of the person. Experience shows that disabled persons and their parents strongly favour defini-tions, paying attention to the handicapping impact of disability on living conditions and quality of life. For them, transactional understanding is the result of personal experience. Confronted with divisive practices and the ongoing judgements of their child as different, parents often strive to keep things as normal as possible. A mother conveys a transactional perspective in this way: 'For me, having Sally at my local school made me feel more like normal – like an ordinary mum. I could concentrate on helping on school committee and being at one school fair, instead of three as before' (Bogard, 1994: 62).

Paying more attention to the functional aspects of disabilities doesn't neces-sarily mean that less attention should be paid to individual aspects, but it surely creates a demand for intermediary research concepts which make it possible to relate personal disability characteristics to contextual characteristics. In other words, the disability concept has to be externally valid, or, maybe more accu-rately, 'ecologically', or contextually, valid, i.e. relevant to the different living environments of the person. As a consequence of paying more attention to social consequence of disabilities, less attention is paid to categories of disability and more attention has been paid – at least rhetorically – to the concept of needs. Needs, however, have to be subjected to transactional understanding. They cannot be determined on the basis of disability *per se*, but must have an external reference to some social goals, and certainly also to the settings in which needs are discovered. Attention to needs underscores that special education is a normative enterprise. The question which has to be raised is: what specific needs ought to be taken as points of departure in special education in order to help disabled persons to reach a specific set of social goals? This is a true transactional question which cannot be answered without considering what should be the most important goals of special education. Hence, the concept of need, too, is relational. Needs must be defined in the interplay between social ideals, which are dependent upon time and location, and the individual characteristics of the disabled person. Education and intervention inspired by the goals of social inclusion and equality would strongly influence definitions of needs. Holistic orientations are also supported by other writers in the field. An American writer defines learning disabilities as

> the result of some unfortunate interaction between the student's neurology, previous experience (both in and out of school), their expectations, interests, personalities, aptitudes, and abilities AND the expectations, experiences, goals, physical characteristics, personalities, aptitudes encountered at school and in other environments.
>
> (Poplin, 1985: 62)

She proposes a holistic model which attempts to combine a 'reductionistic' study of parts with a 'structuralist' approach, taking into account the structuring impact of the whole of a given situation. Such an approach would certainly have important consequences on definition, assessment and instruction. Transactional approaches may help to redefine the concept of learning in special education as shown by the concept of MLE (mediated learning experiences), drawing attention to the relationship between affective and motivational processes for determining cognitive modifiability and the role of human mediators in learning and assessment processes (Tzuriel, 1991; Feuerstein and Feuerstein, 1991). Such an approach demands a variety of paradigms. Furthermore, the fact that different paradigms would focus different units of analysis would demand flexibility of designs and methods and imply that a wide base of theory and knowledge is accessible to researchers. This would be essential in order not to commit the 'reductive fallacy', by which disabilities are treated as a deficiency and an individual category. However, such orientations to disabilities claim openness between sciences and disciplines. An interdisciplinary orientation to disabilities is, however, heavily restricted today by the way sciences are organised and by their traditions. There are also less pronounced barriers to a holistic and relational understanding. Such an understanding would be oriented towards change, and aim to improve the situation for a person in a social context. In order to do this one will necessarily have to consider what ought to be the goals of intervention and criteria of success. However, these are matters which cannot be decided upon on the basis of the disabilities *per se*, but have to do with one's ideological, philosophical and political outlook. Therefore, intervention cannot be decided upon solely on the basis of learning disability research.

A final note

Special education has rightfully been criticised for being too 'functionalist' and 'objectivist'. However, it seems to me that this has been functional within its divisive practices. Modes of practice and modes of science are related to each other. Differentiation and individualisation are complementary processes. By individualisation and reification of disability-making processes, social differentiation has been made legitimate. It is important to keep in mind that these procedures have been based on the 'normal science' of medicine and psychology of the period and that these sciences are subject to much the same critique as special education. This gives us reason to believe that the modes of thought and action in special education are deeply rooted in culture and society. By creating conflicts, new paradigms stimulate consciousness and reflective thought. In this way theory plays an important role in special education. The advent of post-modern thought has created a new 'frame of meaning' for understanding disability and its management. There is a pluralism of voices, and a greater acceptance of all these voices and their relevance of them for this field of theory and practice. On the other hand, there is a growing interest in the concept of 'constructivism', which seems to mean that 'meaning is a personal creation within a social community that accepts the underlying assumptions. There is no right or wrong in an absolute sense' (Singh Dillon, 1995: 2). Even if this line of reasoning may be an important complement to 'materialist' and 'objectivist' ways of thinking there still is a great narrative of segregation and seclusion of disabled and deviant people which should be taken into account, and which resists all post-modernistic diversification. This narrative underscores a need for consistent policies and guidelines for practice.

In the wake of the advent of neo-classical liberalism on the international scene, the metaphor of 'the market place' has also been increasingly used for solving educational problems, and there is a move from the culture of the welfare state based on principles of universal provision to a so-called enterprise culture based on individual responsibility and self-reliance (Olssen and Matthews, 1995). Presently, the adoption of such policies may seem more distant than ever. In this situation it is crucial to ascertain that our way of accumulating knowledge is not governed by this cosmology, but gives room for all relevant discourses and paradigms. Even if deficiency-oriented research may be assumed to be 'normal science' for many years to come, competing paradigms are emerging, creating fruitful conflicts. Such conflicts are true expressions of the complexity of our subject matter.

13

THEORISING SPECIAL EDUCATION

Time to move on?[1]

Catherine Clark, Alan Dyson and Alan Millward

There is a tradition in academic publishing that the editors of a volume retain the right to produce a final chapter which offers an overview of the book as a whole, summarises its various contributions and proffers a view of its field which makes claims to be authoritative. We wish to avail ourselves of this right – but only to a limited extent, and only after recording a number of caveats.

In the introductory chapter to this volume, we asserted our claim that theorising is non-optional and that it is a process. We agreed with Schön (1983a) that any action at the very least *implies* a theory, and the only question is the extent to which such theories are made explicit and coherent. Moreover, we suggested, along with many contributors to this volume, that the development of such explicit and coherent theories inevitably takes place within and reflects a particular sociohistoric context. Put simply, theories are inevitably 'of their time' and reflect the values, assumptions and priorities of that time.

It follows from this that, however powerfully particular theoretical positions may be argued, and however all-embracing and complete they may appear to be, they necessarily emerge out of a *process* of theorising in which particular theories rise and fall as the values, assumptions and priorities which underpin them shift. Recently, Skrtic (1995) has argued for a post-modern approach to theorising special education – an approach which accepts this processual nature of theorising, which problematises the claims of particular theories to be finally 'true', and which sees the essential task of the theorist as being to make the process of deconstructing old theories and constructing new ones as open and explicit as possible.

In essence, this is the task which we have set ourselves in this final chapter. As editors, we are no more in a position to offer an 'ultimate' theory of special education than any of our contributors. Any overview which we chose to provide would be based on values, assumptions and priorities which would be subject to change and, indeed, which would not be shared either by many of our contributors or by some other contemporary theorists. However, we believe that there is a *meta*-theoretical (Ritzer, 1991, 1992) task to perform which is not only valuable but essential. It is both possible and necessary to survey the current state of theorising – as it is represented both in this volume and beyond – and to identify the broad trends which characterise current thinking. These trends tell us something about ourselves: they tell us about the assumptions which we are coming to share, the values which are implicit or explicit in our work and the priorities which we are embodying in our theories. In particular, they indicate to us what we might call the direction of our contemporary gaze. In and through our theorising, we direct our attention towards particular parts of our potential worlds – to particular phenomena, issues and problems. The corollary, of course, is that we at the same time direct our attention *away from* certain other phenomena, issues and problems. Our theories illuminate – but they also conceal, and it is our contention that if we are to see more clearly in (or, indeed, beyond) special education, we must first of all have some idea of what it is that we are currently *not* able to see.

Accordingly, this final chapter sets out to characterise some of the major developments that have taken place in the theorising of special education over the recent decade. In so doing, it will inevitably lose some of the power and subtlety of the particular contributions of individual theorists. However, our aim is not to critique contemporary work – particularly that of our very diverse contributors – in the sense of proving it 'wrong' or 'untrue', but to understand what it is 'collectively' that we have assumed and prioritised. Accordingly, we will use our broad characterisation to suggest what sort of theorising we might now need if we are to be enabled to direct our attention to phenomena, issues and problems that currently elude us. Our aim, in short, is nothing less than to set a new agenda for theorising special education. On the other hand, it is nothing more than to set an agenda which will in turn be deconstructed and superseded in years to come.

The post-positivist paradigm: a contemporary hegemony

There is, in fact, a good deal of consensus in the English-language literature about the history of theorising in special education. Commentators (e.g. Ainscow, 1994b; Clark *et al.*, 1995a; Norwich, 1996; Skrtic, 1995) tend to offer an account which suggests that the early history of special education has been dominated by what has been called the 'psychomedical paradigm' (Clark *et al.*, 1995a).[2] This paradigm has been characterised by a number of features:

- an essentially positivist view of the world, in which differences between learners were taken to be objectively 'real' and susceptible to investigation using the methods of the natural sciences;

- a concern with those differences which were held to take the form of deficits and difficulties and which were understood largely through the disciplines of medicine and, increasingly, educational psychology;
- an essentially functionalist view of special education as a rational response to these difficulties and deficits, developed on the basis of scientific inquiry and offering scientifically proven interventions leading to cure or amelioration.

The literature within this paradigm is considerable, much of it generated by pre-eminent figures such as Burt and Schonell. Implicit in the work of such researchers is a long tradition of theorising about the nature and methodology of scientific inquiry. If the debt to this tradition is not made explicit in the work of Burt, Schonell and others, this is scarcely surprising. The positivist paradigm has been – and to a large extent continues to be – so dominant in the scientific world that it could effectively be taken for granted.

The major shift which is seen to have occurred in the last three decades has been away from this positivist paradigm. In common with other branches of the social sciences (Burrell and Morgan, 1979), a bewildering series of newer theoretical positions have impacted upon special needs education. Skrtic (1995), following Burrell and Morgan, usefully categorises these in terms of three broad approaches – interpretivism, radical structuralism and radical humanism. It is our contention, however, that an emphasis on differences between these newer positions tends to disguise the extent to which they are in fact underpinned by certain common assumptions and, even more noticeably, are united in their critique of the older psychomedical paradigm. Indeed, they can usefully, we believe, be seen as falling within a newer *post-positivist* paradigm, which distances itself from former positions in a number of ways:

Special educational needs as social product

Whereas the psychomedical paradigm saw special needs as arising out of real characteristics of children, these newer positions see special needs as in one sense or another being the product of essentially social processes. These processes are usually seen as encompassing:

- the social use of discourses out of which concepts and categories of need are constructed (e.g. Christensen, 1996; Corbett, 1996; Ware, 1995);
- the functioning of social institutions (schools or education systems as a whole) which generate failure and develop special needs provision as a means of managing that failure (e.g. Ainscow, 1991a, 1994b, 1995a; Fulcher, 1989; Gartner and Lipsky, 1987; Golby and Gulliver, 1979; Skrtic, 1991a, b; Vlachou, 1997);

- structural social and socio-economic processes whereby some groups are systematically disadvantaged and marginalised (e.g. Ballard, 1994; Barton, 1988a, b; Oliver, 1988; Tomlinson, 1982, 1985).

Although these analyses differ considerably in their detail, they all tend to agree that special educational needs cannot be understood simply in terms of the characteristics of individual learners. On the contrary, needs arise within a social context which itself plays an active part in what will be regarded as constituting a 'need' and which needs will be regarded as 'special'. In that sense, special needs are not so much objectively 'real' as socially *produced*, with the corollary that in changed social circumstances (different discourses, different sorts of schools, different social structures), they might simply disappear (Dyson, 1990).

Special education as non-rational

Closely allied to this position is a view of special education as non-rational. As Skrtic (1991a, b) points out, within the psychomedical paradigm, special education could be seen as a rational response to the needs of children – a scientifically guided attempt on the part of benevolent professionals to meet the really-existing needs of learners. However, if needs are socially produced, then special education can be seen as itself part of the processes of social production, helping to sustain the set of social arrangements out of which those processes emerge and the power and privilege of those who benefit from those arrangements. Hence, special education enables schools and education systems to maintain a comfortable status quo .

Not surprisingly, therefore, the commentators who present special education as a social product are frequently able also to identify beneficiaries who are not special education's clients. For Tomlinson (1982, 1985), those beneficiaries are the professional groups such as medics and psychologists who have most to gain in terms of security, status and power in promoting a continual expansion of special education. For Skrtic (1991a, b) it is the mainstream education system itself – and hence, its teachers, administrators and clients – which benefits most by having access to alternatives for children who threaten to disturb its status quo. For others, it is well-resourced and socially advantaged parents who benefit by using special education as a means of saving their children from the stigma of 'backwardness' or 'failure' and securing scarce additional resources for them (Riddell et al., 1994; Slee, 1995a; Sleeter, 1986).

Different as these analyses are, they are united in their view that special education presents a benign and rational façade that is essentially false. There is, in Skrtic's words, something that lies 'behind special education' (Skrtic, 1991a) – a discriminatory, arbitrary and inefficient education system, serving the interests not of the *dis*advantaged but of those who are already well resourced and socially *ad*vantaged.

Liberal values

Underpinning each of these critiques of special needs as a concept and special education as a practice is a particular values orientation which is very different from that in the psychomedical paradigm. In line with the positivist tradition, researchers such as Burt and Schonell saw themselves first and foremost as scientists, governed by the discipline of scientific method. Values were not irrelevant – the scientific enterprise was aimed at benefiting humanity – but values in themselves did not determine the nature and direction of inquiry.

Adherents of the newer paradigm, however, to a greater or lesser extent reject this relationship to questions of value. If something lies 'behind' special education, then commentators and researchers face a choice that is essentially an ethical one. On the one hand, they can accept the claims of special education to rationality and benevolence and work within its founding assumptions. If they do so, however, they are helping to sustain a system that is essentially discriminatory and oppressive. On the other hand, they can seek to critique special education in order to reveal the oppression which lies 'behind' its benevolent face. In order to do this, however, they have to start from the position that special education is indeed oppressive and that appearances to the contrary are no more than a superficial façade. Either way, the analysis of special education requires the adoption of a political and ethical stance; it cannot, therefore, be value-free.

For some, therefore, theorising or any other intellectual inquiry is part of an ongoing struggle against a society which is seen as essentially oppressive (Ballard, 1994, 1995; Oliver, 1992a, b). The whole point of the enterprise is to unmask this oppression and empower oppressed people better to resist it. Taking a principled stand on questions of rights, participation, inclusion, therefore, is the basis on which inquiry is possible and on which the true nature of special education is revealed. Others are, perhaps, less explicit about the role of values in the process of inquiry itself, but nonetheless imply a set of values in their work which are no less strongly held. For a whole range of commentators, there are no hard-and-fast boundaries between the analysis of special education, the advocacy of new responses to difference and the articulation of principled positions (see, for instance, Clough and Barton, 1995). If a prior declaration of values is not the basis for inquiry, it is nonetheless evident that a commitment to particular values shapes the nature of the inquiry and the interpretation of any findings which result.

The values which inform this newer paradigm are, moreover, implicit within the critique of special needs and special education which we have outlined above. If special education is seen as serving the best interests of the advantaged rather than the disadvantaged, this is because adherents of this paradigm see a commitment to the disadvantaged, a promotion of equity, participation in common institutions and non-oppressive practices as being central to their enterprise. Similarly, if special needs as a concept is seen as being discriminatory and devaluing, that is because they also display a commitment to anti-discrimination and the equal valuing of individuals. If, therefore, the older psychomedical paradigm implied somewhat paternalistic values of caring and nurturing (Corbett, 1996), this newer paradigm implies a set of liberal, humane values which have become so fundamental to the field over recent decades that they are now rarely challenged (Clark *et al.*, 1997).

The post-positivist paradigm: some limitations

There can be little doubt that the substantial volume of work which has been undertaken within this post-positivist paradigm has given a new vitality to the field of special needs education. Above all, it has made a major contribution to the rethinking of many accepted 'givens' in this field. It is now virtually impossible to consider provision for individual children, or patterns of provision within national systems, or subjects of inquiry within research without acknowledgement of the highly problematic status of special needs and special education, and without some assessment of how proposed action will or will not further the liberal ideals which the newer paradigm embodies. Indeed, it is arguable – though some would no doubt disagree – that the point has been reached where the newer paradigm exercises the same sort of hegemony over this field that the psychomedical paradigm enjoyed thirty or forty years ago. It is a bold researcher or scholar nowadays who admits to being an unreconstructed positivist! However, the very success of this paradigm produces its own problems. Like all paradigms, it directs attention *towards* certain phenomena and issues and *away from* others; it presents a view of the field of special education which may be coherent but is certainly not the only possible view; and in establishing its hegemony it runs the risk of silencing voices and closing off avenues of inquiry which might yet be productive (Dyson, 1997a).

These limitations are perhaps most immediately obvious when we look at the nature of the work produced within this newer paradigm. That work is, of course, extremely diverse. However, a surprisingly high proportion of it takes the form of an analysis, critique or deconstruction of *existing* conceptualisations of special needs and practices of special education. The overriding concern within the paradigm seems to be for commentators to distance themselves from what they view as the increasingly discredited perspectives of the psychomedical paradigm. At one extreme, a key work such as Tomlinson's (1982) *Sociology of Special Education* consists almost entirely of an attempt to deconstruct special education in terms of the social process which lies 'behind' it. More typically, writers we have cited above, such as Barton and Corbett, or others, such as Slee (1993, 1995b, 1996a, b) and Fulcher (1989, 1993), devote considerable energies to the critique of special education, with more limited attempts to develop some alternative conceptualisation of and response to individual differences. At the very least, there are very few works within this paradigm which do not open with a substantial attack upon what is taken to be the status quo.

In itself, this is not a criticism of these works; critique and deconstruction are reputable and necessary activities which, as Slee (in Chapter 11, this volume) eloquently argues, do much to free us from our preconceptions and to enable us to explore alternative possibilities. However, this preoccupation with critique is, we suggest, indicative of a particular orientation within this paradigm. Since a fundamental claim that the paradigm makes is that special needs and special education are social products, a fundamental activity within it has necessarily to be the 'reduction' (Skidmore, 1996) of those phenomena to that processes out of which they are held to have arisen. This creates problems in terms of the development of alternatives to current conceptualisations and practices. In the first place, the reductionist process creates a momentum within the paradigm from which it can be difficult for commentators to escape. Their orientation towards their subject and the analytical tools which are at their disposal lend themselves inevitably to ever more refined critique which almost becomes an end in itself. It may be significant that many years after the pioneers within this paradigm delivered what might be regarded as intellectually fatal blows to the credibility of the psychomedical paradigm and of the founding assumptions of special education, substantially unchanged recycling of their critiques continues to appear on a regular basis.

More serious than this, however, the orientation towards critique is not simply a matter of personal preference or ease of access to critical tools. Special needs and special education are, as we have seen, assumed within the paradigm to be products of particular social processes rather than descriptions of the reality of children's characteristics or rational responses to those characteristics. There are, therefore, no really-existing 'special needs' which necessarily cause problems for educators and call for some carefully-worked-out response. The process of critical analysis reveals time and again that the special–ordinary distinction in conceptualisation and practice is an unnecessary and non-rational one. It follows that, once that distinction is stripped away through the process of critique, the practices of 'regular' education will, in principle, be capable of responding to the characteristics of all learners. In a sense, therefore, the function of inquiry in special education is to 'do away with itself' (Galletley, 1976). It must deconstruct the object of its inquiry until it disappears – although, in practice, the ongoing forces of social reproduction may well mean that reconstituted forms of special education continually resurface, requiring the attentions of a critical watchdog. To a certain extent this explains the somewhat repetitive nature of work in this field which we noted above.

Beyond this, the belief that processes of discrimination, oppression and exclusion are endemic within social institutions such as schools, and that values such as equity, participation and inclusion are desirable, is not empirically derived. Rather, they are taken within this paradigm as a set of givens, a lens through which the social world must be viewed. It follows that the role of empirical inquiry is very different from the one which it performs in the psychomedical paradigm. For earlier commentators, the world of children and schools was an unknown territory to be explored. In the true manner of the natural scientists, researchers could study children, find out how they worked, test interventions and measure their effectiveness. The process of positivistic inquiry would of itself reveal what the world was like and what should be done within it.

Within the newer paradigm, however, empirical inquiry has a much more limited, illustrative role. The basic conceptual model of the social world is already given; all empirical inquiry can do, therefore, is elaborate and confirm that picture in terms of its details. It is possible, for instance, to identify examples of oppression and to elaborate the ways in which it operates in practice; however, the notion of oppression itself is a priori. There is nothing which empirical inquiry could reveal which would of itself invalidate that concept. By the same token, notions of equity, participation and inclusion are similarly a priori. Studies of schools can certainly reveal the extent to which they embody these values and may well reveal interesting information of how they set about that task. However, such inquiries cannot countermand the imperative of those values or the desirability of schools seeking to embody them.

It is not surprising, therefore, that empirical inquiry is of limited interest for some scholars within this paradigm. Skrtic, for instance, develops a powerful notion of the 'adhocratic school' (Skrtic, 1991a, b, c) with which he clearly intends to influence the practice and configuration of actual schools. Despite this practical orientation, however, the empirical base of his work is almost non-existent, at least in terms of studies of actual schools and their attempt to become inclusive. The conceptual framework which he has at his disposal, in terms of notions of bureaucracy on the one hand and equity on the other, makes it possible for him to delineate the nature of an equitable school not through a study of such schools but by means of a logical tour de force. His argument is not so much that adhocratic schools are in practice more equitable, but that they must, by definition, be so.

The same process can, in a somewhat less extreme form, be observed in the work of many other commentators. Researchers on both sides of the Atlantic (Ainscow, 1994b; Stainback and Stainback, 1990, 1992; Udvari-Solner and Thousand, 1995; Villa and Thousand, 1995; Villa et al., 1992) are certainly very much interested in what schools are actually like and how they set about realising principles of equity, inclusion, and so on. However, at no point do they attempt to derive principles of equity and inclusion from their empirical investigations. The question is not whether such principles actually work for the benefit of children, or whether it is possible for schools to realise them; rather, it is how far and in what ways schools are successful in realising principles that are not susceptible to empirical investigation. The charge that is occasionally levelled at this work, therefore – that it is based on ideal types and idealised models rather than the realities of schools – is not altogether without foundation (Lingard, 1996).

None of this constitutes a criticism of work undertaken within this paradigm.

It is a common tenet of post-positivism that no form of inquiry is entirely free from founding values and assumptions, and that inquiries which make those assumptions clear are greatly to be welcomed. However, this does begin to delineate some of the boundaries of the newer paradigm. One of these is that it is not likely to be predominantly interested in empirical inquiry or in questions which demand empirical answers. More importantly, however, this is a paradigm which is likely to rely heavily on the rehearsal of existing values and assumptions. At its best, this means that inquiry will be principled and wide-ranging. At its worst, however, this means that the paradigm will generate somewhat circular and, indeed, incestuous inquiry in which set positions are rehearsed with no very clear means whereby founding assumptions can be problematised or changed.

This also raises questions about the nature and possibility of development within this paradigm. In a very real sense, all that can be known about the world is already given in the paradigm's founding assumptions. Knowledge can be elaborated and applied, but can scarcely be accumulated in the way that positivists might hope. In practice, what seems to happen is that the critique which commentators develop becomes increasingly reflexive, as evidence of unreconstructed oppression and discrimination is found in previous commentators' work. The consequence is an internal fragmentation within the paradigm as commentators divide themselves into camps engaged as much in critiquing each other's work as in developing educational provision for vulnerable children (see, for instance, Oliver, 1992b).

There are also implications here for the guidance which commentators can offer to the practitioners who must play some part in realising their ideals. The paradigm is, as we have seen, at its strongest in formulating 'ideal types' of provision and practice on the basis of its founding values and its rigorous critique of 'current' provision and practice. It is also capable of identifying instances where these ideal types underpin actual provision and practice to a greater or lesser extent. However, it is, we suggest, less strong in dealing with the problems, difficulties and anomalies which emerge in that actual provision and practice. Because the paradigm makes it possible to develop a powerful critique, such problems are inevitably interpreted in terms of that critique. In other words, they are taken to indicate, not fundamental dilemmas or contradictions within the ideal type itself, but yet further manifestations of the flawed social processes that produced the oppressive and discriminatory phenomenon of special education in the first place.

This has two consequences which we would regard as limiting. First, problems in practice cannot be used for the development of the assumptions and values upon which the paradigm is predicated. Every problem simply lends yet further confirmation to those assumptions. Second, the problems which practitioners experience as realities are treated, if not as illusory, then certainly as artifactual. If, the assumption goes, the underlying social processes – which may actually amount to no more than the constructions of the practitioners themselves – were changed, then the problems would *ipso facto* resolve themselves.

Perhaps the clearest example of this process at work is in the notion of practitioner and organisational problem solving which has been strongly advocated by those commentators who have sought most fully to develop new responses to student diversity (Ainscow, 1994b, 1997; Hart, 1996; Rouse and Florian, 1996; Skrtic, 1991a, b, c). The problems which practitioners face are taken to be soluble if only those practitioners are enabled to work together in a problem-solving mode and thus escape their limiting sets of preconceptions. Whether or not there is *empirical* evidence that this is indeed the case (and we would suggest that such evidence is, at best, ambiguous), it is quite clear that problems in the practice of education are not seen as fundamentally unresolvable. This would contrast, for instance, with another tradition of analysis which sees practitioners as facing a series of complex dilemmas which are, of their very nature, ultimately incapable of solution (Berlak and Berlak, 1981; Norwich, 1993, 1996).

It may be worth adding that there is also an inevitable tendency within this paradigm to offer solutions and proposals that are not clearly located within specific contexts. Because such solutions are developed from first principles, and because the problems that arise in their implementation are argued away, there is no obvious means whereby they can be fully contextualised. It is, we suggest, no accident that proposed ways forward such as 'inclusive education' are taken to apply to *all* groups of learners (Fuchs and Fuchs, 1994) and across *all* national contexts (Ainscow, 1994b; UNESCO, 1994) regardless of the many complex differences that arise in different sites and situations.

This decontextualisation is also reflected in the attitude which commentators tend to take towards human difference. A powerful motor for the development of work within the paradigm has, of course, been a critique of positivist psychology on the grounds that it reifies the constructions of categories of difference that emerge from the practice of certain professional groups – of which educational psychologists are the prime example (Swann, 1982). There is, therefore, an understandable aversion towards developing any 'categorical' notion of difference. Commentators are very content to acknowledge the reality of such difference, but see it as existing at an 'individual' level. Any development of categories, the argument runs, is likely at best to miss the complexity and uniqueness of individuals and, at worst, to lead to responses to those individuals that are arbitrary, discriminatory and even oppressive. It follows that more authentic responses have to be made at the individual level and are by their very nature more *ad hoc* – a further reason for the importance to some commentators of the notion of practitioner problem solving.

Whatever the merits of this approach, it has two consequences in terms of the sorts of knowledge which can and cannot easily be developed within this paradigm. It is, for instance, almost impossible for an explanatory theory of human difference to be generated within this paradigm, at least in so far as such a theory attempts to formalise knowledge gained from individual interactions into overarching categorical frameworks. Similarly, it is almost impossible for pedagogical knowledge to be accumulated and formalised in so far as such knowledge is predicated upon responses to stable dimensions of difference between learners. The nearest approaches to this we have are twofold. First, there is an individual interaction approach which relies upon constructivist models of learning and curriculum (Ware, 1995) and/or on practitioner problem solving to provide the necessary flexibility for an appropriate pedagogy to emerge in an *ad hoc* way in respect of each learner. Second, there is a more formalised and technicist approach to curriculum adaptation, particularly in the USA, which seeks to provide practitioners with a tool kit of techniques for adapting a predetermined curriculum (Lipsky and Gartner, 1997; Udvari-Solner, 1995; Udvari-Solner and Thousand, 1995). Such an approach goes some way towards developing a pedagogical knowledge within special needs education, but that knowledge makes very little use of any fully developed notions of human difference. Its concern is almost exclusively with how the 'curriculum' as a supposedly free-standing entity can be 'adapted', with virtually no reference to the characteristics of the 'learners', in whose interests these adaptations are supposedly taking place. It is not surprising, therefore, that such approaches have been attacked from elsewhere within the post-positivist paradigm as likely simply to reproduce traditional forms of learner categorisation in a new guise (Hart, 1992a; Vlachou, 1997).

An alternative perspective

Our underlying concern about the post-positivist paradigm, at least as it has been applied to special education, centres on whether it has not allowed itself to become too unproblematically and unidimensionally 'millennialist' in its position. By this we mean that in quite properly *deconstructing* the concepts, structures and practices of historical special education, it has *constructed* for itself an image of the world of special needs education in which processes of reconceptualisation, restructuring or political struggle seem capable of removing once and for all the problems, dilemmas and injustices which have hitherto characterised the education system. It appears that, for all commentators within this paradigm, there exists (even if only as a remote goal) the possibility of some ideal state in which principles of equity and participation can be unproblematically realised through restructured educational provision and reconstructed educational practice within a common educational system and common institutions.

Such a promise is indeed attractive, and it is scarcely surprising that it has come to exert a significant influence on education policy internationally – the Salamanca Statement (UNESCO, 1994) being only the most prominent of many examples. However, we confess to finding ourselves not entirely convinced by this promise. It leaves out of count, we suggest, the possibility that what lie 'behind' special education are not only processes of discrimination and oppression which are in principle reversible, but also processes and structures which are somehow endemic to the educational enterprise and which cannot be reversed, restructured or deconstructed. It is to these that we now wish to turn.

The complexities of educational values

The new paradigm has, as we have seen, directed much attention towards exposing the implicit (and often paternalistic) values in special education on the one hand, and developing alternative values – equity, participation, empowerment – on the other. However, we share with Lee (1996) a concern as to whether such values are actually as unproblematic as they may seem. The reasons for this are twofold. First, education systems are rarely if ever charged with realising single values. On the contrary, they are usually asked to deliver multiple values, which may or may not be compatible one with another. The achievement of equity, for instance, is a long-standing goal of many western education systems – but then so too is the maximising of individual achievement and the development of the nation's economic infrastructure. It is not at all clear that these values are mutually compatible.

Second, even single values may not be unidimensional. Again, equity is a case in point. Equity may mean equity of resource distribution, or the equalisation of provision, or of opportunity, or of attainment; it may mean equity as between the genders or between all children of the same age, or children from different socioeconomic backgrounds, or children from different ethnic backgrounds, and so on. It is by no means impossible that one sort of equity may contradict another: for instance, the equity which dictates that the genders should be equally represented in special provision may contradict another version of equity which says that individuals should receive whatever provision they are held to need (see, for instance, Daniels et al., 1996). Again, it is by no means clear that the resolution of such contradictions is either simple or straightforward.

The determinacy of educational provision

We have noted some ambiguities within the new paradigm's approach to specifying the precise nature of the educational provision which is to realise the values that are so powerfully advocated within it. The emphasis on problem solving and 'adhocracy', the focus on mechanistic models of curriculum, the distinctive engagement with (or disengagement from) empirical work are symptomatic of a millennialist perspective which assumes that the detailed structures and practices through which values of equity and inclusion can unproblematically be realised will, in due course, emerge.

We are uneasy with this assumption On the contrary, we suggest that the more determinate the form of any educational provision becomes, the more it becomes one thing rather than another, the less unambiguously and unproblematically it is able to realise 'universal' values. It is inevitable that any curriculum, any form of school organisation, any form of classroom organisation or any pedagogical approach, however structured, will realise different values differentially in respect of different students. What, for instance, is the curriculum within which *all* children can participate equally and within which they can learn equally (Lingard, 1996)? Once the curriculum becomes determinate, it inevitably brings with it discriminations and distinctions: some children learn certain things quickly, others slowly; some engage with some learning tasks, others do not; some find their interests and aptitudes favoured, others find them neglected.

The solution advocated by some theorists within the new paradigm seems to be to leave such matters as indeterminate as possible. Schools and teachers will, the argument goes, through processes of problem solving and reconstruction, invariably find ways of offering the best possible 'deal' to every single student. Our view, however, is that schools, classrooms, curricula and pedagogies have, at some point, to take on determinate form. They become one thing rather than another, and at that point they embody choices to realise some values rather than others, favour some characteristics above others, and advantage some children at the expense of others. The ongoing process of problem solving in respect of disadvantaged children may be both necessary and desirable – but it does not, in the final analysis, make it possible to create a form of educational provision which achieves *everything* for *everyone*.

The nature of educational differences

We have seen how the new paradigm has mounted a telling critique of the categorisation systems of traditional special education, and has demonstrated how such systems are themselves socially constructed and non-necessary. This has opened up the possibility that categorisation itself can be abandoned; the arbitrary distinctions between special and ordinary needs can be superseded by a notion of individual difference in which schools and teachers respond to the unique characteristics of particular students.

We have no argument with this proposition at a level of generality and outside of the specific contexts in which it has to be operationalised. However, it is our contention that, although categories may be constructed, they are not entirely arbitrary. Once education takes on a determinate form, and once it embodies some values rather than others, it necessarily brings about differential responses from students in respect of those values and forms. Some students do well, others less well; some participate fully, others less fully; for some the provision is clearly appropriate, for others it is less so. Whether teachers, and education professionals choose on the basis of these differential responses, to construct categories of student or not, the differences themselves remain. Moreover, they themselves call for differential responses on the part of the education system. In the past, it may well be that such responses have taken the rather crude form of separate special and mainstream provision and that this particular response is no longer in line with prevailing educational values. However, the need for differential response is not itself removed when the special–mainstream distinction is removed.

The sociohistorical dimension of special education

The new paradigm is intensely historical in so far as it mounts a powerful critique of past forms of special education and posits future alternatives. It is also intensely sociological in its outlook in so far as it traces the forms of special education to underlying social processes. However, it is ultimately a-historical and a-sociological in so far as it posits an 'end' to special education. The social and historical processes which have generated special education in the past are, it seems to argue, time limited. At some point in the (near?) future, they will be supplanted by other processes which will make special education redundant.

Once again, the specification of these new processes tends to be rather vague (there is no indication, for instance, of the sort of society out of which they are to emerge). However, this is not our principal quarrel with this proposition. It is, rather, that some at least of the processes which generated separate special education are and will continue to be ongoing. These processes arise, not only out of the reproduction of social and economic advantage to which some commentators correctly point, but also out of the continuing attempt by modern societies to find ways to respond to student diversity within determinate education structures and in the context of complex social values (Gerber, 1995, 1996; Vislie, 1995). Whilst it is possible to see how such societies might become more just and equitable and might thus abandon the special–mainstream divide, it is less easy to see how they resolve the fundamental dilemmas of responding to diversity.

This in turn leads us to adopt a particular perspective on special needs education. Whilst the commentators in the new paradigm tend to see it as the arbitrary product of processes of discrimination – a product which can, therefore, be dismantled once and for all as those processes are challenged – we tend to see it as one resolution in a long sequence of resolutions of fundamental social and educational dilemmas (Clark et al., 1997). For us, societies seek to realise complex and often contradictory values through their education systems. In so doing, they have to create systems which have determinate form – a form which will realise those values differentially. Moreover, they have to realise those values in the context of students who are not identical one with another, whose responses to the available educational provision are diverse, and in respect of whom social values are realised differentially. Although, therefore, we agree wholeheartedly with the new theorists that any given form of provision can be problematised, deconstructed and dismantled, we do not share their apparent optimism that this is a once-for-all process, nor even that it is a process of continuous improvement. Forms of provision can be dismantled, but the dilemmas and complexities out of which they arise cannot.

Towards an alternative theory

In reflecting on our own work, it is apparent that we tend to see human actors as seeking to take 'purposeful action' (Checkland, 1981) in a world which is not easily shaped to their purposes. Although those purposes may be articulated in terms of general values and principles, they have to be realised in complex and ineluctable situations where compromise and subversion are inevitable. In the field of special needs education, therefore, the values of equity and inclusion have to be realised in a situation characterised by real differences between children and in a context of a determinate curriculum, school structure, teaching force, available sets of pedagogical techniques, and so on. Little wonder, then, that the realisation of such values in particular situations is rather different from their articulation in principle – that they are realised in ways that are imperfect and even contradictory. The attempt to understand this process of realisation other than through a reiterated deconstruction of processes of segregation and exclusion is, we suggest, an important item of any new agenda.

In addressing this task, we have found it particularly helpful to think of the choices facing practitioners and policy makers in terms of 'dilemmas' rather than of clearly better or worse alternatives (Clark *et al.*, 1995a, 1997). In situations where overarching values are multiple, complex and frequently contradictory, and where those values have to be realised amidst equally complex realities, human actors are, we suggest, rarely faced with unequivocal choices. On the contrary, because their values are ambiguous and the outcomes of their action unpredictable, they are constantly presented with dilemmas – choices within which each alternative has its own advantages and disadvantages. Thus, we accept, for instance, that inclusion is currently a central value in the development of special needs education – but we also acknowledge the work of those critics (e.g. Fuchs and Fuchs, 1994; Kauffman and Hallahan, 1995; Zigmond and Baker, 1995, 1996) who ask pertinent questions about what happens when practitioners and policy makers attempt to realise inclusion in practice.

Similarly, we have found it helpful to understand special needs education from the perspective of dialectical analysis (Clark *et al.*, 1995a). This does not commit us to a grand Marxian or Hegelian notion of dialectics, but rather to the idea that apparently stable phenomena – such as special needs education in a given national or local context – are actually the product of multiple forces and processes which temporarily find a point of resolution, but which create endemic stresses in that resolution which ultimately cause it to break apart. This has allowed us to include three dimensions in our analysis of special needs education which, we feel, enrich it considerably. First, it allows us to account for 'complexity', since we can relate the complex features of special needs education in practice to the complex processes which produce it. Second, it allows us to include a 'historical' dimension in our analyses, since we can explore the ways in which special needs education has been produced over time and, indeed, speculate about how it might change in the future. Third, it enables us to conduct an analysis of the workings of 'power' in the production of special needs education in so far as the forces at work in the production of special needs education are themselves controlled by one or other social group. It is through these lenses that we have recently attempted to construct an account of the rise of a liberal model of special needs education over the past three decades and to show how and why that model has failed to realise its own ambitions and how it is beginning to give way to alternative models (Clark *et al.*, 1997).

We do not, however, see our theoretical position as replacing the positions adopted within the post-positivist paradigm in any simple way. Our work does not seek to demolish the significant contributions of Tomlinson, Skrtic and others, but rather to draw upon those contributions and set them within an alternative framework. In common, we believe, with a number of other commentators (Skidmore, 1996; Stangvik, Chapter 12, this volume), our principal concern is to avoid reducing the complex phenomenon of special needs education to one or other of its many dimensions.

Such a project has all the advantages – but also all the disadvantages – of any attempt to grapple with complexity. A crucial question for practitioners of special education and for the learners who are its supposed beneficiaries is the relationship between theories of special education and any action which might be derived from such theories. There is an understandable desire for a theory of special needs education which will point unequivocally to a clear course of action. Much recent theorising, we suggest, has attempted to satisfy that desire by premising itself on a set of unproblematic values and/or on some notion of unequivocal progress towards the realisation of those values. Skrtic's (1995) faith in the inevitable progress which will result from democratic processes of inquiry is merely the latest – and, indeed, the most ambitious – attempt of this kind.

The agenda we are proposing, however, does not lend itself to this kind of relationship between theory and action. We direct our attention *away from* the linear relationships between values and the actions which could or should realise them *towards* the more complex and recursive relationships between multiple and competing values and the complex contexts within which they may or may not be realised. Theorising these relationships does not, we suggest, yield simple prescriptions for action which might find themselves embodied in a Salamanca Statement (UNESCO, 1994) or any other 'universal solution' to the problematic nature of special education. Instead, it focuses attention to the particular situations within which such solutions might be attempted and both requires and enables actors within those situations to determine their courses of action on the basis of a fuller realisation of the complexities within which they are enmeshed.

The realisation of complexity, however, is not entirely or necessarily disabling. In the first place, the ambiguity of values and the complexities of the contexts of action do not in the slightest remove the necessity for action which is principled. We do not see our position as entailing either the view that any action is as 'good' as any other, or that some 'objective' analysis of complexity can replace the need for action. Beyond this, moreover, the analysis of complexity makes it possible not simply to understand the context of action, but also to extend action so that it encompasses ever-wider aspects of that context.

There is a specific issue here with which we wish to conclude. At the heart of theorising about special education within the post-positivist paradigm lies a paradox: the more it has sought to deconstruct special education, the more it has confined it to an intellectual ghetto. Having arrived at the important realisation that special education is non-necessary and non-rational, commentators have understandably focused their attention on the ways in which special education is produced and maintained, and the ways in which it might be dismantled. Such concerns are illuminating but they are also, inevitably, concerns which are to do with 'special' education. Certainly commentators have had things to say about the nature of mainstream education, but they have tended to view the mainstream from the perspective of distinctly 'special' concerns.

What this has made very difficult is any connection of the concerns of special education with wider concerns surrounding the education system as a whole. Issues of what children should learn, what education systems should seek to achieve, how education interacts with other aspects of social and economic policy – all have tended either to be entirely absent from debate within special education, or to have appeared only through the lens of 'special' concerns. In this respect, the current enthusiasm for 'inclusive education' is indicative. The inclusive education movement asks some crucial questions about the nature of mainstream education and its relationship to the wider society. However, the perspective of 'inclusion' presupposes a primary concern with those who are 'excluded'; it foregrounds the role of the education system in respect of those groups, but consigns to the background issues to do with groups who are not excluded in this sense, or issues which are not susceptible to analysis within the inclusion/exclusion framework (Gerber, 1995, 1996).

A time to move on?

It is our contention that it is now time to 'reconnect' special education (Dyson, 1997b). We are advocating a theoretical position which emphasises the connection between special education and fundamental educational issues. That position calls for an analysis of special education from a perspective that is broader than the concerns of special education, that is historical and that is situated in the complexities of particular structures and practices at particular times and places. Such a position does not hold out the promise of resolving in some unproblematic way the complexities and contradictions which beset special education. However, it does promise to locate the debate around special education within a much wider context and, thereby, to reinvigorate that debate, 'moving on' beyond the repetitive and sterile arguments within which it has latterly become trapped.

It is in this sense that we believe that it is time to 'move on'. That metaphor, however, is unfortunate in its linearity. Theorising, for us, is not a linear progression towards some unequivocal truth, so much as a continuing process of realignment between values, beliefs and assumptions. What makes that process more than a pointless carousel of ever-changing positions is that it is – or can become – a rational process, seeking both to explicate and justify each new alignment that is proposed. If that process does not lead to some absolute and final 'truth', it may nonetheless open up new ways of understanding, and hence of acting, for particular times and places.

It is in this spirit that we have undertaken not only the articulation of our theoretical position in this chapter, but also the enterprise of this book as a whole. We hope that we and our contributors have opened up for readers some new ways of understanding; in the final analysis, however, the task of theorising special education is one in which each reader must engage on his or her own behalf.

Notes

1 This chapter is developed from Dyson and Millward (1997) 'Theory and practice in special needs education', a paper presented to the international seminar 'Theoretical perspectives on special education', Ålesund, Norway, 25–27 May 1997.

2 The concept of 'paradigm' is one that is always fraught with difficulties. For our purposes here, we simply wish to draw a distinction between 'theories', which are more-or-less clearly articulated and coherent accounts of sets of phenomena, and 'paradigms', which are general predispositions – often only partly articulated – to view some important aspect of the world in a particular way. It is thus possible, say, for fully articulated theories of intelligence or of the causes and treatment of 'dyslexia' or of the causes of 'maladjustment' to arise within a much less clearly articulated psychomedical paradigm. We do not, therefore, see paradigms as having very distinct boundaries, or a high level of internal coherence, or even as having a great deal of stability. Indeed, we find it more helpful to think of paradigms as useful heuristic devices rather than as reified and formalised ways of thinking.

REFERENCES

Abberley, P. (1987) 'The concept of oppression and the development of a social theory of disability', *Disability, Handicap and Society*, 2 (1): 5–19.

—— (1993) 'Disabled people and "normality"', in J. Swain, V. Finkelstein, S. French and M. Oliver (eds) *Disabling Barriers – Enabling Environments*, London: Sage Publications/The Open University.

Adelman, C. (1989) 'The practical ethic takes priority over methodology', in W. Carr (ed.) *Quality of Teaching*, London: Falmer.

Adelman, H. S. (1992) 'Learning disability: the next 25 years', *Journal of Learning Disabilities*, 25: 17–22.

Ainscow, M. (1989) 'Special education in change: themes and issues', in M. Ainscow (ed.) *Special Education in Change*, London: Fulton.

—— (1991a) (ed.) *Effective Schools for All*, London: David Fulton.

—— (1991b) 'Effective schools for all: an alternative approach to special needs in education', in M. Ainscow (ed.) *Effective Schools for All*, London: David Fulton.

—— (1994a) 'Supporting international innovation in teacher education', in H. W. Bradley, C. Connor, G. Southworth (eds) *Developing Teachers, Developing Schools*, London: Fulton.

—— (1994b) *Special Needs in the Classroom: A Teacher Education Guide*, London: Jessica Kingsley Publishers/UNESCO Publishing.

—— (1995a) 'Education for all: making it happen', *Support for Learning*, 10 (4): 147–57.

—— (1995b) 'Helping teachers to respond to educational difficulties', unpublished PhD thesis, University of East Anglia.

—— (1997) 'Towards inclusive schooling', *British Journal of Special Education*, 24 (1): 3–6.

Ainscow, M. and Hart, S. (1992) 'Moving practice forward', *Support for Learning*, 7 (3): 115–20.

Ainscow, M. and Muncey, J. (1989) *Meeting Individual Needs in the Primary School*, London: Fulton.

Ainscow, M. and Southworth, G. (1996) 'School improvement: a study of the roles of leaders and external consultants', *School Effectiveness and School Improvement*, 7 (3): 229–51.

Ainscow, M. and Tweddle, D. (1979) *Preventing Classroom Failure: An Objectives Approach*, Chichester: Wiley.

Ainscow, M., Hargreaves, D. H. and Hopkins, D. (1995) 'Mapping the process of change in schools: the development of six new research techniques', *Evaluation Research in Education*, 9 (2): 75–90.

Allan, J. (1995) 'Pupils with special educational needs in mainstream schools: a Foucauldian analysis of discourses', unpublished PhD thesis, University of Stirling.

—— (1996) 'Foucault and special educational needs: A "box of tools" for analysing children's experiences of mainstreaming', *Disability and Society*, 11 (2): 219–33.

Alltstaedt, I. (1977) *Lernbehinderte. Kritische Entwicklungsgeschichte eines Notstandes: Sonderpädagogik in Deutschland und Schweden*, Hamburg: Rowohlt.

American Psychiatric Association, Task Force on Nomenclature Third Edition (1987) (revised) *Diagnostic and Statistical Manual of Mental Disorder*, Washington DC: American Psychiatric Association.

Angeles, P. (1981) *Dictionary of Philosophy*, New York: Barnes & Noble.

Apple, M. (1982) *Education and Power*, Boston: Routledge & Kegan Paul.

Archibald, W. (1976) 'Psychology, sociology and social psychology – bad fences make bad neighbours', *British Journal of Sociology*, 27: 115–29.

Armstrong, D. and Galloway, D. (1994) 'Special educational needs and problem behaviour: making policy in the classroom', in S. Riddell and S. Brown (eds) *Special Educational Needs Policy in the 1990s: Warnock in the Market Place*, London: Routledge.

Arter, J. A. and Jenkins, J. R. (1977) 'Examining the benefits and prevalence of modality considerations in special education', *Review of Educational Research*, 19: 394–8.

Aspin, D. (1982) 'Towards a concept of the human being as a basis for a philosophy of special education', *Educational Review*, 34 (2): 111–23.

Audit Commission (1992) *Getting in on the Act? Provision for Pupils with Special Education Needs: The National Picture*, London: HMSO.

Bailey, J. G. (1992) 'Australian special education: issues of the eighties, directions for the nineties', *Australasian Journal of Special Education*, 16 (1): 16–25.

—— (1997) 'A proposed measurement and evaluation role for school psychologists', Sydney: unpublished manuscript.

Bailey, J. G. and Bailey, R.A. (1993) 'Towards a comprehensive model of a special education resource consultant', *Support for Learning*, 8 (2): 58–64.

Ball, S. J. (1987) *The Micro-politics of the School: Towards a Theory of School Organisation*, London: Methuen.

—— (1988) 'Comprehensive schooling, effectiveness and control: an analysis of educational discourses', in R. Slee (ed.) *Discipline and Schools: A Curriculum Perspective*, Melbourne: Macmillan.

—— (ed.) (1990) *Foucault and Education: Discipline and Knowledge*, London: Routledge.

—— (1994) *Education Reform: A Critical and Post-structural Approach*, Milton Keynes: Open University Press.

Ball, S. and Goodson, I. (eds) (1985) *Teachers' Lives and Careers*, Lewes: Falmer Press.

Ballard, K. (1994) 'Disability: an introduction', in K. Ballard (ed.) *Disability, Family, Whanau and Society*, Palmerston North: The Dunmore Press.

—— (1995) 'Inclusion, paradigms, power and participation', in C. Clark, A. Dyson and A. Millward (eds) *Towards Inclusive Schools?*, London: David Fulton.

Barnes, C. (1995) 'The case for anti-discriminaton legislation', in Potts, P., Armstrong, F., and Masterton, M. (eds) *Equality and Diversity in Education, National and International Contexts*, London: Routledge.

—— (1996) 'Theories of disability and the origins of the oppression of disabled people in Western Society', in Barton, L. (ed.) *Disability and Society: Emerging Issues and Insights*, London: Longman.

Bartolome, L. I. (1994) 'Beyond the methods fetish: towards a humanising pedagogy', *Harvard Education Review*, 64 (2): 173–94.

Barton, L. (ed.) (1988a) *The Politics of Special Educational Needs*, Lewes: Falmer Press.

—— (1988) 'The politics of special educational needs: an introduction', in L. Barton (ed.) *The Politics of Special Educational Needs*, Lewes: Falmer Press.

—— (1993a) 'The struggle for citizenship: the case of disabled people', *Disability, Handicap and Society*, 8 (3): 235–48.

—— (1993b) 'Labels, markets and inclusive education', in J. Visser and G. Upton (eds) *Special Education in Britain after Warnock*, London: David Fulton.

—— (1994) 'Disability, difference and the politics of definition', *Australian Disability Review*, 3–94: 8–22.

Barton, L. and Clough, P. (1995) 'Conclusion: many urgent voices', in P. Clough and L. Barton (eds) *Making Difficulties: Research and the Construction of SEN*, London: Paul Chapman.

Barton, L. and Landman, M. (1993) 'The politics of integration', in R. Slee (ed.) *Is There A Desk With My Name On It? The Politics of Integration*, London: Falmer.

Barton, L. and Tomlinson, S. (eds) (1981) *Special Education: Policies, Practices and Social Issues*, London: Harper & Row.

Bassey, M. (1990) 'Crocodiles eat children', *CARN Bulletin No. 4*, Cambridge: Cambridge Institute of Education.

Becker, H. (1963) *Outsiders: Studies in the Sociology of Deviance*, New York: The Free Press.

Bell, D. (1993) *Communitarianism and its Critics*, Oxford: Clarendon Press.

Berger, P. and Luckmann, T. (1966) *The Social Construction of Reality*, Harmondsworth: Penguin.

Berlak, A. and Berlak, H. (1981) *Dilemmas of Schooling: Teaching and Social Change*, London: Methuen.

Bernstein, B. (1996) *Pedagogy, Symbolic Control and Identity: Theory, Research, Critique*, London: Taylor & Francis.

Bernstein, R.J. (1983) *Beyond Objectivity and Relativity: Science, Hermeneutics and Praxis*, Philadelphia: University of Pennsylvania Press.

Bertness, H. J. (1976) 'Progressive inclusion: the mainstream movement in Tacoma', in J. B. Jordan (ed.) *Teacher Please Don't Close The Door: The Exceptional Child in the Mainstream*, Reston, Virginia: Council for Exceptional Children.

Best, S. and Kellner, D. (1991) *Postmodern Theory: Critical Interrogations*, New York: Guilford Press.

Bhabha, H. (1994) *The Location of Culture*, London: Routledge.

Bhaskar, R. (1986) *Scientific Realism and Human Emancipation*, London: Verso.

Bhavnani, K. (1990) 'What's power got to do with it? Empowerment and social research', in I. Parker and J. Shotter (eds) *Deconstructing Social Psychology*, London: Routledge.

Biklen, D. (1988) 'The myth of clinical judgement', *Journal of Social Issues*, 44: 127–40.

Blake, N. (1995) 'Ideal speech conditions, modern discourse and education', *Journal of Philosophy of Education*, 29 (3): 355–67.

Bleidick, U. K. (1974) *Padagogik der Behinderten*, Berlin-Charlottenburg: Marhold.

REFERENCES

Blenkin, G. and Kelly, A.V. (1983) *The Primary Curriculum in Action: A Process Approach to Educational Practice*, London: Harper & Row.

Bodna, B. (1987) 'People with intellectual disability and the criminal justice system', in D. Challinger (ed.) *Intellectually Disabled Offenders*, Canberra: Australian Institute of Criminology.

Bogard, M. (1994) 'Sally and Mel', in K. Ballard (ed.) *Disability, Family, Whanau and Society*, Palmerston North: The Dunmore Press.

Bonder, B. (1991) *Psychopathology and Function*, New Jersey: Slack.

Booth, T. (1981) 'Demystifying integration', in W. Swann (ed.) *The Practice of Special Education*, Oxford: Basil Blackwell/The Open University.

—— (1985a) 'Labels and their consequences', in Lane, D. and Stafford, B. (eds) *Current Approaches to Down Syndrome*, New York: Rinchart and Wilson.

—— (1985b) 'Training and progress in special education', in J. Sayer and N. Jones (eds) *Teacher Training and Special Educational Needs*, London: Croom Helm.

—— (1988) 'Challenging conceptions of integration', in L. Barton (ed.) *The Politics of Special Educational Needs*, London: Falmer.

—— (1991) 'Integration, disability and commitment: a response to Marten Soder', *European Journal of Special Needs Education*, 6 (1): 1–16.

—— (1992a) *Reading Critically, Unit 10 of Learning for All*, Milton Keynes: Open University.

—— (ed.) (1992b) *Curricula for Diversity in Special Education*, London: Routledge.

—— (1996a) 'Stories of exclusion: natural and unnatural selection', in E. Blyth and J. Milner (eds) *Exclusion from School*, London: Routledge.

—— (1996b) 'Changing views of research on integration: the inclusion of students with "special needs" or participation for all?', in A. Sigston, P. Curran, A. Labram and S. Wolfendale (eds) *Psychology in Practice with Young People, Families and Schools*, London: Fulton.

Borsay, A. (1986) 'Personal trouble or private issue? Towards a model of policy for people with physical and mental disabilities', *Disability, Handicap and Society*, 1 (2): 179–95.

Bourne, J., Bridges, L. and Searle, C. (1994) *Outcast England – How Schools Exclude Black Children*, London: Institute of Race Relations.

Branson, J. and Miller, D. (1989) 'Beyond integration policy – the deconstruction of disability', in L. Barton (ed.) *Integration – Myth or Reality?*, Lewes: Falmer Press.

Bricker, D. (1978) 'A rationale for the integration of handicapped and non-handicapped pre-school children', in M. Guralnick (ed) *Early Intervention and the Integration of Handicapped and Non-handicapped Children*, Baltimore: University Park Press.

Brock, S. (1995) 'Accidental emancipatory action? The evolution of a project in which I learned how to work with shifting sands', in P. Potts, F. Armstrong and M. Masterton, (eds) *Equality and Diversity in Education 2, National and International Contexts*, London: Routledge.

Bronfenbrenner, R. U. (1979) *The Ecology of Human Development*, Cambridge, Massachusetts: Harvard University Press.

Brown, A. L. and Campione, J. C. (1986) 'Psychological theory and the study of learning disabilities', *American Psychologist*, 14: 1059–68.

Brown, C. (1994) 'Parents and professionals further directions', in K. Ballard (ed.) *Disability, Family, Whanau and Society*, Palmerston North: The Dunmore Press.

Brown, H. (1990) *Rationality*, London: Routledge.

177

Burbules, D. (1996) 'Deconstructing difference and the difference it makes', paper presented at the 30th Annual Conference of the Philosophy of Education Society of Great Britain, Oxford, March.

Burgess, R. G. (1982) 'Keeping a research diary', *Cambridge Journal of Education*, 11 (1): 75–83.

Burrell, G. and Morgan, G. (1979) *Sociological Paradigms and Organisational Analysis*, Aldershot: Gower.

Callewaert, S. (1992) *Kultur, pedagogik og videnskab. Om Pierre Bourdieus habitusbegreb og praktikteori*, København: Akademisk Forlag.

Campione, J. (1981) 'The instruction of reading comprehension', paper presented at the Second Annual Conference on Reading Research of the Study of Reading, New Orleans, April.

Capra, F. (1975) *The Tao of Physics: An Exploration of the Parallels between Modern Physics and Eastern Mysticism*, London: Wildwood House.

—— (1982) *The Turning Point: Science, Society and the Rising Culture*, London: Wildwood House.

—— (1996) *The Web of Life*, London: HarperCollins.

Carr, W. and Hartnett, A. (1996) *Education and the Struggle for Democracy: The Politics of Educational Ideas*, Buckingham: Open University Press.

Carr, W. and Kemmis, S. (1986) *Becoming Critical: Knowing Through Action Research*, London: Falmer.

Casti, J. (1994) *Complexification – Explaining a Paradoxical World Through the Science of Surprise*, London: Abacus.

Chasty, H. (1993) 'A skills development approach to literacy', Proceedings of the British Dyslexia Association Conference, London: Hornsby International Centre, September,

Checkland, P. (1981) *Systems Thinking, Systems Practice*, Chichester: John Wiley.

Chewning, B. and Sleath, B. (1996) 'Medication decision-making and management: a client-centered model', *Social Science Medicine*, 42 (3): 389–98.

Choate, J. S., Enright, B. E., Miller, L. J., Poteet, J. A. and Rakes, T. A. (1995) *Curriculum-Based Assessment and Programming*, Boston: Allyn & Bacon.

Chomsky, N. (1965) *Aspects of the Theory of Syntax*, Cambridge, Massachusetts: MIT.

Christensen, C. (1996) 'Disabled, handicapped or disordered: "What's in a name?"', in C. Christensen and F. Rizvi (eds) *Disability and the Dilemmas of Education and Justice*, Buckingham: Open University Press.

Clark, C., Dyson, A. and Millward, A. (1995a) *Towards Inclusive Schools?* London: David Fulton.

Clark, C., Dyson, A., Millward, A. and Skidmore, D. (1995b) 'Theorising special education', paper presented at the International Special Education Congress, Birmingham, 12 April.

—— (1995c) 'Dialectical analysis, special needs and schools as organisations', in C. Clark, A. Dyson, and A. Millward (eds) *Towards Inclusive Schools?*, London: David Fulton.

—— (1997) *New Directions in Special Needs: Innovations in Mainstream Schools*, London: Cassell.

Claxton, G. (1990) *Teaching to Learn: A Direction for Education*, London: Cassell.

Clough, P. (1995) 'Problems of identity and method in the investigation of special educational needs', in P. Clough and L. Barton (eds) *Making Difficulties: Research and the Construction of Special Education Needs*, London: Paul Chapman.

Clough, P. and Barton, L. (eds) (1995) *Making Difficulties: Research and the Construction of Special Educational Needs*, London: Paul Chapman.

Codd, J. (1994) 'Educational reform and the contradictory discourses of evaluation', *Evaluation and Research in Education*, 8 (1 and 2): 41–54.

Cole, E. and Siegel, J. A. (1990) *Effective Consultation in School Psychology*, Toronto: Hogrefe & Huber Publishers.

Cooper, P. (1993) *Effective Schools for Disaffected Students: Integration and Segregation*, London: Routledge.

Cooper, P. and Ideus, K. (1995) 'Is attention deficit hyperactivity disorder a Trojan Horse?', *Support for Learning*, 10 (1): 29–34.

Cooper, P. and Upton, G. (1991) 'Controlling the urge to control: an ecosystemic approach to problem behaviour in schools', *Support for Learning*, 6 (10: 22–6.

Cooper, R. and Burrell, G. (1988) 'Modernism, postmodernism and organizational analysis', *Journal of Organizational Studies*, 9 (1): 91–112.

Corbett, J. (1993) 'Postmodernism and the "special needs" metaphors', *Oxford Review of Education*, 19 (4): 547–53.

—— (1994) 'Special language and political correctness', *British Journal of Special Education*, 21 (1): 17–19.

—— (1996) *Bad Mouthing – The Language of Special Needs*, London: Cassell.

Coveney, P. and Highfield, R. (1995) *Frontiers of Complexity: The Search for Order in a Chaotic World*, London: Faber & Faber.

Crawford, N. (1978) *Curriculum Planning for the ESN(s) Child*, Kidderminster: British Institute of Mental Handicap.

Cromer, R. (1991) *Language and Thought in Normal and Handicapped Children*, Oxford: Blackwell.

Crossley, N. (1996) *Intersubjectivity: The Fabric of Social Becoming*, London: Sage.

Csapo, M. (1982) 'Concerns related to the education of Romany students in Hungary, Austria and Finland', *Comparative Education*, 18 (2): 205–17.

Daniels, H., Hey, V. and Leonard, D. (1996) *Gender and Special Needs Provision in Mainstream Schooling*, Report to ESRC.

Davidson, A. (1986) 'Archaeology, genealogy, ethics', in D. Hoy (ed.) *Foucault: A Critical Reader*, Oxford: Basil Blackwell.

Deem, R. (1996) 'Chartered status for educational researchers?', *Research Intelligence*, 56: 22–23 April.

Delamont, S. (1992) *Fieldwork in Educational Settings*, London: Falmer.

Department for Education (1994) *The Code of Practice on the Identification and Assessment of Special Educational Needs*, London: HMSO.

Department of Education and Science (1978) *Report of the Committee of Enquiry into Special Educational Needs*, London: HMSO.

Dessent, T. (1987) *Making the Ordinary School Special*, London: Falmer.

Dreyfus, H. and Rabinow, P. (1983) *Michel Foucault. Beyond Structuralism and Hermeneutics*, Chicago: University of Chicago Press.

Dumont, J. J. (1994) *Leerstoornissen 1, theorie en model*, Rotterdam: Lemniscaat.

Dyson, A. (1990) 'Special educational needs and the concept of change', *Oxford Review of Education*, 16 (1): 55–66.

—— (1997a) 'Professional intellectuals from powerful groups: wrong from the start?', in British Educational Research Association Annual Conference, University of York, 11–14 September.

—— (1997b) 'Social and educational disadvantage: reconnecting special needs education', *British Journal of Special Education*, 24 (4): 152–7.

Dyson, A. and Millward, A. (1997) 'Theory and practice in special needs education', a paper presented to the international seminar 'Theoretical perspectives on special education', Ålesund, Norway, 25–27 May 1997.

Eastman, N. (1992) 'Psychiatric, psychological, and legal models of man', *International Journal of Law and Psychiatry*, 15: 157– 69.

Ebbutt, D. (1983) *Education Action Research: Some General Concerns and Specific Quibbles*, Cambridge Institute of Education, mimeo.

Eding, M. L., Loykens, E. H. M., van den Bos, K. P. and Van Gemert, G. H. (1994) 'A decision model for the treatment of learning problems', in J. E. Rink, R. C. Vos, K. P. van den Bos, R. van Wijck and P. L. Vriesema (eds) *The Limits of Orthopedagogy: Changing Perspectives*, Part 2, Leuven: Garant.

Edwards, B. (1996) 'Suspension regulations in Victorian government schools', unpublished M Ed thesis, Bundoora, LaTrobe University.

Elkins, J. (1990) 'Integration', in A. Ashman and J. Elkins (eds) *Educating Children with Special Needs*, Sydney: Prentice-Hall.

Eliott, J. (1981) *Action Research: A Framework for Self-evaluation in Schools*, Cambridge Institute of Education, mimeo.

Ewing, R. and Brecht, R. (1977) 'Diagnostic–prescriptive instruction: a reconsideration of some issues', *The Journal of Special Education*, 11: 323–7.

Fairclough, N. (1992) *Discourse and Social Change*, Cambridge: Polity Press.

Ferguson, M. (1981) *The Aquarian Conspiracy: Personal and Social Transformation for the 1980s*, London: Routledge & Kegan Paul.

Feuerstein, R. and Feuerstein, S. (1991) 'Mediated learning experience: a theoretical review', in R. Feuerstein, P. S. Klein and A. J. Tannenbaum (eds) *Mediated Learning Experience (MLE): Theoretical, Psychosocial, and Learning Implications*, London: Freud Publishing House.

Feyerabend, P. (1975) *Against Method: Outline of an Anarchistic Theory of Knowledge*, London: New Left Books.

Finkelstein, V. (1980) *Attitudes and Disabled People: Some Issues for Discussion*, New York: World Rehabilitation Fund.

—— (1993) 'Workbook 1: being disabled' in *The Disabling Society (K665)*', Milton Keynes: Open University Press.

—— (1996) 'Outside "Inside Out"', public dissemination paper.

Fish, J. and Evans, J. (1995) *Managing Special Education – Codes, Charters and Competition*, Buckingham: Open University Press.

Forest, M. and Pierpoint, J. (1991) *Two Roads: Inclusion or Exclusion?*, Toronto: Centre for Integrated Education, McGill University.

Foucault, M. (1967) *Madness and Civilisation: A History of Madness in the Age of Reason*, London: Tavistock.

—— (1973) *The Birth of the Clinic*, London: Routledge & Kegan Paul.

—— (1976) *The History of Sexuality*, Harmondsworth: Penguin.

—— (1977a) 'Intellectuals and power: a conversation between Michel Foucault and Giles Deleuze', in Bouchard, D. (ed) *Langauge, Counter-memory, Practice: Selected Essays and Interviews by Michel Foucault*, London: Basil Blackwell.

—— (1977b) *Discipline and Punish: The Birth of the Prison*, Harmondsworth: Penguin.

—— (1982) 'The subject and power', in H. Dreyfus and P. Rabinow (eds) *Michel Foucault: Beyond Structuralism and Hermeneutics*, Brighton: Harvester.

—— (1987) 'The ethic of care for the self as a practice of freedom', in *The Final Foucault, Philosophy and Social Criticism (special issue)*, 12: 2–3.

—— (1988) 'Technologies of the self', in L. Martin, H. Gutman and P. Hutton (eds) *Technologies of the Self: A Seminar with Michel Foucault*, London: Tavistock.

Fuchs, D. and Fuchs, L. S. (1994) 'Inclusive schools movement and the radicalisation of special education reform', *Exceptional Children*, 60, 4: 294–309.

Fulcher, G. (1989) *Disabling Policies? A Comparative Approach to Education Policy and Disability*, London: The Falmer Press.

—— (1993) 'Schools and contests: a reframing of the effective schools debate?', in R. Slee (ed.) *Is There A Desk With My Name On It? The Politics of Integration*, London: Falmer Press.

Gadamer, H. (1989) *Truth and Method*, London: Sheed & Ward.

Gale, A. (1991) 'The school as organisation: new roles for psychologists in education', *Educational Psychology in Practice*, 7, 2: 67–73.

Gallagher, J. and Reid, K. (1981) *The Learning Theory of Piaget and Inhelder*, Austin, Texas: PRO-ED.

Gallas, K. (1994) *Languages of Learning: How Children Talk, Write, Dance, Draw and Sing Their Understanding of the World*, New York: Teachers College Press.

Galletley, I. (1976) 'How to do away with yourself', *Remedial Education*, 11 (3): 149–52.

Galloway, D., Armstrong, D. and Tomlinson, S. (1994) *The Assessment of Special Educational Needs: Whose Problem?*, London: Longman.

Garner, P. and Sandow, S. (1995) *Advocacy and Self-advocacy and Special Needs*, London: David Fulton.

Gartner, A. and Lipsky, D. K. (1987) 'Beyond special education: toward a quality system for all students', *Harvard Educational Review*, 57 (4): 367–95.

Gerber, M. M. (1995) 'Inclusion at the high-water mark? Some thoughts on Zigmond and Baker's case studies of inclusive educational programs', *Journal of Special Education*, 29 (2): 181–91.

—— (1996) 'Reforming special education: beyond "inclusion"', in C. Christensen and F. Rizvi (eds) *Disability and the Dilemmas of Education and Justice*, Milton Keynes: Open University Press.

Gewirtz, S., Ball, S. J. and Bowe, R. (1996) *Markets, Choice and Equity in Education*, Milton Keynes: Open University Press.

Giddens, A. (1993) *New Rules of Sociological Method*, 2nd edn, Cambridge: Polity Press.

Gilborn, D. (1995) *Racism and Antiracism in Real Schools*, Milton Keynes: Open University Press.

Goddard, A. (1983) 'Processes in special education', in G. Blenkin and A. V. Kelly (eds) *The Primary Curriculum in Action: A Process Approach to Educational Practice*, London: Harper & Row.

Goffman, E. (1961) *Asylums: Essays on the Social Situation of Mental Patients and Other Inmates*, New York: Anchor Books.

—— (1963) *Stigma: Notes on the Management of Spoiled Identity*, Harmondsworth: Pelican.

—— (1971) *Relations in Public*, Harmondsworth: Pelican.

Golby, M. and Gulliver, R. J. (1979) 'Whose remedies, whose ills? A critical review of remedial education', *Remedial Education*, 11 (2): 137–47.

Goodley, D. (1996) 'Tales of hidden lives: a critical examination of life history research with people who have learning difficulties', *Disability and Society*, 11 (3): 333–48.

Gould, S. J. (1992) *The Mismeasure of Man*, Harmondsworth: Penguin.

Gramsci, A. (1971) *Selections from the Prison Notebooks of Antonio Gramsci*, London: Lawrence & Wishart.

Gregoire, N. and Prigogine, I. (1989) *Exploring Complexity*, New York: Freeman.

Gregory, S. (1996) 'The disabled self', in M. Wetherall (ed.) *Identities, Groups and Social Issues*, London: Sage/Open University.

Griffiths, M. (1996) 'Social justice in educational practice', paper presented at the 30th Annual Conference of the Philosophy of Education Society of Great Britain, Oxford.

Griffiths, M. and Davies, C. (1995) *In Fairness to Children: Working for Social Justice in the Primary School*, London: David Fulton.

Gross, R. (1990) *Psychology: The Science of Mind and Behaviour*, 8th edn, London: Hodder & Stoughton.

Hamilton, D. (1996) 'Peddling feel-good fictions', *Forum*, 38 (2): 54–6.

Hammersley, M. (1992) *What's Wrong with Ethnography?'*, London: Routledge.

Hargreaves, A. (1994) *Changing Teachers, Changing Times*, London: Cassell.

Hargreaves, D. (1996) 'Teaching as a research based profession: possibilities and prospects', Teacher Training Agency Annual Lecture.

Harre, R. (1981) 'The positivist–empiricist approach and its alternative', in P. Reason and J. Rowan (eds) *Human Inquiry*, Chichester: Wiley.

Harris, K. and Graham, S. (eds) (1994) 'Constructivism: principles, paradigms and integration', *Journal of Special Education*, 28: 3 (special issue).

Hart, S. (1992a) 'Differentiation – way forward or retreat?', *British Journal of Special Education*, 19 (1): 10–12.

—— (1992b) 'Differentiation. Part of the problem or part of the solution?', *The Curriculum Journal*, 3 (2): 131–42.

—— (1996) *Beyond Special Needs: Enhancing Children's Learning Through Innovative Thinking*, London: Paul Chapman.

Hassan, I. (1987) *The Postmodern Turn: Essays in Postmodern Theory and Culture*, Columbus: Ohio State University Press.

Haycock, C. (1995) 'Drama for all in a primary school', in P. Potts, F. Armstrong and M. Masterton (eds) *Equality and Diversity in Education 2, National and International Contexts*, London: Routledge.

Hayden, C. (1996) 'Primary school exclusions: the need for integrated solutions', in E. Blyth and J. Milner (eds) *Exclusions from School: Interprofessional Issues in Policy and Practice*, London: Routledge.

Helfer, R. E. (1985) 'The medical model: in search of a definition', *Child Abuse and Neglect*, 9: 299–300.

Helmke, A. (1989) 'Affective student characteristics and cognitive development: problems, pitfalls, perspectives', *International Journal of Education Research*, 13 (8): 895–913.

Heshusius, L. (1989) 'The Newtonian mechanistic paradigm, special education and contours of alternatives', *Journal of Learning Disabilities*, 22 (7): 403–15.

—— (1995) 'Holism and special education: there is no substitute for real life purposes and processes', in T. Skrtic (ed.) *Disability and Democracy*, New York: Teachers College Press.

Hevey, D. (1992) *The Creatures that Time Forgot – Photography and Disability Imagery*, London: Routledge.

Hinshaw, S. (1994) *Attention Deficits and Hyperactivity in Children*, London: Sage.

Holden, R. J. (1990) 'Models, muddles and medicine', *International Journal of Nursing Studies*, 27 (3): 223–34.

Holly, M. L. (1989) 'Reflective writing and the spirit of enquiry', *Cambridge Journal of Education*, 19 (1): 71–80.

Hopkins, D., Ainscow, M. and West, M. (1994) *School Improvement in an Era of Change*, London: Cassell.

Hornby, G. (1992) 'Integration of children with special educational needs: is it time for a policy review?', *Support for Learning*, 7 (3): 130– 4.

Hornsby, B. and Shear, F. (1974) *Alpha to Omega – The Teaching of Reading, Writing and Spelling*, London: Heinemann.

House, E., Lapan, S. and Mathison, S. (1989) 'Teacher inference', *Cambridge Journal of Education*, 19, 1: 53–8.

Huberty, T. and Huebner, E. (1988) 'A national survey of burnout among school psychologists', *Psychology in the Schools*, 25 (1): 54–61.

Iano, R. P. (1986) 'The study and development of teaching: with implications for the advancement of special education', *Remedial and Special Education*, 7 (5): 50–61.

Jackson, P. (1968) *Life in Classrooms*, New York: Holt, Rinehart & Winston.

Jackson, S. E., Schwab, R. L. and Schuler, R. S. (1986) 'Towards an understanding of the burnout phenomenon', *Journal of Applied Psychology*, 71 (4): 630ff.

Jagger, A. (1983) *Feminist Politics and Human Nature*, Totowa, New Jersey: Rowman & Allanheld.

Jenkins, R. (1991) 'Disability and social stratification', *British Journal of Sociology*, 42 (4): 557–76.

Johnson, T. J. (1972) *Professions and Power*, London: Macmillan.

Jones, R. (1995) *The Child–School Interface: Environment and Behaviour*, London: Cassell.

Kanner, L. (1959) 'Johann Jakob Guggenbuhl and the Abendberg', *Bulletin of the History of Medicine*, 33: 6.

Kauffman, J. K. and Hallahan, D. P. (eds) (1995) *The Illusion of Full Inclusion*, Austin, Texas: PRO-ED.

Kemmis, S. and McTaggart, R. (1982) *The Action Research Planner*, Victoria: Deakin University Press.

Kivinen, O. and Kivirauma, J. (1988) 'Deviance as deficiency. The classification of special education students in Finnish compulsory education 1910–1985', *Nordisk Pedagogik*, 8 (4): 203–9.

Kobi. E. E. (1977) 'Modellen und Paradigmen in der heilpäsagogischen Threoriebildung', in A. Bürli (hrsg.) *Sonderpädagogische Theoriebildung*, Luzern: Schweizerische Zentralstelle für Heilpädagogik.

Kuhn, T. (1970) *The Structure of Scientific Revolutions*, Chicago: University of Chicago Press.

Lakatos, I. (1978) *Philosophical Papers, Vol. I, The Methodology of Scientific Research Programmes*, Cambridge: Cambridge University Press.

Lanzara, G. F. (1991) 'Shifting stones: learning from a reflective experiment in a design process', in D. A. Schön (ed.) *The Reflective Turn*, New York: Teachers College Press.

Lather, P. (1986) 'Research as a praxis', *Harvard Educational Review*, 56 (3): 110–29.

—— (1990) 'Reinscribing otherwise: the play of values in the practices of the human sciences', in E. G. Guba (ed.) *The Paradigm Dialogue*, Newbury Park, CA: Sage.

Lee, C. (1993) *Faking It: A Look into the Mind of a Creative Learner*, London: Cassell.

Lee, T. (1996) *The Search for Equity: The Funding of Additional Educational Needs under LMS*, Aldershot: Avebury.

Levin, H. M. (1993) 'Empowerment evaluation and accelerated schools', paper presented at the American Evaluation Association Annual Meeting, Dallas.

Levinson, E. (1990) 'Actual/desired role functioning, perceived control over role functioning, and job satisfaction among school psychologists', *Psychology in the Schools*, 27 (1): 64–74.

Lewin, K. (1946) 'Action research and minority problems', *Journal of Social Issues*, 2: 34–6.

Lewis, D. R., Johnson, D. R., Erickson, R. N. and Bruinincks, R. H. (1994) 'Multiattribute evaluation of program alternatives within special education', *Journal of Disability Policy Studies*, 5 (1): 77–112.

Lewis, E. and Gilling, R. (1985) *A Celebration of Differences – A Book for Physically Handicapped People*, Bristol: Bristol Broadsides.

Lewis, J. (1989) 'Removing the grit: the development of special education in Victoria 1887–1947', unpublished PhD thesis, Bundoora, LaTrobe University.

Lewis, J. P. (1984) 'Towards a broader perspective on special education', unpublished M Ed thesis, University of Nottingham.

Lieberman, L. (1980) 'The implications of a non-categorical special education', *Journal of Learning Disabilities*, 13 (2): 65–8.

Lincoln, Y. S. and Guba, E. G. (1985) *Naturalistic Inquiry*, Beverly Hills: Sage.

Lingard, T. (1996) 'Why our theoretical models of integration are inhibiting effective integration', *Emotional and Behavioural Difficulties*, 1 (2): 39–45.

Linzey, T. (1991) 'Metaphors and theoretical innovations in human development', in J. Morss and T. Linzey (eds) *Growing Up: The Politics of Human Learning*, Auckland: Longman Paul.

Lipsky, D. K. and Gartner, A. (1997) *Inclusion and School Reform: Transforming America's Classrooms*, Baltimore: Paul H. Brookes.

Lovitt, T. (1977) *In Spite of All My Resistance I've Learned from Children*, Columbus: Merrill.

MacCracken, M. (1974) *A Circle of Children*, London: Gollancz.

—— (1987) *Turnabout Children: Overcoming Dyslexia and Other Learning Disabilities*, New York: Signet.

Macdonald-Ross, M. (1973) 'Behavioural objectives: a critical review', in M. Golby (ed.) *Curriculum Design*, London: Croom Helm.

MacIntyre, A. (1981) *After Virtue*, London: Gerald Duckworth.

Maclure, M. (1994) 'Language and discourse: the embrace of uncertainty', *British Journal of Sociology of Education*, 15 (2): 283–300.

McMillan, M. (1917) *The Camp School*, London: George Allen & Unwin.

Mandelson, P. and Liddle, R. (1996) *The Blair Revolution: Can New Labour Deliver?*, London: Faber & Faber.

Marginson, S. (1993) *Education and Public Policy in Australia*, Cambridge: Cambridge University Press.

Marks, G. (1994) '"Armed now with hope . . . ": the construction of the subjectivity of students within integration', *Disability and Society*, 9 (1): 71–84.

Marshall, J. (1996) 'Personal autonomy and liberal education: a Foucauldian critique', in Peters, M., Hope, W., and Webster, S. (eds) *Personal Autonomy and Liberal Education*, Palmerston North: The Dunmore Press.

Martin, J. (1980) 'Syndrome delineation in communication disorders', in L. A. Hersov and M. Berger (eds) *Language and Language Disorders in Childhood*, Oxford: Pergamon.

Mertens, D. and McLaughlin, J. (1995) *Research Methods in Special Education*, Thousand Oaks, California: Sage.

Mills, Wright C. (1959/1970) *The Sociological Imagination*, reprinted 1970, London: Penguin.

Molnar, A. and Lindquist, B. (1989) *Changing Problem Behaviour in Schools*, San Francisco: Jossey-Bass.

Mongon, D. (1988) 'Behaviour units, "maladjustment" and student control', in R. Slee (ed.) *Discipline and Schools: A Curriculum Perspective*, Melbourne: Macmillan.

Moore, J. (1992) 'Good planning is the key', *British Journal of Special Education*, 19 (1): 16–19.

Morris, J. (1991) *Pride Against Prejudice: Transforming Attitudes to Disability*, London: The Women's Press.

—— (1992) 'Personal and political: a feminist perspective on researching physical disability', *Disability, Handicap and Society*, 7 (2): 157–66.

Morss, J. R. (1996) *Growing Critical: Alternatives to Developmental Psychology*, London: Routledge.

Myers, P. I. and Hammill, D. D. (1969) *Methods for Learning Disorders*, New York: John Wiley & Sons Inc.

Nias, J. (1987) 'Learning from difference: a collegial approach to change', in J. Smyth (ed.) *Educating Teachers: Changing the Nature of Pedagogical Knowledge*, London: Falmer.

Nirje, B. (1970) 'The Normalisation Principle: implications and comments', *British Journal of Mental Subnormality*, 16: 62–70.

Nissen, E. and Tylén, T. (1981) 'Specialpædagogik i ungdomsuddannelserne', *Skrifter fra SEL, nr. 2,1981*, Statens erhvervspædagogiske læreruddannelse.

Norwich, B. (1990) *Re-appraising Special Needs Education*, London: Cassell.

—— (1993) 'Ideological dilemmas in special needs education: practitioners' views', *Oxford Review of Education*, 19 (4): 527–46.

—— (1994) *Segregation Statistics*, London: CSIE.

—— (1996) 'Special needs education or education for all: connective specialisation and ideological impurity', *British Journal of Special Education*, 23 (3): 100–4.

Oates, R. K. (1996) 'It's time to have another look at the medical model', *Child Abuse and Neglect*, 20 (1): 3–5.

Oliver, M. (1988) 'The social and political context of educational policy: the case of special needs', in L. Barton (ed.) *The Politics of Special Educational Needs*, Lewes: Falmer Press.

—— (1990a) 'Politics and language: the need for a new understanding', *International Rehabilitation Review*, XL (3): 10.

—— (1990b) *The Politics of Disablement*, London: Macmillan.

—— (1992a) 'Changing the social relations of research production', *Disability, Handicap and Society*, 7 (2): 101–14.

—— (1992b) 'Intellectual masturbation: a rejoinder to Soder and Booth', *European Journal of Special Needs Education*, 7 (1): 20–8.

—— (1996) *Understanding Disability: From Theory to Practice*, London: Macmillan Press.

Olssen, M. (1995) *Beyond Marx and Gramsci: Considering Foucault as Historical Materialist*, New Zealand, University of Otago: Education Department.

Olssen, M. and Matthews, K. M. (1995) 'Education, democracy and reform: an introduction', in M. Olssen and K. M. Matthews (eds) *Education, Democracy and Reform*, University of Auckland, New Zealand: Rume Publication.

Parsons, C., Hailes, J., Howlett, K., Davies, A., Driscoll, P. and Ross, L. (1995) *National Survey of Local Education Authorities' Policies and Procedures for the Identification of, and Provision for, Children Who are Out of School by Reasons of Exclusion or Otherwise*, London: DfEE.

Patton, M. Q. (1980) *Qualitative Evaluation Methodology*, London: Sage Publications.

Pearl, A. (1988) 'The requirements of a democratic education', in R. Slee (ed.) *Discipline and Schools: A Curriculum Perspective*, Melbourne: Macmillan.

Pendleton, D. and Hasler, J. (eds) (1983) *Doctor–Patient Communication*, London: Academic Press.

Penrose, R. (1989) *The Emperor's New Mind: Concerning Computers, Minds and the Laws of Physics*, London: Vintage.

Persson, B. (1995) *Specialpedagogiskt arbete i skolan. En studie av f"rutsättningar, genomförande och verksamhetsinriktning*, Specialpedagogiska Rapporter, nr. 4, Göteborgs Universitet: Institutionen för Pedagogik.

Peters, S. (1995) 'Disability baggage: changing the educational research train', in P. Clough and L. Barton (eds) *Making Difficulties: Research and the Construction of Special Educational Needs*, London: Paul Chapman.

Piaget, J. (1971) *Biology and Knowledge*, Oxford: Oxford University Press.

Polanyi, M. (1958) *Personal Knowledge: Towards A Post-critical Philosophy*, London: Routledge & Kegan Paul.

Polk, K. and Tait, D. (1990) 'Changing youth labour markets and youth lifestyles', *Youth Studies*, 9 (1): 17–23.

Polkinghorne, D. (1983) *Methodology of the Human Sciences*, Albany: State University of New York Press.

Poplin, M. (1985) 'Reductionism from the medical model to the classroom: the past, present and future of learning disabilities', *Research Communications in Psychology, Psychiatry and Behaviour*, 10: 1–2.

—— (1988a) 'The reductionist fallacy in learning disabilities: replicating the past by reducing the present', *Journal of Learning Disabilities*, 21 (7): 389–400.

—— (1988b) 'Holistic/constructivist principles of the teaching/learning process. Implications for the field of learning disabilities', *Journal of Learning Disabilities*, 21 (7): 401–16.

Poplin, M. and Weeres, J. (1992) *Voices from the Inside: A Report on Schooling from Inside the Classroom*, Claremont, California: Institute for Education in Transformation.

Popper, K. (1972) *Objective Knowledge: An Evolutionary Approach*, Oxford: Clarendon Press.

Prigogine, I. and Stengers, I. (1984) *Order out of Chaos: Man's New Dialogue with Nature*, New York: Bantam Books.

Pullis, M. E. (1988) 'Fostering independence and managing behaviour problems', in D. K. Reid (ed.) *Teaching the Learning Disabled: A Cognitive Developmental Approach*, Boston: Allyn & Bacon, Inc.

Pyke, N. (1992) 'Into the exclusion zone', *Times Educational Supplement*, 26 June.

Reason, P. and Rowan, J. (1981) *Human Inquiry: A Sourcebook for New Paradigm Research*, Chichester: Wiley.

—— (1988) *Human Inquiry in Action: Developments in New Paradigm Research*, London: Sage.

Reed, J. and Watson, D. (1994) 'The impact of the medical model on nursing practice and assessment', *International Journal of Nursing Studies*, 31 (1): 57–66.

Reid, D. K. (ed.) (1988) *Teaching the Learning Disabled: A Cognitive Developmental Approach*, Boston: Allyn & Bacon, Inc.

Reid, D. K. and Hresko, W. P (1981) *A Cognitive Approach to Learning Disabilities*, London: McGraw-Hill.

Reindal, S. M. (1995) 'Discussing disability – an investigation into theories of disability', *European Journal of Special Needs Education*, 10 (1): 58–69.

Reynolds, D. (1995) 'Using school effectiveness knowledge for children with special needs – the problems and possibilities', in C. Clark, A. Dyson and A. Millward (eds) *Towards Inclusive Schools?*, London: Fulton.

Reynolds, D. and Ramasut, A. (1993) 'Developing effective whole school approaches to special educational needs: from school effectiveness theory to school development practice', in R. Slee (ed.) *Is There A Desk With My Name On It? The Politics of Integration*, London: Falmer Press.

Riddell, S. (1994) 'Education and the struggle for empowerment of young people with special educational needs', *International Studies in Sociology of Education*, 4 (1): 77–96.

—— (1996) 'Theorising special educational needs in a changing political climate', in L. Barton (ed.) *The Sociology of Disability: Emerging Issues and Insights*, London: Longman.

Riddell, S. and Brown, S. (1994) *Special Educational Needs Policy in the 1990s: Warnock in the Market Place*, London: Routledge.

Riddell, S., Brown, S. and Duffield, J. (1994) 'Parental power and special educational needs: the case of specific learning difficulties', *British Educational Research Journal*, 20 (3): 327–44.

Riddick, B. (1995) 'Dyslexia: dispelling the myths', *Disability and Society*, 10 (4): 457–73.

Rispens, J. (1990) 'Traditie en vernieuwing', *Tijdschrift voor Orthopedagogiek*, 29: 36–51.

Ritzer, G. (1991) *Metatheorising in Sociology*, Lexington, Massachusetts: Lexington Books.

—— (1992) *Metatheorising*, Newbury Park, California: Sage.

Rogers, C. and Freiberg, J. (1994) *Freedom to Learn*, 3rd edn, Columbus, Ohio: Merrill.

Rorty, R. (1989) *Contingency, Irony and Solidarity*, Cambridge: Cambridge University Press.

—— (1990) 'Foucault, Dewey, Nietzsche', *Raritan*, 9 (4): 1–8.

Rose, N. (1989) *Governing the Soul*, London: Routledge.

Roszak, T. (1978) *Person–Planet: The Creative Disintegration of Industrial Society*, New York: Anchor Press.

Roth, J. (1992) 'Of what help is he? A review of *Foucault and Education*', *American Educational Research Journal*, 29 (4): 683–94.

Rouse, M. and Florian, L. (1996) 'Effective inclusive schools: a study in two countries', *Cambridge Journal of Education*, 26 (1): 71–85.

REFERENCES

Ryan, J. (1991) 'Observing and normalising: Foucault, discipline and inequality in schooling', *The Journal of Educational Thought*, 25 (2): 104–19.

Salvia, J. and Ysseldyke, J. (1991) *Assessment*, New Jersey: Houghton Mifflin.

Sandow, S. (1994) *Whose Special Need?*, London: Paul Chapman.

Sandy, L. R. (1986) 'The descriptive–collaborative approach to psychological report writing', *Psychology in the Schools*, 23: 395–400.

Sarason, S, B. and Doris, J. (1979) *Educational Handicap, Public Policy, and Social History*, New York: The Free Press.

Schindele, R. (1985) 'Research methodology in special education: a framework approach to special problems and solutions', in S. Hegarty and P. Evans (eds) *Research and Evaluation Methods in Special Education*, Windsor: NFER-Nelson.

Schön, D. A. (1983a) *The Reflective Practitioner*, New York: Basic Books.

—— (1983b) 'Organisational learning', in G. Morgan (ed.) *Beyond Method: Strategies for Social Research*, Newbury Park: Sage.

Schrift, A. (1995) 'Reconfiguring the subject as a process of self', *Michel Foucault: J'accuse'*, *New Formations*, 25 (special issue): 8–39.

Schroeder, C. (1994) 'Community partnerships and medical models of health? I don't think so . . . ', *Public Health Nursing*, 11 (5): 283–4.

Sebba, J. and Ainscow, M. (1996) 'International developments in inclusive schooling: mapping the issues', *Cambridge Journal of Education*, 26 (1): 5–18.

Shakespeare, T. (1994) 'Cultural representation of disabled people: dustbins for disavowal?', *Disability and Society*, 9 (3): 283–99.

—— (1996) 'Rules of engagement: doing disability research', *Disability and Society*, 11 (1): 115–19.

Shakespeare, T. and Watson, N. (1995) '"The Boy Line controversy": a new direction for disability studies?', unpublished paper presented at the Sociology and Disability Studies Conference, Hull, UK.

Shapiro, J. (1981) 'Disability and the politics of constitutive rules', in G. L. Albrecht (ed.) *Cross-national Rehabilitation Policies*, California: Sage Publications.

—— (1993) *No Pity: People with Disabilities Forging a New Civil Rights Movement*, New York: Times Books.

Shumway, D. (1989) *Michel Foucault*, Charlottesville: University Press of Virginia.

Siegel, G. M., Spradlin, J. E. (1978) 'Programmes for language and communication therapy', in Shiefelbusch, R. L. (ed) *Language Intervention Strategies*, Baltimore: University Park Press.

Sigston, A. (1996) 'Research and practice worlds apart?', in A. Sigston, P. Curran, A. Labram and S. Wolfendale (eds) *Psychology in Practice With Young People, Families and Schools*, London: David Fulton.

Simons, J. (1995) *Foucault and the Political*, London: Routledge.

Singh Dillon, A. (1995) 'Science, constructism and science education', *Access: Critical Perspectives on Cultural and Policy Studies in Education*, 13 (2): 1–20.

Sinha, C. (1981) 'The role of psychological research in special education', in W. Swann (ed.) *The Practice of Special Education*, Oxford: Basil Blackwell.

Skidmore, D. (1996) 'Towards an integrated theoretical framework for research into special educational needs', *European Journal of Special Needs Education*, 11 (1): 33–47.

Skrtic, T. M. (1986) 'The crisis in special education knowledge: a perspective on perspectives', *Focus on Exceptional Children*, 18 (9): 1–15.

188

—— (1991a) *Behind Special Education: A Critical Analysis of Professional Culture and School Organisation*, Denver: Love Publishing.

—— (1991b) 'The special education paradox: equity as the way to excellence', *Harvard Educational Review*, 61 (2): 148–206.

—— (1991c) 'Students with special educational needs: artifacts of the traditional curriculum', in M. Ainscow (ed.) *Effective Schools for All*, London: David Fulton.

—— (ed.) (1995) *Disability and Democracy: Reconstructing (Special) Education for Post-modernity*, New York: Teachers College Press.

Slee, R. (1991) 'Learning initiatives to include all students in regular schools', in M. Ainscow (ed.) *Effective Schools for All*, London: David Fulton.

—— (1992) *Discipline in Australian Public Education: Changing Policies and Practice*, Hawthorn: Australian Council for Educational Research.

—— (ed.) (1993) *Is There A Desk With My Name On It? The Politics of Integration*, London: Falmer Press.

—— (1995a) *Changing Theories and Practices of Discipline*, London: Falmer Press.

—— (1995b) 'Inclusive education: from policy to school implementation', in C. Clark, A. Dyson and A. Millward (eds) *Towards Inclusive Schools?*, London: David Fulton.

—— (1996a) 'Disability, class and poverty: school structures and policing identities', in C. Christensen and F. Rizvi (eds) *Disability and the Dilemmas of Education and Justice*, Milton Keynes: Open University Press.

—— (1996b) 'Inclusive schooling in Australia? Not yet!', *Cambridge Journal of Education*, 26 (1): 19–32.

Sleeter, C. E. (1986) 'Learning disabilities: the social construction of a special education category', *Exceptional Children*, 53 (1): 46–54.

Smead, V. S. (1977) 'Ability training and task analysis in diagnostic–prescriptive teaching', *The Journal of Special Education*, 11: 113–25.

Soder, M. (1989) 'Disability as a social construct: the labelling approach revisited', *European Journal of Special Needs Education*, 4 (2): 117–29.

Special Educational Needs Training Consortium (SENTC) (1996) *Professional Development to Meet Special Educational Needs*, Stafford: SENTC.

Stainback, W. and Stainback, S. (eds) (1990) *Support Networks for Inclusive Schooling*, Baltimore: Paul H. Brookes.

—— (eds) (1992) *Curriculum Considerations in Inclusive Classrooms: Facilitating Learning for All Students*, Baltimore: Paul H. Brookes.

Stambolovic, V. (1996) 'Human rights and health within the dominant paradigm', *Social Science Medicine*, 42 (3): 301–3.

Stangvik, G. (1979) *Self Concept and School Segregation*, Göteborg Studies of Educational Sciences 27, Acta Universitatis Gothoburgensis: University of Göteborg.

—— (1993) 'Etatskultur og handlingsstrategi', in G. Stangvik (ed.) *Notater fra prosjektet Kommunal kompetanse for forbedring av funksjnoshemmedes livskvalitet, ALH-rapport 1993:5*, Høgskolen i Finnmark.

—— (1994) *Funksjonshemmede inn i lokalsamfunnet*, Oslo: Universitetsforlaget.

Stenhouse, L. (1975) *An Introduction to Curriculum Research and Development*, London: Heinemann.

Stuffelbeam, D. (1977) 'Needs assessment in evaluation', paper presented at the AERA Evaluation Conference, San Francisco, California.

Sugarman, L. (1986) *Life-span Development: Concepts, Theories and Interventions*, London: Methuen.

Swann, W. (1982) *Psychology and Special Education: Course E241, Unit 12*, Milton Keynes: Open University Press.

Taylor, E. (1994) 'Hyperactivity as a special educational need', *Therapeutic Care and Education* (Special issue on ADHD), 4 (2): 130–44.

Ter Horst, W. (1980) *Algemene Orthopedagogiek*, Kampen: Kok.

Thomas, G. (1995) 'Special needs at risk?', *Support for Learning*, 10 (3): 104–12.

Thomas, S. (1995) 'Parents' perspectives: towards positive support for disabled children and those who experience difficulties in learning', in P. Potts, F. Armstrong and M. Masterton (eds) *Equality and Diversity in Education 2. National and International Contexts*, London: Routledge.

Tomlinson, S. (1982) *A Sociology of Special Education*, London: Routledge & Kegan Paul.

—— (1985) 'The expansion of special education', *Oxford Review of Education*, 11 (2): 157–65.

—— (1993) 'Conflicts and dilemmas for professionals in special education', paper presented at the Social Justice, Equity and Dilemmas of Disability in Education International Working Conference, Brisbane.

Torgesen, J. K. (1979) 'What shall we do with psychological processes?', *Journal of Learning Disabilities*, 12: 514–21.

—— (1986) 'Learning disabilities theory: its current state and future prospects', *Journal of Learning Disabilities*, 19: 399–407.

Troyna, B. (1993) *Racism and Education: Research Perspectives*, Milton Keynes: Open University Press.

—— (1994) 'Blind faith? Empowerment and educational research', paper presented at the International Sociology of Education Conference, University of Sheffield.

—— (1995) 'Beyond reasonable doubt? Researching "race" in educational settings', *Oxford Review of Education*, 21 (4): 395–408.

Tzuriel, D. (1991) 'Cognitive modifiability, mediated learning experience and affective–motivational processes: a transactional approach', in R. Feuerstein, P. S. Klein and A. J. Tannenbaum (eds) *Mediated Learning Experience (MLE): Theoretical, Psychosocial, and Learning Implications*, London: Freud Publishing House.

Udvari-Solner, A. (1995) 'A process for adapting curriculum in inclusive classrooms', in R. A. Villa and J. S. Thousand (eds) *Creating an Inclusive School*, Alexandria, Virginia: ASCD (Association for Supervision and Curriculum Development).

Udvari-Solner, A. and Thousand, J. (1995) 'Effective organisational, instructional and curricular practices in inclusive schools and classrooms', in C. Clark, A. Dyson and A. Millward (eds) *Towards Inclusive Schools?* London: David Fulton.

UNESCO (1994) *The Salamanca Statement and Framework on Special Needs Education*, Paris: UNESCO.

Van Strien, P. J. (1975) 'Naar een methodologie van het praktijkdenken in de sociale wetenschappen', *Nederlands Tijdschrift voor de Psychologie*, 30: 601–19.

—— (1984) 'Naar een verwetenschappelijking van de praktijk', *Tijdschrift voor Orthopedagogiek*, 13: 161–80.

Villa, R. and Thousand, J. S. (eds) (1995) *Creating an Inclusive School*, Alexandria, Virginia: Association for Supervision and Curriculum Development.

REFERENCES

Villa, R. A., Thousand, J. S., Stainback, W. and Stainback, S. (eds) (1992) *Restructuring for Caring and Effective Education: An Administrative Guide to Creating Heterogeneous Schools*, Baltimore: Paul H. Brookes.

Vislie, L. (1995) 'Integration policies, school reforms and the organisation of schooling for handicapped pupils in western societies', in C. Clark, A. Dyson and A. Millward (eds) *Towards Inclusive Schools?* London: David Fulton.

Vlachou, A. D. (1997) *Struggles for Inclusive Education: An Ethnographic Study*, Milton Keynes: Open University Press.

Vliegenthart, W. E. (1972) *Inleiding in de orthopedagogiek*, Groningen: Wolters-Noordhof.

Wang, M. (1992) *Adaptive Education Strategies – Building on Diversity*, New York: Paul Brookes.

Ward, J. and Center, Y. (1987) 'Attitudes to integration of disabled children into regular classes – a factor analysis of functional characteristics', *British Journal of Educational Psychology*, 57: 221–4.

Ware, L. (1995) 'The aftermath of the articulate debate: the invention of inclusive education', in C. Clark, A. Dyson and A. Millward (eds) *Towards Inclusive Schooling?*, London: David Fulton.

Warner, D. (1991) 'The operation of a postcompulsory college', in T. Seddon and C. E. Deer (eds) *A Curriculum for the Senior Secondary Years*, Hawthorn: Australian Council for Educational Research.

Wasley, P., Hampel, R. and Clark, R. (1996) 'Collaborative inquiry: a method for the reform minded', paper presented at the Annual Meeting of the American Educational Research Association, New York.

Waterland, L. (1994) *Not a Perfect Offering: A New School Year*, Stroud: Thimble Press.

Webb, N. (1989) 'Peer interaction and learning in small groups', *International Journal of Educational Research*, 13 (1): 21–40.

Weber, M. (1948) *From Max Weber: Essays in Sociology*, (translated, edited and with an introduction by H. H. Gerth and C. Wright Mills), London: Routledge & Kegan Paul.

Wedell, K. (1981) 'Concepts of special educational needs', *Education Today*, 31: 3–9.

West, M., Ainscow, M. and Hopkins, D. (1997) 'Making sense of school development from the inside', paper presented at the International Conference on School Effectiveness and Improvement, Memphis, USA.

Wilkie, T. (1993) *Perilous Knowledge – the Human Genome Project and Its Implications*, London: Faber & Faber.

Williams, R. (1976) *Keywords*, London: Fontana.

Winter, R. (1989) *Learning from Experience: Principles and Practice in Action Research*, Lewes: Falmer Press.

Wolfendale, S. (1992) *Empowering Parents and Teachers. Working for Children*, London: Cassell.

Wong, B. Y. L. (1986) 'Problems and issues in the definition of learning disabilities', in J. K. Torgesen and B. Y. L. Wong (eds) *Psychological and Educational Perspectives on Learning Disabilities*, San Diego: Academic Press.

Wood, P. (1981) *International Classification of Impairments, Disabilities and Handicaps*, Geneva: World Health Organisation.

Worthen, B.R. and Spandel, V. (1991) 'Putting the standardised test debate in perspective', *Educational Leadership*, 48 (5): 65–9.

Yeatman, A. (1994) *Postmodern Revisionings of the Political*, New York: Routledge.

REFERENCES

Yin, Q. and White, G. (1994) 'The "marketisation" of Chinese higher education: a critical assessment', *Comparative Education*, 30 (3): 217–37.

Young, R. (1989) *A Critical Theory of Education: Habermas and Our Children's Future*, Hemel Hempstead: Harvester Wheatsheaf.

Ysseldyke, J. E. (1973) 'Diagnostic–prescriptive teaching: two models', *Exceptional Children*, 41: 181–5.

Zeichner, K. and Liston, D. (1987) 'Teaching student teachers to reflect', *Harvard Educational Review*, 57 (1): 23–48.

Ziegler, E. and Valentine, J. (eds) (1979) *Project Headstart: A Legacy of the War on Poverty*, New York: Free Press.

Zigmond, N. and Baker, J. M. (1995) 'Concluding comments: current and future practices in inclusive schooling', *Journal of Special Education*, 29 (2): 245–50.

—— (1996) 'Full inclusion for students with learning disabilities: too much of a good thing?', *Theory into Practice*, 35 (1): 26–34.

INDEX

193